TE&

TRIBULATIONS:

A Year in Andalucía

TAPAS, TEARS & TRIBULATIONS:
A Year in Andalucía

Drew Johnson

To my dear wife, soulmate, best friend and partner in this foreign adventure, Chris. Thank you for continuing to make such wonderful memories with me and allowing me to retell some of them here. You have been a constant support throughout the writing process, and for that (and much, much more) I love you

This book is based on actual events and actual people, although the names of all Spanish characters have been altered as a courtesy. All other characters are real-life family members or friends who are happy to be exposed for their association with the author – more fool them!

"There is no night life in Spain.
They stay up late but they get up late.
That is not night life.
That is delaying the day."
(Ernest Hemingway)

CONTENTS

1

No Going Back

Dumping the overnight bags on the twin beds of the tiny cabin, I gazed out of the porthole at the battleship grey outline of the Type 82 destroyer resting at dock across the harbour and wondered out loud to my harassed wife, Chris, 'Do you think the cabins are any bigger on that one?'

It was a cool, overcast afternoon in early September 2016, and we'd just boarded the *Pont-Aven*, one of Brittany Ferries' passenger ships covering the Portsmouth to Santander route. Having booked it quite late, this twenty-four-hour, one-way voyage with a twin-berth outside cabin had cost us the thick end of six hundred pounds, and I was hoping it wasn't going to be the worst six hundred pounds I'd ever spent.

In hindsight, the worst six hundred pounds I ever spent was on a 1977 Mark I 2.0 litre Ford Granada in candy apple red that I rather foolishly acquired in 1987. To be fair, the seller did tell me the gearbox was knackered when I bought it, but I wouldn't listen – it was a nice, shiny, lolloping beast of a car that was going to leave me with some much-needed cash in my pocket after flogging my mint condition, unfailingly reliable, 1.6 litre Nissan Sunny Coupe via Auto Trader. Although, given the state of the Granada, that 'cash in my pocket' didn't last long, as it happened.

The warship I was looking at was HMS *Bristol*, a familiar sight on the dockside at Portsmouth. It had been in service for forty-three years now – ten years fewer than me – and it still looked as imposing as the day it was launched – which was more than could be said of me. These days it was used only for training after being let out to pasture following the Falklands War. It was a unique ship. Not in a particularly good way, apparently … it was unique in that it was the only one of its type ever built, when the rest of the Navy's order was cancelled after Harold Wilson's Labour-led 1966 Strategic Defence Review shrunk the defence budget.

In contrast, the German built *Pont-Aven* was only twelve years old and the flagship of Brittany Ferries' fleet of cruise ferries, so maybe things would look up a bit once we went 'topside' – or 'outside', to those of us that prefer to have soil under our feet.

'It'll be fine,' Chris said. 'It's only for one night. Let's go and wave goodbye to dreary old Britain.'

Up on deck, we perched ourselves alongside the rail and looked out across the windswept landscape of Whale Island. Thanks in no small part to free labour from a bunch of press-ganged French prisoners during the Napoleonic Wars, the island had grown to its present size during the nineteenth century using reclaimed land dredged out of the harbour. Whale Island was now home to HMS *Excellent*, the Royal Navy's Command Headquarters. So, if anyone ever asks you, 'What have the bloody French ever done for us?', you'll be able to tell them now.

'Ooh! I think we're moving,' Chris said.

And sure enough, good old England, the country of our birth – well, my birth actually as Chris is Scottish – slipped gently away from the boat. Or at least that's how it felt from where I was standing.

I raised a hand to my temple in mock salute, and as I did so, a seagull dropped a little departure gift from above onto the handrail next to me, and as a parting gesture to the cold, cloud-filled September skies of Hampshire, I couldn't think of a more fitting farewell. So I let the moment linger and simply watched as the grey watery gap between us and Blighty grew steadily wider.

The boat, and our big foreign adventure, were both underway – we were emigrating to the Costa del Sol.

Our love affair with Spain and the Spanish lifestyle had started many years earlier, way back in the late nineties, when we would load up the car in the middle of the night for the long drive down to Spain and our annual two-week summer camping holiday. Setting off at two in the morning with three of our four sleepy daughters in the back, the twelve-hundred-mile road trip would take us around forty hours to get from Bury in the northwest of England to what we affectionately referred to as 'our second home', a Keycamp tent on the Costa Brava's Camping Castell Montgri site in the beautiful resort of Estartit.

Now you might be wondering what our fourth daughter had done to miss out on this 'trip of a lifetime' with us – well, with ten years between her and our youngest, she was hellbent on enjoying a quite different kind of holiday with her mates in one of Europe's fleshpot, hedonist resorts.

And apart from anything else, she wouldn't have fitted in the car.

Anyway, leaving aside my painful memories of handling the mood swings of a stroppy pubescent teenage girl, I believe we made this same pilgrimage for eight straight summers, although for most of those years with just the two youngest girls in tow, as we were able to shed the dead weight of another stroppy teenager after the first two years.

To make it a bit more interesting, we would vary our route through France each year, staying overnight somewhere along the way – usually another Keycamp site a half-hour detour off our chosen route – a route which was made much easier by the opening of the Eurotunnel.

Despite what to many would seem like one hell of a drive, you'd be surprised how many British families did exactly the same as us every year, and many of them to the same magnificent holiday park. We tried to get the kids thinking the journey was all part of the adventure, and to be fair to them, they kept the 'Are we nearly there yet?' questions to a minimum.

We even extended the trip to three weeks one year and did a European tour that took us through seven other countries before reaching Spain. In eight years, we drove over twenty thousand miles in three different cars … and we only crashed once, when we got a bit lost driving out of Barcelona one night.

As usual, during that fateful daytrip, I expected the Spaniard in front to ignore the amber traffic light and hurtle through it like any self-respecting Catalan would. Thinking I might get through it myself too, I went for the accelerator, just about the same time he hit the brakes.

He was genuinely very nice about it, actually, after I'd shunted him several yards beyond the red light and into the oncoming morass of a six-street intersection. Surprisingly, there wasn't a scratch on the bumper of his car, whereas one of the headlights on my Renault Laguna was now lighting up the living room of the woman in the third-floor flat opposite.

With no chance of getting a replacement right-hand drive lamp before our return, I just had to patch it up as best I could with a bit of sticky tape. On the journey home a week later, the Spanish border guard decided it was worth a closer inspection and indicated for me to pull over. I just waved at him, put on a 'stupid foreigner' expression, and ploughed on into France – oh, the delights of the Schengen Agreement!

Eighteen years after our first lifechanging Spanish holiday, our dream of moving to the Iberian Peninsula had now become a reality … although, thankfully, this time our destination wasn't a blue and yellow tent on the Costa Brava.

And the kids weren't coming.

* * *

As the ferry moved out into The Solent, our journey began to take on an air of finality about it, and I was minded to recall Mark Twain, who once said, 'Twenty years from now you will be more disappointed by the things that you didn't do than by the ones you did do. So, throw off the bowlines, sail away from safe harbour, catch the trade winds in your sails. Explore, Dream, Discover'. It sounded like an advert for Saga Cruises, but we were on our way and there was no going back.

Having rounded the Isle of Wight and scanned the shoreline at Ventnor to see if my brother was waving at us – he wasn't – we went 'midships' for a spot of dinner in the ship's restaurant, after which we had an early night and headed below decks to our quarters – or more like eighths – in 'steerage'.

The rest of the trip across to Santander was uneventful and much better than we could have hoped for. For one thing, the weather out at sea was in our favour, and the *Pont-Aven* gently rolled over the waves as if it were gliding majestically across a shag pile carpet.

I'm afraid I don't have fond memories of crossing any serious expanse of water. As a youngster, I learned to play the trumpet and joined the local schools' concert band. On a few occasions, the teaching staff were naive enough to fill a fifty-six-seater coach with testosterone-filled boys and hormonal girls from Salford and take them on a foreign musical exchange trip for a week.

One year, they took us all to Jersey on the ferry in conditions I would never want to experience ever again. The captain on that occasion appeared to have cast himself as George Clooney in *The Perfect Storm* as the ferry ploughed relentlessly on to its destination in conditions that reportedly measured gale force nine on the Beaufort scale. And, judging by one of the onboard tannoy announcements halfway across, the owner of a Rolls Royce Corniche would have been feverishly checking their insurance was up to date.

Only one of our party suffered no ill effects from the journey, while the rest of us endured a sleepless night, vomiting at regular intervals in the toilets, the floor of which soon resembled an ocean itself; sadly not of saltwater, but the remains of everyone's dinner, sloshing merrily from side to side as you were bent double over the toilet bowl or a vacant sink … or the waste bin, for that matter.

In case you were wondering, that's why you have to step over a six-inch lip to enter the toilets on a ferry – it's designed to keep all forms of bodily waste within the confines of the toilet area. Although I can testify now that it does depend on the severity of the prevailing seas, and that it's not, in fact, entirely foolproof.

Our distressed state was hardly assuaged by the sneering salty dog of a tuba player who'd seated himself outside the entrance to the toilets so he could shout, 'Greasy sausages. Blaargh!', at anyone leaving, and then belly-laugh to himself as they immediately dashed back inside.

Bearing in mind this was in the mid-seventies when flared jeans were the trouser of choice for the discerning young man about town, you can imagine what state the bottom of those were in after wading in and out of a roiling tide of sick all night.

The following morning we'd arrived in Jersey much the worse for wear. Our instruments had gone on ahead in a minibus on the earlier ferry which had made it into Guernsey harbour but not out again, so we were without the instruments for the first twenty-four hours of our Channel Islands stay. And much to our hosts' chagrin, the rather splendid buffet they'd laid on for us at the welcoming reception party remained untouched by all but our hardy tuba player, but even he couldn't eat for sixty of us, despite first impressions.

Add to that a rough Hull-Zeebrugge crossing in later life and a failed cross-channel, charity jet ski attempt in my twenties in inclement conditions, you can begin to imagine my fear and loathing of a life on the ocean waves.

However, on this occasion, we were barely troubled on the crossing beyond the English Channel and down through the Bay of Biscay, which is known for its brutal seas and violent Atlantic storms. Ask any member of the yachting fraternity about this stretch of water and they will eagerly warn you of its fearsome reputation. Thankfully, Chris and I were only planning on doing this trip once, and it looked like we were sneaking through on a good day.

The boat itself was quite pleasant, actually. The food on board was very tasty, and given we were a captive audience, the drinks were reasonably priced too. By way of comparison, I would say it was akin to whiling away a few happy, relaxed hours at a French service station, which is not something you'd want to do at a British one.

After a decent breakfast and a quick stretch of the legs, I spent most of the day drinking red wine and reading *Driving Over Lemons*, the first of Chris Stewart's wildly entertaining Spanish travelogues. I was thankful that we weren't going to be quite as adventurous as Mr Stewart and take over a run-down farm in the

Alpujarras. Ours was to be a life of sun, sea and sangria, or so we thought.

The only minor mishap on this part of the journey was when Chris plugged her hairdryer into my recently purchased Swiss world travel adapter and blew the fuse. I felt like giving her the full Charlie Croker and saying, 'You're only supposed to blow the bloody doors off!'

Never mind, eh? Spilt milk, and all that.

2

Welcome to Spain

As the afternoon sun began to drop ever more quickly in the sky, the Cantabrian coastline and the port of Santander hove into view.

'*Bienvenido a España*,' Chris said, a beaming smile across her chops as she gazed longingly at the Spanish mainland from the front bit of the boat – I think they call that the foredeck, or something like that.

Before long, the tannoy call informed us we'd be coming into port soon and that we should think about making our way down to the cars. So we collected our bags from the cabin and joined the throng of people clambering down the steep stairwell to the car deck to be reunited with their motor vehicles.

We spotted our car quite easily, as it wasn't what you'd call inconspicuous.

We'd made the journey thus far in Chris's 2005 Mini Cooper, a fetching little number in sky blue with a white roof and white bonnet stripes. This was her pride and joy, and (in her words) she couldn't wait to 'let it loose on the winding Spanish roads'.

Not that she'd be doing much 'throwing it round corners' just yet – it was currently crammed with thousands of pounds worth of my most prized possessions, from trumpets and flugelhorns to cameras and computer equipment.

Other than that, we had a suitcase of clothes each, and that was it. The rest of our (less valuable) worldly goods had been loaded into a removal van a few days earlier as we bade a tearful farewell to our modest three-bedroom family home of twenty-two years, which had previously been Chris's parents' house and her own childhood home.

After disembarking the boat, we had a short ride west to our hotel for the night, an uninspiring but conveniently located golf hotel not too far from the city. It felt good to finally set foot in Spain and not be here just for a brief holiday.

After a few trips to and from the car to disgorge some of my most precious belongings, we headed down to the bar for something to eat. Over a long relaxing dinner – and another welcome glass or two of Spanish red – we reminisced about the UK lives, home and family we'd just left behind.

Eventually, as our eyes glazed over from our reminiscing – or more accurately a *vino tinto* haze – we emptied our glasses, agreed that home is where the heart is, but that Spain is where the sun and cheap plonk is, and we took ourselves off to bed.

* * *

'Happy fifty-third birthday,' Chris said, as I regained consciousness and wondered where the hell I was for a moment.

Maybe I shouldn't have drunk so much red wine the night before. I made a mental note to bear that in mind (maybe) ... after my birthday celebrations, of course.

Today was the day I'd really been looking forward to since we set off three days ago, having stayed the first night in a nice country house hotel outside Rugby, and the second night onboard ship.

My unbridled excitement, however, was nothing to do with the fact it was my birthday – I can't even remember what present Chris bought me – but because the next overnight stop on our journey south to the mountains of Andalucía was to be at the rather magnificent Hacienda Zorita Wine Hotel & Spa, perched on the banks of the river Tormes, just outside Salamanca.

This stunning five-star hotel is a little spot of paradise, with its own organic farm and, more importantly for me, its own vineyards further up the valley on the edge of the Valladolid section of the renowned Ribera del Duero wine region. The Rio Duero, which starts high up in the Picos de Urbión and runs for 460 miles into Portugal before flowing into the Atlantic Ocean at

Porto, is commonly referred to as the longest 'wine river' in the world – a river full of wine? … now you're talking my language.

Now, I love a good bottle of Rioja. I mean, who doesn't? But I noticed on my business travels in Spain that whenever I was wined and dined by my Spanish hosts, they always chose Ribera del Duero. Without fail.

It's no surprise, therefore, that Ribera has become my wine region of choice in Spain ever since, and the opportunity to spend my birthday at such a wonderful hotel was too good to miss. My only regret was that we didn't have time to go and explore Salamanca, as I'm told it's a particularly beautiful city. But it's good to have an excuse to revisit the place another time.

The Hacienda Zorita is teeming with history, dating back over eight hundred years to 1185. At various times in its long and illustrious existence it has been the home of a close friend of Constanza, the Queen and wife of King Fernando IV in the fourteenth century, before the owner, a noblewoman by the name of Inés de Limoges, donated the entire estate to the Dominican Friars in the vain hope it might save her dearly departed husband's soul. God knows what the fool had done, but it wasn't uncommon, I suppose, in those times to think that a late act of contrition, sacrifice or generosity to The Church might smooth one's passage to the more comfortable side of the afterlife.

The Zorita's more impressive historical claim to fame, though, came when the Italian explorer, Christopher Columbus, came to stay here in the middle part of the 1480s during the Valcuevo Conferences of the time. He was there to try and convince the then Queen Isabel and assorted other Catholic Kings to finance his explorations of the New World – no doubt over a bottle or three of Ribera. We like a good drink us Catholics … it's the altar wine, you see, it's so addictive.

Columbus was ultimately aiming to find a trading route to the East Indies, to counter his compatriot Marco Polo's eastern route to China. Or rather, his goal was to loot as much gold as possible because he'd been promised a ten percent cut by the Spanish Crown. He sailed westward across the Atlantic, believing correctly that the world is round, and when he reached land, he thought he'd arrived in India.

Unfortunately for the indigenous tribes of the region, the murderous swine ended up in The Bahamas instead, and later named the region the West Indies. Further voyages led him to establish Spanish colonies in other Caribbean islands, and beyond there to the northern regions of South America and the eastern edges of Central America. In fact, Columbia is named after him.

In typical colonial fashion, the local tribes were of course subjugated, their womenfolk ravaged, and their gold and other precious metals looted to enrich the personal fortunes of the European Monarchs and the Catholic Church. Don't you just love the way religion brings everyone together peacefully?

As we arrived at the hotel late that morning, the last thing on our minds was a ransacking of the place (with the possible exception of the minibar, naturally).

Stepping from the car, our welcome couldn't have been any warmer as we were greeted personally by the General Manager himself, who took our cases from us and presented us with complimentary wide-brimmed straw hats to protect us from the midday sun. This personal service is available to all guests, of course, not just those that have a birthday that day.

Walking towards the hotel was a feast for the eyes. The tall, elegant cypresses that framed the gardens against the local, golden Villamayor stonework gave the place an almost Tuscan flavour (although I've never been to Tuscany ... but I've seen it on the telly, so I know what I'm talking about).

'Ooh, look,' Chris squealed, as we ambled along behind our host.

'What? What? Where?'

'There,' she pointed. 'It's a huge stork's nest.'

And it was. A stork's nest. Without stork. But it was huge. At least six feet across, sitting atop one of the towers.

We were ushered into reception and given a chilled glass of cava whilst the hotel and its various facilities were described to us in detail. If we wanted exclusive use of the spa then that was all part of the service, we just had to choose a time. Not being partial to a rubdown from an oily-handed stranger and my feet messed about with, we graciously declined. We did book an early evening wine-tasting slot, though – it'd be rude not to.

Our first-floor room was delightful and opened onto a huge private balcony that was larger than the room itself, complete with sunloungers and a view of the river Tormes which ran directly under the hotel beneath our room. Inside the room was a complementary bottle of rosé cava on ice and a well-stocked wine fridge. This was no Travelodge.

We really couldn't have asked for a more marvellous introduction to our new country of residence than this, our first full day in Spain. We lunched like Catholic Kings on a sharing platter of local cheeses, meats and a bottle of Ribera down by the river – the raw milk cheese made from the endangered Varata goat was particularly moreish. This place is sometimes referred to as the *tierra del pan y del vino*, the land of bread and wine, and it's easy to see why – they've been growing vines on the site since 1366.

Afterwards, we headed upstairs to crack open the cava, which was followed by an unplanned siesta on the terrace, a habit I'm sure I could get used to. After a couple of coffees and a quick wash and brush-up, we headed down to enjoy one of the most amazing wine-tasting experiences.

We were treated to a highly informative session on a mezzanine floor above the wine cellar, and we sampled a good range of both whites and reds, the latter being our tipple of choice. After ripening under a Spanish sun – yes, it's a different sun to the one we get in the UK – the predominantly tempranillo grapes are matured in French and American oak barrels for twelve to eighteen months, before being bottled, uncorked and poured down my grateful throat.

It was then back to the room for another coffee, a quick splash and back out for an excellent dinner in the hotel's restaurant, accompanied of course by yet more of their delicious Ribera. Sadly, Chris had a bit of an iffy tummy next morning – not the wine, surely – so I breakfasted alone before reluctantly checking out.

Today was to be the last leg of our long journey south, but unlike the migratory birds we'd be following, we hung a left at

Seville and went southeast to Málaga, while they carried on to The Strait of Gibraltar and, ultimately, Africa.

3

We've Arrived

Are we nearly there, yet?' Chris asked, as we turned a corner, followed immediately afterwards by, 'Haven't we just been down this road?'

'Erm. I think so. This must be it here,' I replied, less than convincingly, my eyes glued to Google Maps.

'Is that her there, waving at us?' she said, pointing across the street to a woman standing in the doorway of the apartment block.

'Yeah, must be.'

Chris pulled the Mini over, it's cooling system working overtime in the afternoon heat, protesting at what we'd put her through these last four days – the poor little car clearly wasn't used to carrying a full load in these temperatures.

I'm pleased to report that, despite the old girl's age – the car, not Chris – the journey had been car-trouble-free, and apart from a momentary lapse in concentration at Cannock that put us on the M6 Toll, we had avoided every other toll road on the way down. Not only that, since disembarking the ferry and driving over six hundred miles through central Spain, we hadn't seen a single set of roadworks or a single bloody traffic cone – now you can't say that about England.

'Hi, Drew,' shouted Tamara, our hostess.

I should point out that an apartment block with screaming kids round the pool was *not* where we were planning to spend our retirement. Nice as the place was – in comparison to Bury, at least – this wasn't what we'd packed up our lives for and driven over a thousand miles to find. This was just another temporary layover, our home for the next few weeks at least: an Airbnb apartment on the Miraflores development in Calahonda.

'Welcome, welcome,' Tamara effused. 'You must be tired from the long drive. Let me grab a couple of things from you.'

We all struggled up the stairwell, laden with bags. After a whistle-stop tour of the well-appointed two-bedroom apartment, Tamara stood in the doorway swinging the keys.

'I'm off to play nine holes,' she said. 'Here's the keys. Call me if you have any problems.'

And with that, she was gone.

We both looked on as Tamara's head disappeared from view down the stairwell.

'She didn't hang about,' Chris said.

'She didn't, did she? Come on,' I said, turning to go back inside, 'let's crack open a bottle and chill out on the terrace for a bit.'

Opening a bottle of Hacienda Zorita's Ribera that we'd liberated from the hotel's wine fridge that morning, Chris went in search of wine glasses.

We relaxed on the terrace for a while, admiring our view of the Mediterranean, and savoured the rich tapestry of flavours teasing our taste buds. Two glasses in, we thought it might be wise to empty the car before we dozed off and it got broken into. For all we knew, this might be the rough end of Calahonda, although it didn't appear so.

* * *

The search for our new home in the sun had begun in the January. Chris had just taken early retirement at fifty-five, after a life spent nursing the good folk of Salford – and some of the bad ones too. I'd just been made redundant at Christmas, which didn't come as too great a surprise to me at the time, although I thought it was a bit unnecessary that I had to fly over to Malmö for lunch just so my boss could give me the bad news. I'd have much rather had the few hundred pounds it cost them to do that given to me as a Christmas bonus, but hey ho.

To be fair, I walked away with a decent package, and they delayed my termination date by a month so the company's private health insurance would still pick up the tab for my imminent hernia operation.

'You win some, you lose some,' I'd said to Chris when I broke the news from Sweden.

'Oh well, never mind,' she said. 'We were going to move to Spain next year anyway.'

So, in January, to celebrate Chris's birthday and the start of her retirement, we'd booked ourselves into a penthouse apartment for two weeks overlooking the main square in Mijas Pueblo, one of the prettiest whitewashed towns on the Costas. From there, we explored Andalucía, visiting different towns and villages in an effort to decide where to live.

We'd originally planned to move to the Costa Brava as we knew that area so well, but we ultimately felt it was going to be too damned cold in the winter months, with many places also closing down out of the peak tourist season. The much warmer southerly climes of the Costa del Sol, therefore, seemed the wiser choice for all-year-round living.

We learned a lot on that scoping out trip …

We learned that the Costa del Sol is bloody freezing at night in the winter months. That was a revelation. After getting back to the apartment after dinner, we'd both be huddled round a portable gas fire for warmth before giving up and climbing into bed shivering.

We learned that Spanish plumbing isn't the best. The place we'd chosen had one of those over-the-bath showers that gurgled when you turned on the tap, and then sent a pitiful trickle of water dribbling down, which by the time it hit your body had cooled down again to a temperature close to the freezing point of mercury. And the second person in the shower got what was left of the under-sized eight-litre tank. This was a three-bedroom flat for goodness' sake.

We learned that it's always wise to read the small print on Airbnb listings. 'What do you mean, there's no Wi-Fi?' Chris had said, aghast. So when we needed to browse online estate agent listings, we had to sit in the pub to use their Wi-Fi, which was at least a bit warmer than sitting in the apartment.

We learned that being able to order a *cerveza* in a bar wasn't much use when you urgently needed to see a dentist with only a smattering of Spanish. Thankfully, an English-speaking dentist on the coast sorted me out after my first failed attempt to give the local Spanish dentists my business. Thanks to my overly zealous consumption of a boiled sweet on Boxing Day, I'd rushed into my dental practice at home, only for the locum dentist to make a rather ham-fisted job of extracting my cracked tooth. A week later, with the drugs having no effect on my pain, the dentist in Fuengirola had to finish the job off. Chris told me to stop being soft, as growing up on army camps, she was (mis)treated by army dentists – which is all well and good, but she now has a phobia of dentists and hasn't been to see one for years.

We also learned that donkeys live in houses at night. Or they do in Mijas Pueblo. We saw them most nights filing into one of the houses off the back street by the entrance to our apartment after a long day ferrying selfie-stick-obsessed Asian tourists round the cobbled streets.

And finally, we rather crushingly learned that we couldn't afford a sea view! Not unless we wanted to rent a two-bed apartment rather than a three-bed villa with private pool.

We weren't quite as bad as some of those tyre-kickers you see on *A Place in the Sun* that have never been to Spain before or have holidayed in a different province. You know the ones I mean: the ones that want to buy a villa in a quiet location, yet close to bars and restaurants, with a private pool, sea views and a bloody rooftop solarium they'll never use, with a budget of forty grand. Do these fools know how hot it gets here in the summer? They'll be diving for the shade after ten minutes.

Our expectations on the other hand were far more reasonable. We were looking to rent somewhere for up to a thousand euros a month – with a nice shady terrace – whilst renting out our home in Bury to cover most of the costs. The only thing was, we'd have to be on the other side of the mountain.

That wasn't such a hardship, we agreed. Sure, a sea view would have been nice to wake up to, but there appeared to be a lot of decent-sized private villas in the Guadalhorce Valley that were within budget, and you wouldn't be paying tourist prices in the restaurants either.

With that in mind, we spent a fair amount of time on this trip navigating the treacherous Mijas mountain road to get to and from the town of Alhaurín El Grande on the other side. It seemed like a good place to base ourselves going forward. It was a typical Spanish working town of a reasonable size that meant everywhere was open throughout the year; unlike Mijas Pueblo, where we'd found many of the restaurants were closed in the winter evenings after the coaches had spirited away the hordes of day-trippers.

Alhaurín El Grande was also within a thirty-minute drive of Málaga city, the airport and the coastal towns of La Cala de Mijas, Marbella and Fuengirola. Ideal then, we thought.

The estate agents weren't really interested in entertaining our enquiries at such an early stage as we didn't plan to move over until the summer, so we contented ourselves with visits to different parts of the valley so that we had a rough idea of where we'd be happy to live.

Once the location was agreed, we reverted to holiday mode, vowing to work on our Spanish before moving over in the summer.

'*Hasta pronto*,' we said, hoping to return soon, as the plane left the tarmac, and we craned our necks to see if we could spot the mountain town of Alhaurín El Grande, somewhere down there on our left.

* * *

But here we were now. For real. In the words of the inimitable Peter Kay, we'd 'booked it, packed it, …' – well, you know how the phrase ends!

We woke up in Calahonda with a spring in our step … and went furniture shopping.

The removal van was setting off from Preston that day, and pretty soon we'd be in our rented villa with only half of it furnished. We needed terrace furniture – as there wasn't much call for that sort of thing in Bury – and at least one more of the three bedrooms kitted out if we planned to have guests staying over any time soon.

Before we'd decamped from Bury, we'd gotten rid of all but the essential things. We had detailed plans of the new place and knew what fitted where, so we'd sold half of our living room suite and variously given away or dumped the contents of two bedrooms and a garage.

I'd even done a car boot sale to get rid of some of the stuff, which is an enlightening experience. Especially 'up north', where they do like a bargain.

'How much do you want for that, mate?' an interested punter asked me, fingering a bedside lamp.

'Yours for two quid, mate,' I said, safe in the knowledge I hadn't pitched it at an unreasonable price.

I could see he was considering it.

'It's priced to sell,' I continued. 'That woman was just having a look at it too,' I added, trying to ramp up the pressure a little, like I was selling him Marbella timeshare options.

'It won't be here in ten minutes at this rate,' I gambled.

'I'll give you twenty pence.'

'I'll take fifty.'

'What about thirty?'

'It's yours, mate.'

Who said I was no good at this selling malarky?

'I don't suppose you want an Ainsley Harriet cookery book for another ten, do you?' I said hopefully, as he moved aside a wad of twenty-pound notes while he rummaged for thirty pence in coppers.

'God loves a trier, son,' the old boy sneered, before sloping off with his ill-gotten gains.

'Yeah, well watch you don't run into him sooner than you think,' I muttered under my breath.

Chris was in her element in the furniture shops. She likes nothing more than picking out a nice new piece of furniture or cushion for the house, and she was clearly revelling in the idea of kitting out the villa.

First up was a three-piece rattan suite to go at one end of the terrace, and we soon found what we were looking for in one of the big DIY outlets. That was the first purchase in the bag then, a good old Ted Rogers 3-2-1 – a three-seater, two-seater and single-seater, with a pouffe and matching glass-topped coffee table.

Next up, the second bedroom.

We were perusing a Danish furniture store, looking at double beds.

'This one's nice,' Chris said, giving the mattress a quick bum test.

We were looking at an oak bedframe with a headboard, a nice deep comfortable thermo mattress, and matching side tables. Out came the tape measure just to be sure.

'Yep. That'll fit,' I said. 'Let's order one.'

The assistant came over and Chris, whose Spanish runs to more than ordering food and drink, told the woman we'd like this bed, the mattress, and two of the matching side tables.

The woman noted our request then fired a question back at us. And that's where it began to unravel.

Anyone who has a smattering of any foreign language will tell you that they're fine ordering stuff and making up sentences, given a few seconds to find the right words. What they're not so good at is anticipating a question coming back at them. It's made doubly difficult when that question is asked not in the Queen's English – or in this case the King's Spanish – but in the local dialect.

Now the official language in Spain is Castilian Spanish, or *castellano* as they call it over here. But what they speak in Málaga Province is Andalusian. There's a school of thought that reckons Andalusian is not just a dialect, but a language in its own right, and we were starting to believe that to be the case.

'*¿Perdón?*' Chris said.

The woman repeated the question, possibly using the same words as the first time, but possibly not – it was difficult to tell. And from the blank look on our faces I think she got the message that we didn't have a clue what she was asking us. So she cut the question down to its essential parts and spoke very slowly and with clear diction.

'*So-m-ier,*' she said, pointing at the wall. '*¿Qué somier?*'

'I think she wants us to choose a base for the bed,' Chris said.

I followed the woman's finger and took in the range of bed bases and slats hanging off the wall, each with its own hefty price tag.

'What?' I said. 'You don't get the bottom bit with the bed? That's ridiculous. The mattress would be on the floor.'

Now according to this store's website, the mattress and bed springs are an 'incomparable duo'. In my view, the bloody bed frame and bed base should be an incomparable duo, or rather an 'inseparable duo', i.e. you can't have one without the other, and they most definitely shouldn't be priced individually.

It'd be like going in Curry's and choosing a 50" television and the assistant asking you if you'd like a remote control for it – 'well of course, I bloody would, and I don't expect to pay extra for it, neither', I'd have been shouting at them.

'Well that's how they must sell them over here,' Chris said.

'Marvellous.'

So what I thought was going to cost us about six hundred and fifty euros for a bed in the second bedroom that would be slept in a few times a year, was now going cost us eight hundred and fifty euros. No wonder the Danes were the happiest nation on earth – they had all our bloody money. At this point I was considering boycotting Danish bacon. But then I had a word with myself and resolved not to do anything too hasty.

'Thank God the wine's cheap over here,' I said, as I handed the woman my credit card.

And so to cheer myself up, that's where we went next: wine shopping.

4

Collecting the Keys

Two days later, and we were at the new place collecting the keys. But hang on a minute, haven't we only been in Calahonda three days?

Well, yes.

And haven't we booked that place for a month?

Erm, yes.

Then what's going on?

Ah, well. A bit of horse, cart, piss-up, brewery situation, as it happens. Or more accurately, our first experience of Spanish bureaucracy and the *mañana* attitude.

Allow me to explain …

* * *

After our January scouting trip, we returned in June for a proper look, giving ourselves eight days to secure a place and do all the necessary paperwork.

We'd already done the usual online property searches for long-term rentals in our price range and been left disappointed by our initial interactions with Spanish estate agents. Some of them have loads of villas listed, but when you enquire about them, they don't exist. They say they can't be bothered taking them off the website because they'll probably be back on the market again a year later.

It seems we'd wasted endless nights searching online, making a shortlist, and trying to pinpoint property locations.

You see, the other thing they do over here is they don't tell you where the property is. Oh no, that would be far too easy. They just drop a pin in the middle of the countryside and say it's not far from there, when in fact it could be miles away. We'd therefore become quite adept at spotting the house from the air using Google Earth – usually from the shape of the pool and its position in relation to the house.

The day after our arrival we'd arranged to view five properties, four of them with the one agent, Sofía. Having said that, we could have seen all five with Sofía, as the other quirk of the property market in Spain is that houses are often listed with several agents.

Confused? Yes, so were we.

The first place we went to see was with the other agent: a spacious two-storey house with a nice garden, a pool at the front and a balcony off the main bedroom. From the online photos it looked amazing. The reality was altogether different.

When we arrived, the gate was hanging off, the previous occupant had removed all the lightbulbs and lampshades, the owner had a section of one room partitioned off to keep his own stuff in, and the place needed painting. It was also on an urbanisation, with little privacy to the garden and over budget. My spirits slumped, as this one had been my favourite. So off we went to meet Sofía.

Sofía was really lovely and took us to see Chris's personal favourite first, a new villa with wonderful views up to the town and the Sierra de Mijas. It was new because the owner, Olivia, had apparently knocked down her Dad's old place and built a single-storey, white, three-bedroom finca there instead. It stood in the middle of an acre of land with lots of fruit trees and an olive grove – just what Chris had dreamed of for years.

And here was me thinking we weren't taking on a farm.

As soon as we walked in the place, I loved the light-coloured floor tiles and white walls – in estate agent speak, it was 'light, bright and airy'. There was only one bathroom, which was a bit of a compromise, and a shower rather than a bath, but I couldn't remember the last time I'd used the bath in Bury – except to clean my trumpets in, but don't tell Chris that.

I knew Chris was loving it too. Stepping onto the terrace to admire the mountain, with Alhaurín El Grande gleaming white halfway up it, we looked at one another and knew what the other was thinking: that's a pretty special view.

'What do you think?' Sofía said.

'It's beautiful,' Chris said. 'What kind of fruit trees are those?'

There was a brief exchange of Spanish with Olivia.

'You've got lots of oranges, some lemons, figs, pomegranates, plums, apples, peaches, avocados—'

'Wow!'

'And the olives, of course.'

'It's great. And the pool?' I said, looking down into a dirty big hole in the ground beside the finca.

'That will have white tiles and pool lights when it's finished.'

Chris and I wandered all around the property and were getting quite excited. The land looked manageable, all the trees were on irrigation pipes, and there were just a few plants at the front that would need watering by hand.

'The villa at the back belongs to Olivia's sister and her husband,' Sofía said, as she followed us round. 'And the house on the other side belongs to a local farmer, who comes down now and again to tend the land.'

'Does it have air conditioning?' I asked, as I hadn't seen any units on the walls inside.

'There are vents built into the lounge and bedrooms, but if you want air con then you'll need to buy the unit to go on the outside.'

'And roughly how much would that cost us?'

'Oh, I'm not sure. Maybe about eight hundred euros. And Olivia is waiting for the electricity to be connected.'

I turned to face Sofía. 'It has no electricity?'

'Yes, it does, but just enough for the builder at the moment.'

Apparently, they have what's called 'builder's electric' over here, which is a single-phase electricity supply for the builder to use, but once it becomes occupied, it needs to be switched to a bigger, more expensive, three-phase supply.

24

'Ok,' I said slowly, mulling it over. 'And how long before the pool is finished, and the electricity is connected?'

'The owner's applied for the electricity, and the pool should be finished next month.'

'Great. Shall we go and look at the other properties now?'

The next place we went to see was up on the side of a hill, and on the approach, it looked like another contender. As we got out of the cars, we were accosted by two dogs.

'Oh, the dogs come with the house,' Sofía said.

'Sorry?'

'The dogs. If you want them. They're yours. The owner doesn't want them.'

Who the hell moves out of a house and doesn't take their dogs? No wonder there are dog rescue centres all along the Costas.

'Aw. They're lovely,' Chris said. 'But we hadn't planned on having dogs. Not yet anyway.'

The outside space here was a lot smaller and more manageable. The garden was landscaped, the pool was nice, there was a wine cellar under the pool and there were marvellous views of the mountain and the valley ... however, the house was tiny inside, and all done out in pine. Definitely not to our taste.

Rejoining our cars, Sofía said we wouldn't like the third property, so it was off to see the fourth one on our list. But as we drove there, Chris and I decided that Olivia's house was perfect for us, and the last one would have to be pretty special to beat it.

As it happened, the owner never turned up to let us in, so we just told Sofía to take us back to Olivia's for another look.

And that was it, all done and dusted in the space of an hour.

We agreed the rental price, which was bang on budget, and Sofía said we needed to pay two month's deposit to secure it. Then, on completion, a month's rent in advance, and half of her agent's fee, equivalent to half a month's rent. That's how it works over here most of the time – the renters usually have to pay half of the agency fees. And that's why the owners have several agents marketing the same property, usually at different prices too.

We agreed to move over in the middle of August, with two weeks' leeway either side, dependent on the pool being finished and the electricity being connected.

And that was it.

We'd found our dream home.

* * *

So why are we now living in an apartment in Calahonda? Well, by the end of July, and with most of Spain's workers going on holiday in August, the electricity company still hadn't upgraded the supply – Olivia had even enlisted the mayor's help to put some pressure on. And we didn't want to miss the end of the Spanish summer. So, in desperation, we just booked the ferry, put our house up for rent, organised the removal van for early September and booked an apartment for a month.

Then sod's law kicked in: soon after we'd booked everything, the villa got its long-awaited electricity supply connected in the middle of August – miracle of miracles – and was ready for us. But by this time, we'd paid for a month in Calahonda.

And that's why we're in Spain now, with two houses to live in. Maybe we could have one each! ... although I'd have to drop my washing off every week, of course.

The house we *wanted* to live in was an empty shell, our furniture was in transit, and my Mum and Dad would arrive in two days.

Don't panic Mr Mainwaring! Don't Panic!

I'm not panicking. The situation just requires a cool head.

Right, here's what we did: we signed the final contract (for eleven months – that story can wait) ... we got a quick tour from Olivia (in Spanish) of the workings of the pool pump and fuse box ... we found out the villa had no mains sewerage but was connected to a septic tank instead (which explained the periscope sticking out of the ground halfway down the garden) – always ask the right questions before committing! ... we paid Olivia a month's rent ... we paid Sofía half her fee ... we shared a glass of cava on the terrace with them both before waving them off ... we had the internet man round within the hour (that story can wait too) ... and then we jumped in the pool ...

5

I've Gone Back

… and then I went to the airport and flew to the UK.

Believe it or not, that's exactly what happened.

I'd only left the country six days earlier, and now I was back in the UK – in grey, miserable Luton, of all places.

You see, when I said, 'no going back', I didn't really mean it. Not just yet anyway.

Thankfully, I'd only come back on business, but boy, was that a whirlwind of a week. From Bury to Portsmouth to Santander to Málaga and back over to Luton.

And this was going to be my life until my work contract finished at the end of October. But then I was jacking it all in.

So, I'd just left my lovely wife on her own in a foreign country, in an Airbnb, without her furniture, and with no friends or family for support, while I went back to work in the UK.

And to bring into sharp relief what we'd left behind here, this morning we'd received a picture of our granddaughter, Jessica, looking resplendent and pleased as punch in her uniform on her first day at school.

On our way down to Portsmouth last week, we'd detoured via Luton Airport to drop my car off so I could use it this week.

So, while I was settling into my room at the Holiday Inn Luton South, waiting for the kettle to boil and wrestling with the lid of a tiny carton of UHT milk, Chris was sitting on the terrace in Calahonda, enjoying the heady scent of jasmine mixed with the Mediterranean sea air and finishing off another bottle of red.

Over the coming weeks, whenever we were apart, we had to content ourselves with long telephone conversations and shared photographs of the weather and what we were eating and drinking.

Two days after I'd deserted Chris, though, she at least had some company when my parents arrived in Málaga to stay with her. The apartment had everything they needed and was a nice place to relax in the evening – that was until the karaoke started up in the poolside bar. We still don't know who the wailing banshee was, or indeed what sex it was, but it wasn't pleasant, the few times I had to endure it. And they didn't mention that in the brochure.

This first business trip away soon ended. I'd been working abroad for years, usually in mainland Europe on large IT contracts, and I typically flew out on a Monday for three nights. So it was that I found myself at Luton Airport that first Thursday evening, looking forward to getting back to Chris and my parents and having a couple of glasses on the terrace. It was our wedding anniversary, so I didn't want to hang around.

As a seasoned business traveller, I knew how to pack within the airline's guidelines and avoid unnecessary delays by having to wait at the luggage carousel. So, I had my regulation wheelie case, I was waiting to board the flight (which was already an hour late), and I could see the airline assistant working her way down the line attaching baggage tags to cases like mine.

This was a new airline ploy I'd heard about but hadn't seen in action before, as up to now, I'd been driving to Luton for this contract. Before she reached me, I could feel the red mist descending.

The upshot was she wanted to put my bag in the hold. There was only room for forty-five bags in the overhead bins, she said. How ridiculous. Unless the scheduled one-hundred-and-eighty-seat A320 had been swapped for a twin-prop Cessna, that was a blatant lie. Despite my protestations, she put the tag on and moved on to have the same argument with the woman behind me.

Now anyone who knows me will happily tell you that I'm a very even-tempered, easy-going sort of guy. It takes a lot to upset me usually, but this check-in clerk was doing a fine job. I don't know if airline staff are trained to provoke the passengers – or 'self-loading cargo', as they apparently call us – or if they occasionally misinterpret their own airline's ever-changing baggage guidelines, but I wasn't a happy bunny.

I shuffled through the gate with all the late-season holidaymakers, and crossing the tarmac, I reached down and ripped off the tag, putting it discreetly in my pocket. I looked over my shoulder, half-expecting the attendant to come racing after me, but there was no sign of her.

Despite being one of the last to board, on entering the aircraft, I found the luggage bins practically empty – no surprise – and so I stowed my bag and took my seat. The woman who boarded in front of me was even more brazen – she didn't even bother taking the tag off her bag.

And so began my membership of the speedy boarding scheme. At least I'd only have to suffer this routine for another six weeks … or so I thought.

I dashed out of the airport at Málaga and got straight in a taxi, but I didn't make it back to the apartment before the clock struck midnight. I'd missed our wedding anniversary after all. But at least the taxi hadn't turned into a pumpkin, and I hadn't lost a shoe on the way … and there was some of that Ribera waiting for me.

6

Moving In

The following morning, we were up early with my folks and drove them up the mountain road to Alhaurín and our new villa. The removal van was arriving, and we were excited to be putting furniture in the house.

My parents liked the place – although they're the type of people who wouldn't have told us if they didn't, anyway. Or maybe Dad would and then been told off by Mum. So, overall, yes, I think they liked the place. I think Dad was already planning his next trip so he could lie in the Spanish sun all day, which is generally his preferred pastime.

My Dad lives for his holidays. He's a holidaying pioneer in many respects – he was the inventor of the two-centre holiday. It's true! One summer in the early seventies, he took my mother and us three kids up to Loch Lomond in the caravan, where after enduring a solid week of wall-to-wall rain, he decided to hitch up the caravan and drive us four hundred miles south to East Anglia for a second week of beachside sunny heaven. Nothing comes between my Dad and that big fuzzy ball of orange warmness in the sky.

'I see the hole in the wall is fixed?' I said to Chris, as I stood on the terrace.

'Yes, Olivia's cousin repaired it. Apparently, it was him who built the place.'

'How much did it cost?'

'Nothing. He wouldn't take any money from me.'

'Aw. That was nice of him,' I said.

And you know, I've often found this with Spanish workmen. If the job's no big deal, they won't take any money from you. Our Spanish mechanic, Paco, is the same if it's something and nothing. We took the Mini in once for its annual service, and when we went back later to collect it, he said it hadn't needed one. He'd compared the current mileage to last year's – which admittedly was only about eight hundred miles – and decided nothing needed doing. If that had been one of the expat Brit garages, they'd probably have serviced it and charged us an arm and a leg … or perhaps not serviced it and still charged us an arm and a leg.

Paco got a fiver anyway for his honesty, which he tried to shrug off.

Since we've lived in Spain, we've heard a lot of stories about people being ripped off by expat workers, so it pays to shop locally and learn the lingo. In fact, before Paco was recommended to me, I'd used an English mechanic. I thought one of my tyres might have been low on tread. The lad said it probably had another thousand miles on it and that I should come back in a few weeks.

As it happened, the tyre sailed through it's first Spanish MOT three months and two thousand miles later, and Paco was amused that I kept calling by every couple of months and asking him to double-check it. He'd have a quick look and shake his head, laughing, and off I'd go again. It was about a year and six thousand miles later before it needed changing.

'How come you had a hole in the wall?' Dad asked.

'It was the internet guy,' I said. 'I could have killed the pillock. We'd only been in the place an hour, and he comes round, drills a hole from the inside to the outside, gives his drill a good hard shove at the end and takes a bloody big chunk out of the cement.'

'We were mortified,' Chris chipped in. 'We had to ring the estate agent, Sofía, and ask her to apologise profusely to Olivia. She came straight round and told us not to worry, and that she'd send someone round to repair it.'

'And you know the worst thing about it?' I said. 'When Olivia came round, she pointed out the wiring ducts that ran all through the house from the rear. He could have come in at the back of the house, apparently, and used pull-throughs to get the wire to this side for the router, instead of drilling through the front of the villa.'

'Yeah,' said Chris. 'I wish she'd have still been here when he came. We had no idea. She'd turned a few people away who wanted to rent the house from her because she didn't like the look of them. Sofía said Olivia really liked us when she met us and knew we'd look after the place for her. And what's the first thing we do? Put a hole in the wall.'

The rest of the day went without a hitch, thankfully.

The removal van arrived, and as the boxes were offloaded and dumped in the relevant rooms, I made a beeline for the ones containing my precious audio equipment. So while Chris was busy in the kitchen unpacking pots and pans with my Mum – and my Dad was sitting on the terrace sunbathing – *my* focus was entirely on setting up the sound system in the living room, which consisted of a set of Bowers & Wilkins speakers, a turntable for an impressive selection of jazz records I'd been collecting since the age of thirteen, and a digital audio media player containing hundreds of digitised CDs.

After toiling away for half an hour and making sure all the wiring was neatly tucked out of sight, it was time to see if I'd made all the right connections. Like a kid in a sweet shop, I rolled an appreciative finger over my extensive twelve-inch vinyl collection. It had to be something special for the first play, and my eyes were drawn to Steely Dan's 1980 classic album, *Gaucho*. I slipped it carefully out of its sleeve, blew a few dust particles off it, spun it around between my fingers and placed it gently over the spindle. Not even having the patience to close the lid, I hit the play button and watched, mesmerised, as the disc began to rotate, and the needle began to lift from its cradle … only to be stopped in its tracks by the in-transit retaining arm.

Bugger.

That's like watching your football team score the winning goal in the dying moments of the game, only for the fat linesman on the far side (who couldn't possibly have been keeping up with the play) to raise his flag for offside.

At the second time of asking – with the operator having corrected his earlier schoolboy error – the referee blew for a penalty kick in the opposition box. The crowd hushed as the striker strode forward, and there was that scintillating crackle of static before the ball was struck sweetly into the back of the net, and the drummer heralded in the opening bars of *Babylon Sisters*. A full forty-five seconds later, the unmistakable voice of Donald Fagen poured out of the B&Ws like lava down a mountain and singed my toes.

This track was later described on the renowned music review website, Pitchfork, as a 'melody that creeps into the room like toxic fog', and here it was now, swirling round my ankles like some mythical sea mist.

The illusion was short-lived, however.

'What're you doing?' Chris said, hands on her hips in the kitchen doorway.

'Just listening to Steely Dan,' I sheepishly replied, with that face you have when you're supposed to have been hoovering and she comes home to find you watching Sky Sports.

'Well make yourself useful and go and assemble the bed.'

'OK.'

'Oh, and turn that rubbish off!'

The cheek of it. Well they say that opposites attract.

When I'd stopped messing around and located my toolbox, the house gradually began to take shape. The removal firm we used were brilliant. And to our great relief, every single piece of furniture, crockery and glassware – and jazz album – arrived in perfect condition. It wasn't cheap to ship it all over, but this Spanish finca was looking more like a home to us now it had our furniture in it.

As soon as the removal lads had finished, Mum stripped down to her swimming costume and got in the pool. It was so nice to see the old girl enjoying herself in a swimming pool ... in my garden ... in Spain.

Today was definitely one of life's good days.

And then we locked up and went back to Calahonda. Well we couldn't all sleep here yet, could we? There was only one bed.

The next morning, we went furniture shopping. Again.

Oh, joy! This time we bought a dining set for the other side of the terrace from the first shop we went in. And with that one in the bag nice and early, we went down to the beach for the rest of the day.

Back at the apartment, I made seafood paella for everyone, using the new paella pan Chris had bought me for our anniversary – I like a good kitchen accessory. We washed it down with a big jug of homemade sangria, a recipe that's been perfected over the years, the basics of which came from watching a loose-wristed barman make it in Fuerteventura.

Incidentally, the Canary Island of Fuerteventura is often thought to mean 'strong winds', hence its appeal to kitesurfers, but it actually translates as 'strong fortune'. In contrast, due to the prevalence of strong winds, it was the Costa del Sol that was originally dubbed the Costa del Viento (*viento* means wind) by the Andalusians who lived in the small fishing villages that dotted the shoreline. It was only in the 1950s when Franco wanted to attract tourists that they started referring to it in holiday brochures as the Costa del Sol (*sol* of course meaning sun). The afternoon winds that more often than not roar down the Guadalhorce Valley and shake the palm trees are quite legendary in these parts.

That evening, we watched in amazement as a Waning Gibbous Moon rose over Calahonda to paint a shimmering seascape before our eyes, and all was well with the world once again.

7

First Night

The next few weeks passed in a blur of flights in the midst of an unreasonably crammed schedule. After another week in Luton, I'd first of all nipped over to Dublin for a stag weekend (thankfully with no significant casualties). Back in Spain, Chris had packed up the apartment, my parents had returned home, and we were ready to take up residence in the villa on my return.

I landed in Málaga on the Sunday afternoon. But as Jennifer Hudson sang in *Dreamgirls*, it was for 'One Night Only', and she very kindly came to the airport to collect me – Chris that is, not Jennifer – and then we duly got lost on the way back in Málaga's version of spaghetti junction.

Road signage is not something they do terribly well in Spain – you often come across motorways that suddenly split into two with the same city names above both bits, and you have to quickly decide how you roll the dice – and this was the first time Chris had driven from the airport to Alhaurín. At this early stage in our adventure we hadn't learned all the road numbers yet, or the names of the other towns you had to head for when you were trying to go somewhere else in that general direction. After a half-hour detour round the suburbs of the city, we finally got back on track and headed inland.

On the way home, Chris was telling me more about her online friend, Kim, who along with her husband Martin and their labrador had emigrated to Spain the day before us. They were now the proud owners of a finca up in the mountains on the eastern side of Málaga in a small town called Árchez, population three men and a dog – make that four men, a woman and two dogs now. Chris and Kim had struck up a friendship on Facebook after sharing thoughts on a Spanish expat forum.

They were apparently getting on like a house on fire, which is an unfortunate way of putting it, as fires are an all-too-common occurrence along the Costas. Like me, Martin worked abroad all week, and so the two of them found themselves isolated and alone for a few days each week and would send messages of support to each other. I was delighted Chris had found someone else to share this new Spanish experience with while I was away from home.

As we turned off the main road and headed down the single lane track that led to our house, Chris blurted out, 'Oh, there are some weird sounds in our garden at night.'

'What kind of weird sounds?'

'Just odd noises when I'm sitting on the terrace. I'm sure something had a dip in our pool. I heard a definite splash.'

'Did you go and investigate?'

'Are you kidding? I was going to put the pool lights on but thought I might regret it. I think I'd rather not know what's out there when I'm sitting here on my own.'

'I thought I was the wuss,' I said.

'You are,' she laughed. 'Even Alicia next door was surprised I didn't have a dog, living out here on my own during the week. Oh, and I've bought some big candles for the terrace. It's all about the ambience,' she said.

I thought it was all about the bass, myself, but what do I know?

When we made it home, we cracked open a bottle of champagne and relaxed on the terrace under a clear Spanish sky, with the pool lights providing illumination for a chorus of stridulating cicadas. It was one of those moments in your lifetime that you never forget.

We'd made it at last: our first night in our very own (erm, rented) *Place in the Sun*.

'We've come a long way together, haven't we?' Chris said, as I was topping up her glass, and she made no attempt to remove the smug smile from her face.

'We have,' I said, as I reflected on the twelve hundred miles I'd just flown to be there with her.

And then I jumped on a plane the next day and flew another twelve hundred back to Dublin, although this time I was just transiting through the place on my way to a ten-day stint in Chicago on business, an eventful trip that included a suicide jumper from the top floor balcony of my hotel.

When I finally landed back in Spain, exhausted from the transatlantic flight via Heathrow, there was a storm brewing. Theresa May might have just told the Conservative Party Conference that she planned to trigger Article 50 by the end of March 2017 to formally start the Brexit withdrawal process, but that wasn't what had set the cat amongst the pigeons – the Spanish had much bigger fish to fry ... people were calling it 'Paella Gate'. Jamie Oliver had committed the cardinal sin – according to the Spanish – of putting chorizo in a paella. The Spanish media were calling him a culinary terrorist, and Jamie even received death threats from some Iberian bedroom-dwelling keyboard warriors – usually blokes with no girlfriend who haven't washed for a month and live with their mum. When Chris picked me up from the airport, she swore me to secrecy.

'Don't ever tell any of our Spanish neighbours we sometimes put chorizo in the paella,' she said.

'Don't worry,' I said. 'You're secret's safe with me. What's for dinner anyway?'

'Chicken and chorizo paella,' she said, cracking up.

8

First Guest

As we ate dinner on the terrace that evening, we could hear the neighbours having some sort of row. Or maybe it was just Alicia on the phone again. If it was a row, whoever it was with was definitely losing.

Alicia's house was about eighty yards away – across open land and a wire fence, so there was a clear line of sight – and when Alicia used the phone you knew about it. If the person she was talking to was up in the village, they didn't need to bother ringing, as I'm sure they could have heard her from there.

Her husband, José, was a hardworking old fella – and henpecked by the sound of it. His age was a bit of a mystery, but we reckoned he was in his late sixties or early seventies. Either that or he'd had a really tough life. He was a farmer with a small two-acre plot who busied himself in his garden a few days a week, planting and watering all kinds of fruit and vegetables. He had a gorgeous old cat with a shiny black coat that followed him around the garden like a dog, and several other cats that he left food out for too. The more the merrier, it seemed, to keep the pests and rodents off his crops.

The black cat would come and happily sit on the terrace with us in the evening, allowing us to stroke her. She was clearly the matriarch to the others, a motley bunch of cats of all colours. The rest of them hadn't had human contact soon enough as kittens so were quite feral. They wouldn't let you stroke them, but they didn't turn their noses up at the odd tin of tuna.

We were cat people ourselves. I had never had pets growing up – unless you count two goldfish from a passing fair – but Chris had dogs and cats as a child. Together, we had a few cats, in ones and twos over the years. If they could avoid doing anything daft like getting run over then they generally lived to a ripe old age. In fact, we might have moved to Spain sooner had our last cat, Liquorice, not lived so long. But we didn't want to upset her by bringing her to a new country. She hung on for another year in the end to reach the age of twenty, like her stepsister, Barney, before her. It was poor old Charlie that met a premature death crossing the road, sadly.

Given that we planned to return to the UK regularly to visit family, we felt we shouldn't rush into taking on pets of our own, but we were more than happy to share José's.

He was a lovely old thing – José as well as the cat. He didn't move very fast and walked with a stick, so I felt sorry for him toiling away in the heat sometimes. He had a nasty cough, which Chris reckoned was probably chronic bronchitis. He also had a proper broad Andalusian accent, so it was difficult knowing what he was talking about sometimes.

We'd usually bump into each other while I was out doing a bit of weeding. His opening gambit as he came over to the fence was *mucho trabajo*. Yes, it is a lot of work, I would concur. And then he'd usually have a whinge about the government and taxes (I think).

I couldn't really see what his beef was, as he and Alicia were both of retirement age. I could only think it was the property taxes he was moaning about. He had this house in the *campo* (Spanish countryside) and a townhouse up in the village, as do a lot of Spaniards in the area. They used to live in town once it started getting a bit colder, as the *campo* houses are detached with no insulation. I know he sold a bit of his fruit and veg to the local petrol stations, and as long as they had their Spanish pensions coming in – which are much more generous than our UK state pensions – then he shouldn't have been short of a few bob.

After a while, I'd look forward to my interactions with José. And Luis on the other side, who was a retired doctor. Luis's wife, Rosa, was the landlady's sister, but you couldn't hear her on the telephone.

The following day, we had to prepare for the arrival of our first guest at the villa. Our eldest daughter, Steph, was coming to stay with us for a few days – and no doubt check we weren't frittering away her inheritance too quickly.

As a result, we had to be up and about to tidy the house and garden. I didn't know why that should involve me, as I'd only spent one brief night here in the last three weeks, so I couldn't have made the place untidy.

Chris said I made the place look untidy just by being there. Charming. I was also still feeling a bit jetlagged too.

The house and terrace were Chris's responsibility. The garden was mine. So, oddly, Chris began by cleaning the pool, but I wasn't complaining.

The first time she'd cleaned the pool was while I was in the US. Olivia had popped round to show her what to do, although I don't know why, as Olivia had never had a pool herself before. Chris said it was like the blind leading the blind, and to make it worse, it had been done in a foreign language, of course – Andalusian again, I presume.

To be fair to Olivia, she did have a few words of English, but we'd insisted to her that it was important for our education that we conversed in Spanish, which from our end usually involved a lot of nodding and '*sí, sí, sí*'-ing, followed by a pregnant pause while Olivia waited for a reply to the question she'd just asked that didn't warrant a yes or no reply. That was my standard response to most things Olivia said to me: '*sí*' – for all I knew, she could have been asking me if it was ok to double the rent, and I would have been happily nodding and smiling like an idiot, going '*sí, sí*'.

Chris had taken on board everything Olivia had said about cleaning the pool – or the bits she understood – and then she'd gone online to get some proper instructions off YouTube.

And she did a grand job of cleaning it too – it looked immaculate when she'd finished. Although I wasn't allowed in, just in case I got it dirty again before Steph arrived.

Meanwhile, I cracked on with the garden.

I'd brought a bit of basic gardening equipment with me from England: a spade, a fork, a rake, etc. – I'd left the lawn mower and strimmer at the old house for our future tenants to use – so I couldn't tackle anything too ambitious. The pool was set back three metres from the side of the terrace, so you had to traverse a bit of earth to get to it. We thought we might put a small lawn around it so you could go from pool to terrace with wet feet if you wanted to. I therefore cracked on with weeding and levelling that part of the garden ready for some grass seed in the spring.

The following morning, it was off to the airport to collect Steph. On arriving back at the villa, we gave her the guided tour, and she was bowled over ... until we got to the bathroom.

'Oh, by the way,' I said. 'We've no mains sewerage, so use the waste basket for toilet paper, please.'

'Really?'

'Yes, if it didn't come out of you, it doesn't go down the loo!' I waxed lyrically.

And so was born my favourite phrase for all new guests.

That weekend, we showed Steph round the area, trying out some of the local eateries with her, and generally frolicking in the pool and languishing in the glorious sunshine. We might have overdone the celebratory mood on the first night, though, as she didn't surface again until the afternoon – we even had to go in and wake her up. Which was surprising seeing as we hadn't taken delivery of the most expensive bed in Spain yet and so she was having to sleep on an inflatable mattress.

In her defence, she'd left the UK at the crack of dawn and had a demanding job as a nurse – that was her excuse anyway. Nothing to do with the half-empty bottle of brandy then. We didn't begrudge her the lie in, we were just concerned about her. As parents, you're always worrying about your kids, even when they're thirty-six.

And as I'd found since being here, you get a bloody great night's sleep. We weren't near any main roads, farms, dog kennels or noisy neighbours – apart from when Alicia was on the phone – and we'd moved to a very peaceful location at the end of a single-lane road. And the blinds – or *persianas* as they're called here – are brilliant. All the houses seem to have them; mainly to block out the sunlight in the heat of the day, but when you wake up in the morning, you've no idea if it's night or day until you open them.

In fact, it's so dark with the *persianas* down that you can't see your hand in front of your face. Which is fine until you want to quietly get up in the night for a wee and have to walk round the bed, avoiding the furniture on memory alone – the sharp corners of an oak bed do wonders for restoring any memory lapses. Thankfully, unless I've been drinking several pints, the need to get up in the night is a relatively rare occurrence. For now, at least.

That evening, we were relaxing on the terrace in the glow from the candlelight, listening to the sounds of the *campo*. Earlier on, we'd been laughing about a scary virtual reality game that Chris and I had tried out a few weeks ago on my phone.

'Dad, can I try out that VR *Sisters* game?' Steph asked me.

'Are you sure you can handle it? You know what you're like with scary experiences,' I said.

'Ha! You can talk,' she said. 'I remember you running and screaming like a baby at The Forbidden Corner in Yorkshire when that skeleton popped out from behind the door.'

'I only ran because you lot were screaming and running towards me.'

'Yeah, course you were.'

I went and dug out the VR headset and set the game up on my phone for her. I gave her my Bluetooth headphones too to make it even more immersive. Describing the game online, you're warned to 'be careful where you look, because something doesn't want you here'.

'Is it really bad?' Steph asked.

'Why, are you having second thoughts now?'

'No. And you're not going to touch me, are you?'

'No, I promise,' I said. What did she take me for? I knew what was coming, so I didn't need to add another dimension of horror myself. I slotted the phone into the headset after pressing play, and we watched as she perched on the edge of her seat, looking all around and behind her in nervous anticipation.

The premise of the game is you're sitting in a dark spooky house, all alone, with a lightning storm going on outside and sinister music playing. Steph can't hear us, but we can hear her, of course, and we're rolling about laughing at her.

'I don't like this,' she said. 'I think there's someone in here with me.' Then a few moments later, 'Argh! I can hear a girl's voice, and there's a spooky doll over there.'

She continued to move around the sofa all of a jitter, looking over her shoulder every few seconds.

'That doll's gone,' she said, even more concerned now.

I knew what was coming next and knew when she looked down to her side it was going to be sitting on the sofa with her. Then she jumped up out of her seat and let out a blood-curdling scream, ripping off the headset as she did so. My headphones flew one way, and my phone the other, landing a few yards away on the driveway. With the noise she made, it's a wonder nobody called the *policía*.

'I've had enough of that,' she said. 'I don't like it.'

I must admit, it is quite unsettling. For some reason, though, my girls love egging each other on to do things like stay the night in haunted houses or go to late night Halloween experiences where men with chainsaws jump out and chase you. They're all mad!

Of all of our four daughters, I think it was Steph who was the most vocal about us not leaving the family behind in the UK. She's very close to her Mum, as are the other three, but I do recall she made the most fuss.

A few days before we left the UK, we hosted a big celebratory dinner for a large group of our nearest and dearest friends and family at a local restaurant. The food and wine flowed freely – well it would do because I was paying for it – and towards the end of the evening, the four girls invited us outside for a moment.

As I stepped outside the restaurant, I was rather hoping there'd be a little red two seater sports car in the car park with a big ribbon on it, but they just wanted to tell us both how much they loved us … and to try and talk us out of going.

The girls presented us with a little memento to remember them by – as if we were going to forget them in a hurry – and then we all went back in the restaurant to continue getting drunk.

Having seen how happy we both were to have finally pursued our dream and to be taking it easy in Spain – by the way, at this point of course, I was far from 'taking it easy' just yet – Steph was convinced we'd done the right thing, and that, given half a chance, she wouldn't have been too far behind us.

The following day, Chris dropped us both off in town where I rode in a taxi with Steph to the airport. Unfortunately, we both still had jobs to go to.

This time, while Steph flew back to Manchester, I boarded a flight to Liverpool to pick up my car from the long stay car park – if I could remember which row I'd parked it in weeks ago on the way to that stag party in Dublin – and then drive two hundred miles south to Luton again.

Oh, what joy.

9

Short Back and Sides

During that last brief stay in Spain, and while Steph was with us, I thought I'd better try and get my hair cut – I couldn't put it off any longer. After all my recent globetrotting and not being able to see my usual barber back home anymore, my hair was beginning to look a bit untidy, so it was off to throw myself headfirst – literally – into another daunting new experience … finding a Spanish barber and trying to convey to them that I wanted a number two up the back and sides and left short and spiky on top, with a bit of hair gel to finish off.

'Good luck,' Chris called out, as I borrowed her car keys.

'I'm gonna need it,' I replied.

At this point, I had no idea if I needed an appointment or not, so I just had to wing it. I had a quick look online for barbers and there were several to choose from. I plumped for one with five-star reviews and headed out to find it. Peering through the window I could see two barbers hard at work and nobody waiting. In I went and took a seat, pretending to read a Spanish motorbike magazine while I waited.

Occasionally, I'd look furtively at my phone and start talking to myself. They must have thought they had a right nutter just walk in. All I was trying to do was memorise these new Spanish words that Professor Google was telling me were the ones I needed. Then another punter walked in and took a seat opposite me.

Before long, one of the barbers had finished. In the UK, the protocol is first in the door, next in the chair. I put the magazine down on the table, then the other lad got up and walked over to the chair. I was starting to worry I'd gotten the protocol wrong, and I needed an appointment. Five minutes later, the other barber finishes and it's just me now in the waiting area.

Another quick look at Google Translate, and I waited patiently. The young barber turned and gestured for me to take my place in the hot seat. It was now or never.

I seated myself down and he started to cloak me up. I was praying he wasn't the chatty type.

'*¿Qué quiere?*' he said.

Here we go, I thought, he's asking me how I want it. My big moment had arrived.

'*Número dos y puntiagudo en la parte superior,*' I mumbled back in response.

Why is it that when you're not confident in what you're saying, especially in a foreign language, you turn the volume down to a whisper?

'*¿Qué?*' he enquired.

'*Número dos y puntiagudo en la parte superior,*' I said, a little louder this time, but no more confident. I mean, had Professor Google even ever had his haircut? I didn't know, did I? I knew the number two bit was right, but as for the rest of it, it was anyone's guess. I could have just asked him to put blonde highlights in.

The barber returned an even blanker look than the first time.

'*¿Qué?*' he said, again, screwing his eyes up.

Was I speaking a foreign language or something? Well clearly, I was, but I thought it was the same language he'd been using from birth. I supposed I had to make allowances for the fact I wasn't fluent in Andalusian yet, but why is it that when you go in a barber shop, they don't seem to know what your usual style is, when it's clearly there, staring them in the face? The evidence is on your head, albeit a bit longer than you like it. How hard can that be? I've not come in for a bloody perm, have I?

That was it. I'd failed vocally. I could have either got up and walked out or soldiered on. So I resorted to hand gestures. An arm appeared from under my cloak, and I motioned round the back of my head.

'*Número dos*,' I said for the third time, checking in the mirror to see if he was getting my drift or not. And then my hand moved to the top of my head, and I did a passable impression of Stan Laurel, pulling my hair up with my fingers. I was on the *puntiagudo* bit, and I bravely added *con gel* to inform him I'd need it gelling at the end for it to be spiky, although I pronounced *gel* as *jel* (as you would) and not *hel* as I should have done.

It was a bloody minefield this foreign language malarkey.

The young lad seemed to have got the message anyway. Either that or he'd just lost interest. All the same, he reached for his razor and off he went up the back and sides. I started to relax a little as clumps of hair fell about my shoulders.

I don't know about you, but I love having my hair cut. It feels great getting it all neat and tidy again. And the young lad seemed to at least know what he was doing.

Having said that, experience is no guarantee of a good quality haircut. When I was a teenager and trying to make a splash on the music scene, I used an old barber underneath the railway arches opposite the Haçienda nightclub in Manchester. One of the lads in our eighties' pop band dragged me there once and said the fella did a decent job, although thinking back, my mate had a bald head at the time, until he turned up to a gig one day with a pioneering weave!

This old boy would have BBC Radio 4 on, and he'd be listening to *Play for Today* and be totally oblivious to whoever was sitting in the chair. When your turn came, he'd sit you down, get the razor out, and give you a number one up the back and sides first. Then he'd remember you were a paying customer and might have some preference for how the top bit looked at least, so only then would he ask you how you wanted it cutting. I think his style range was somewhat limited, thanks in no small part to his previous occupation, I'm guessing. Apparently, he used to shave dead bodies in the army during the Second World War. He swore blind he never had any complaints back then, and you couldn't disagree with him on that point.

The young Spanish lad went about my head with gusto – which was rather appropriate as it means 'pleasure' in Spanish – and he was cutting it from every angle possible, and some angles more than once. He got through his full range of razors, including the cut-throat one, for which I was pleased he hadn't been trained by Sweeney Todd. Finally, and with some measure of relief, he reached for the hair gel, which he applied to my satisfaction … and I was about to get out of the chair and pay the lad when he pushed me back down, grabbed the hairdryer and undid all his good work at the end by blow-drying it.

Maybe he thought the style I'd asked for was better suited to a younger man. Or maybe *puntiagudo* means blow-dry – who knows?! Ah well, I could always sort it out myself when I got home. At least he wasn't the chatty type, which would have been a nightmare. He did rabbit on to the other barber, though, in his Andalusian drawl, and I picked up maybe one word in twenty. I paid the lad seven euros and threw in another euro for his effort and left.

'Who cut that for you?' Steph laughed when I got back, who incidentally was an award-winning colourist in an earlier career.

'It's fine,' I said. 'He just didn't need to blow-dry it at the end.'

'Why didn't you tell him, then?'

'Don't push it. I think I've done well to come back with any sort of haircut.'

And with that, off I popped to the bathroom to sort it out.

I still don't know if *puntiagudo* is the correct term, so now I usually just tell him to not cut it too short on the top, and then I fix it how I like it when I get home.

10

Keep Cool and Carry On

During one of my early stints away from home, I had to leave Chris in charge of supervising the installation of the air conditioning. We'd invited quotes from a couple of reputable companies, and sure enough, Sofía's 'wet finger in the air' estimate of about eight hundred euros proved to be about as accurate a prediction as Saddam Hussein having a cache of WMDs on a forty-five-minute launch sequence. The figures were coming in at two thousand six hundred euros plus VAT – or IVA as they call it over here. I could have bought a bloody WMD for that.

This was clearly a significant investment in a property that wasn't ours, and that we only had an eleven-month contract for – more on that shortly.

Alive to the perils of the fickle Spanish rental market, we decided this was a risk we weren't prepared to take, not without establishing some legal assurances about us recouping the money in the event we were asked to move out. So we had a separate agreement drawn up with Olivia so that if she asked us to leave in the first three years, then she'd repay us proportionately for the cost of the air conditioning installation. After three years the unit could be considered part of the house, which I thought was fair. This was signed without a fuss, which gave us the reassurance we were looking for.

The next thing we needed to do was get the price down. The unit we'd been quoted for was the right size to cover the entire property, but as there would only be two of us living here for most of the year, we didn't need the spare bedrooms cooling down if no guests were staying. So if we could close off the bedroom vents when not in use then a smaller unit should suffice.

Also, we didn't like having the aircon on in our own bedroom overnight as it tended to dry out the air and leave you with a sore throat in the morning. We much preferred the cooling effect of having a fan blowing the warm night air across the bed instead. So a smaller unit was found, the price negotiated down a few hundred euros, and a deal was done.

After the fiasco of the hole in the wall from the internet installation, we decided it would be wise for Olivia to be present when the air con went in, as in addition to the outdoor fan unit you tend to see on buildings, this was a split system with an internal unit that had to be concealed above the bathroom's false ceiling to feed the air vents.

For some reason, and I don't know if it's another Spanish idiosyncrasy or not, the large tiles suspended in the false ceiling grid in the bathroom were heavy ceramic ones. So heavy in fact, that if one fell on your head, it would probably kill you.

Afterwards, Chris reported that there'd been an 'incident'. Apparently, Olivia had been round to speak to the installation team, who explained to her what they planned to do in the bathroom. She was happy with their explanation and left.

'And then there was an almighty crash,' Chris explained over the phone.

'What do you mean?'

'Half the ceiling fell down. It's a wonder nobody was killed.'

'How did that happen?'

'They were removing some of the tiles to get access to the ceiling void and the metal grid that supports them wasn't connected up to anything.'

It turned out the tiles were just loosely held in place by a floating set of metal strips forming a grid shape but with no integral strength to the framework, so the more tiles you removed, the more unstable it became.

'Was anyone hurt?' I asked.

'No, thankfully.'

'Any damage to the bathroom?'

'Miraculously, just a small chip in the corner of one of the ceiling tiles. Oh, and our bathroom scales are dented. But other than that, nothing.'

It sounded like the lads had a lucky escape, and the damage to the tile wasn't obvious unless you knew where to look. The dent in the bathroom scales serves as a permanent reminder, though.

Chris said she heard them muttering something about 'cheap Chinese crap' and then cracked on with the job.

* * *

Now a quick note about that eleven-month rental contract nonsense.

Anyone who has rented a property over here in the last forty years will tell you that it's a notoriously common clause in rental contracts, particularly on the Costa del Sol. It's been used here for years because many landlords and estate agents have the misconception that by including it, the tenants have fewer legal rights if the landlord wishes to evict them. In actual fact, the clause is meaningless now in law and wouldn't stand up in court.

At the time we moved in, long-term tenants renting from private landlords were permitted to stay for up to three years at their discretion, and longer with the landlord's approval, and this has since been extended to five years. However, despite this, it didn't stop suspicious landlords adding the eleven-month clause into contracts.

Our landlady seemed very pleasant, so we didn't anticipate having any problems with her, and were happy to ignore this unenforceable clause in our own contract.

'It's just what they do here,' Sofía had said when we queried it.

They also stab bulls and can't drive very well, I thought, neither of which should be a reason to continue doing so.

11

Formalities

Approaching the end of our first two months in Spain, we were sitting on the terrace with a glass of red wine and a bowl of olives, reflecting on our experiences to date and talking through the logistics of the next few months. October had been almost as hectic as September, and there didn't appear to be an end in sight in the short term.

My mate, Gary, was getting married in Wales soon and I was on best man duties, plus my IT contract should have been entering its last week but had been extended to the end of December due to unforeseen project delays. This was a blow to our plans and meant Chris spending yet more time alone in Spain – since landing at Santander fifty-four days ago, I'd only spent twenty-seven of those in Spain myself. And so we were looking at two more months of the same routine. At least I'd still be earning for a while longer and topping up my pension fund.

Which was just as well, because the other thing that hadn't quite gone according to plan, was that our UK house hadn't been rented out yet.

We'd left the place in immaculate condition, done all the promotional photos for the agent ourselves, and put it on the market at what we felt was an achievable price, albeit a little more than the agent had suggested. With the country voting for Brexit in June, the pound had dropped from 1.30 to 1.11 euros, losing fifteen percent in the process, and I guess we were tempted to try and achieve that little bit extra from the property to cover more of our costs in Spain.

We'd had some viewings, but no sensible offers as yet. The first people to view it were of Eastern European origin, according to the agent, and they wanted to pay cash as they had no UK bank account. They had no references, and a credit check couldn't be completed. Now they may have been quite lovely people, but it was too much of a risk. For all we knew, they might have been planning to turn the house into a production site for marijuana, so the offer was met with a firm rebuttal.

Another couple to view it were a French footballer and his wife. I'd never watched ITV's *Footballers' Wives* drama in the earlier part of the millennium, but I somehow couldn't imagine our modest three-bed detached house living up to the expectations of a Premier League footballer and his wife. At one point, I even mused what the going rate was for location fees if they used our house in a future series.

I knew Paul Pogba had recently returned for a second spell at Manchester United, but I couldn't see him walking into Bury every morning to get the tram to the training ground. As it turned out, the young footballer in question was coming to play for one of the lower league clubs so I needn't have worried. It mustn't have met their requirements in the end as they didn't pursue their interest further.

With Christmas on the horizon, viewings had all but dried up generally in the rental market, and so we would have to wait a while longer for our first tenants.

Our new home in Spain, meanwhile, had taken shape, and all three bedrooms were fully furnished, with two sets of garden furniture spread across the south-facing terrace. The pool was cooling down a bit, and it wouldn't be long before we'd be goading each other to 'stop being a pussy and jump in'.

Living in the *campo*, albeit only a mile or so from the centre of town, there was no postal service to the house, so we'd hired a PO Box in town. And in doing so, we discovered they still use carbon paper in Spain, which is rather a novelty. The chap probably had a drawer full of it and was determined to use it all up before he was seduced to come over to the dark side and go digital.

And so began the laborious process of updating our address with all the relevant companies, from HMRC and our UK banks, to all those online accounts one accumulates for everything from car hire firms to airlines and hotel chains. We'd even been using a curry ingredient delivery service in the UK who very kindly agreed to continue delivering those little packs of spicy deliciousness to Spain for us – great stuff, Friday night was still going to be 'Curry Night'.

Our euro cash reserves had dried up pretty quickly, and so we'd opened a joint Spanish bank account together, which was a bit weird, as I'd never had a joint account with anyone before – no more hidden purchases perhaps, although I still had my UK credit card. At least the bank had gone digital, although we lost count of the number of forms we had to sign to open the damn thing.

Apart from paying a fee to activate our bank cards, the operation of the account was free of charge, and by using a carefully selected money transfer broker, there would be no bank transfer fees. That all seemed relatively straightforward, and the lady in the bank was really lovely to deal with, speaking good English, which was a relief at this early stage in our Spanish lives.

After opening the account with just our passport numbers as reference, we were informed we needed to obtain NIE numbers. An NIE number – *Número de Identidad de Extranjero* – is a foreigner's ID number in the Spanish system. You need one to reside in Spain or if you're buying property as a non-resident. It's a bit like your National Insurance number in the UK and remains with you for life. Without one, the Spanish Tax Authority can't collect your taxes ... or do things like embargo your bank account without warning so they can help themselves to some of your hard-earned money for some spurious reason.

We asked Felipe, who operates the PO Box service, to help us obtain our NIE numbers, as this was one of the additional services he offered his expat clients. This would be our first meaningful encounter with the Spanish authorities on any level.

Felipe booked appointments for us over the phone with the police station at Fuengirola, and when the time came, Bruno, his assistant, took us down to the coast to be processed.

Anyone needing to do *anything* with the Spanish authorities is well advised to seek out and pay for assistance from a native speaker or translator, and that person should be someone who knows the law, and more specifically, the procedures involved in getting registered for everything from an NIE number to a Resident's Permit and Driving Licence.

In Spain, such a person is formally known as a *gestor*, which is usually someone who has legal and financial knowledge and a suitable degree. Other individuals who are not legally trained also offer their services to help foreign clients navigate the complex bureaucratic paperwork and procedures involved. It's advisable to use a *gestor* or accountant to help file your tax returns, but obtaining documentation that legalises your position in Spain can be done quite easily by people with the experience necessary. For such people, read Felipe and Bruno.

If you're wondering why local assistance is essential, apart from the obvious language barrier, then typing 'Spanish red tape' into the search box in YouTube and watching the first video in the list will prove enlightening. It's hilarious, but oh so true …

A young woman is applying for a work permit, and her nemesis, a black-shirted, matchstick-chewing, obstructive administration clerk, asks her for copies of this and that, all of which she produces from her handbag, duly completed. The guy is trying to find any excuse to refuse her a permit. He thinks he has her at the end when she needs to have two forms stapled together and he won't let her use the office stapler, but then she retrieves her own staple gun from up her sleeve and the guy is beaten. It all plays out like a Wild West showdown, with the pair staring each other down throughout. You'll be surprised how accurate it is when you come face to face with the Spanish authorities.

With the video fresh in our minds, we headed to Fuengirola with Bruno. We had with us the completed NIE application forms, passport photos, our rental contract and our passports … and photocopies of all of the above … and a staple gun in Chris's handbag – we weren't mugs, they weren't going to catch us out so easily. All the same, having watched the video, the nervous anticipation of approaching this task was like chucking a ferret down your trousers and wondering which bollock it was going to sink its teeth into first!

As it happened, the process went smoothly, although it was a little chaotic in the police station. We certainly would have struggled doing it on our own. With the process complete, we stepped out into the sunshine and breathed a sigh of relief.

'So, when do we get our NIE numbers?' I asked Bruno.

'In about a week,' he said. 'Don't worry. I can come back on my own and collect them.'

'Why don't they just print them off while we're here?' I said, my brain involuntarily trying to reengineer the process like the time-served business analyst I was. 'That would surely save everyone a lot of time.'

'Ah. That would be far too simple,' Bruno smiled. 'Welcome to Spanish bureaucracy.'

A week came and went, and we popped in to check the post. Sure enough, there was our paperwork. We were now 'in the system', although we wouldn't have to become tax resident until the following financial year, which in Spain runs from 1st January.

On returning home and reviewing the documents more closely, we noticed that Chris's paperwork listed her as first name then surname, whereas mine was the other way around. There was no indication on the document to say which one was your *apellido* (surname), so I emailed Felipe to ask him. I suggested the policeman had made a mistake in registering one of us and asked if it needed correcting. He happily reassured me and told me not to worry; in fact, his exact words were: 'They do it sometimes and we went to ask several times, but they always told us that it is not a problem'.

So there it was in black and white – or blue and white in the case of the email reply. One of us – we later discovered it to be me – had been registered with our names back to front. But hey, I needn't worry, because it seemed I wasn't the first and I wouldn't be the last. And according to the police, it wasn't a problem. Only time will tell how accurate that statement is.

I wondered if the error was a genuine mistake or done deliberately by the humourless police officer that processed us. I tried to recall the guy's face now in that video, to see if there was a familial resemblance – perhaps it was him after all, and he was still smarting from being outwitted by the young girl.

12

Learning the Lingo

'¡Hola! Mi nombre es Drew.'

I was introducing myself to a bunch of strangers with a beer in my hand and felt I should really continue that sentence with '*y soy alcohólico*', but my Spanish wasn't good enough at that point.

We were sheltering from the sun under the shady terrace of the bar at the end of the road. Happily, we weren't attending a meeting of the Alhaurín El Grande branch of Alcoholics Anonymous but having our first Spanish lesson since moving to Spain.

Having previously completed part of an Open University Spanish course, Chris's *español* was better than mine, despite me attending four terms of Spanish night school with her a few years earlier. Prior to that, my Spanish was restricted mainly to ordering off a menu. We might have continued with night school but for my job getting in the way at the time, and the realisation that unless we were using it daily, we would forget most of it – and of course, I had.

In a bid to get us back on track, Chris had enrolled us in this Spanish Beginners' class which was taking place on our doorstep. It was to be a regular Friday afternoon affair, which fitted in nicely with my current travel plans. It was just a bit surreal doing it with a beer in my hand, but I wasn't complaining.

It was a small class of five, with my classmates reminding me of the cast of an Agatha Christie murder mystery. There was the slightly batty older woman who had lived in the area almost half her life and knew less Spanish than I did. Her main objective appeared to be to run the clock down on our allotted time by talking in English about anything other than what we were learning. Then there was another curious couple at that first lesson who had, like us, recently relocated to Spain, but that's where the similarities ended. They were clearly going to struggle, especially the husband, who was out of his depth at *hola*.

Thankfully, our Brummie teacher, Michelle – whose accent was more Solihull than Dudley, happily – had the patience of a saint and soldiered on. It wasn't long before I was able to appreciate that her previous experience as a psychiatric nurse was going to come in very handy with this bunch of misfits … myself and Chris excluded, of course. If we'd have been doing this at school, the batty one would have been a regular visitor to the headmaster's office for disrupting the class, and the other fella would have been kept down a year, I'm sure.

As the class wore on, it became obvious the married couple weren't going to see the course through. The poor chap was wading through treacle and just didn't have the confidence to continue, despite his wife trying to make a go of it. And sure enough, after a couple more weeks of stuttering 'progress', they called it a day and we never saw them again.

Unfortunately for our own progress, the batty one stuck around for nearly two years, remarkably without getting appreciably better. I think she just wanted to get out of the house myself. We had other people come and go over the following months, but while they tried and failed to master it, we found ourselves gradually improving our understanding of the language and grammar rules.

As far as pronunciation goes, the Spanish language is very phonetic, or in the words of Roy Walker, 'Say what you see. Say what you see'. This is in stark contrast to English, where the mere coupling of letters is no guarantee of how the word is pronounced. For instance, in English, the word *bass* can be a fish or a musical instrument, both spelt the same but pronounced differently. Likewise, the word *content* has different meanings if you place the stress on the *con-* part as opposed to stressing the -*tent* part.

In Spanish, because it's phonetic, you should be able to look at a word and know how to pronounce it; they even stick one of those acute accents over one of the vowels if it's not obvious where the stress should be. Sometimes, pronunciation can be a bugger, though, as they seem to like a good tongue twister, especially with all the lisping you have to do if you want to speak authentic Spanish and not the South American version. And while we're on that subject, the insensitive academic who came up with the word *lisp* to describe the poor souls afflicted with that condition clearly had a wicked sense of humour.

There are some words I've always found really hard to pronounce, like the word for exercise, *ejercicio* (e-her-thi-thi-oh), where the *j* is pronounced as *h* and *c* pronounced *th*. Try saying that with dentures in (although, for the record, that's a challenge I don't have to deal with just yet).

I also can't roll my *r*'s, which hinders my pronunciation sometimes – as a trumpet player, that's been a constant source of embarrassment when I'm trying to produce a rasping growl out of the thing. And speaking of embarrassment, don't make the mistake I did when trying to tell someone I was embarrassed. So many Spanish words are similar to the English equivalent, and when you're struggling to remember the correct one, it's tempting to throw in your best guess. Be warned though, the word *embarazada* means you're pregnant, which as a fifty-something male can of course be more than a little embarrassing.

Although to be fair, such an embarrassment pales into insignificance when compared to the most embarrassing moment in my life. I was about eight years old and was competing in a swimming gala at our local pool, Seedley Baths. This old Victorian swimming pool had individual changing cubicles running the length of each side of the pool. I was a keen swimmer and was really hyped up for my upcoming race. I got changed at the very end of the pool and was confidently strolling along the poolside towards the shallow end when a voice I recognised pierced the deafening noise of splashing water and screaming kids.

60

'Andrew! You've no trunks on!' my Mum was yelling from the other side of the pool.

And sure enough, to my horror, I'd stepped out of the cubicle stark bollock naked.

Oh, the ignominy of it all.

To add insult to injury, after winning my race, I ran over to my Mum brandishing my hard-earned prize: a Marathon bar – or to anyone born in the UK since 1990, a Snickers – and as she turned around to see what her needy middle child wanted her for, she inadvertently knocked it out of my hand, where it came to rest in the shallow end. Story of my life, right there.

I'm no stranger to making a fool of myself, as Chris never tires of reminding me, much to her amusement. There's the time I walked straight into a plate glass window at the chippy as she watched on from the car.

Or the time I was hurrying for an excursion coach in Mexico and slipped on some standing water, whereupon I proceeded to do one of those cartoon-like scrabbles with my feet before falling flat on my back. On that occasion, the Hanna-Barbera sound effects wouldn't have been out of place as it all seemed to happen in slow motion, with me kicking at the air in vain.

I think it's more embarrassing, though, when you do something stupid in front of a stranger, and I seem to have a habit of making a fool of myself when speaking to the locals in their native tongue. After the first few weeks of Spanish lessons, I went to the bar of our local to order another glass of red wine for Chris.

'*Otra copa de vino tinto para mi esposo,*' I requested confidently, feeling bullish at my improved grasp of the language.

As the barman picked up the bottle and began filling the glass, I continued in the local tongue and asked him if he thought my Spanish was improving. Breaking into English, he cut me down to size with ease.

'Not unless you wanted to order wine for your husband,' he laughed.

Damn – I was one letter out … *esposa* not *esposo*.

One phrase to avoid in a restaurant when you want to order chicken and chips is asking for *polla con patatas fritas* instead of *pollo con patatas fritas* – with the first one, by getting just that one vowel wrong, you've just asked for 'dick and chips'. Thankfully, that's one mistake I haven't made myself yet.

And if you fancy eggs, it's advisable to avoid using the phrase *tienes huevos* which, although separately translated, means 'do you have eggs?' when used together over here it means 'do you have balls?' So unless you're asking the waiter to step outside for a dust-up, it's better to ask him if 'there are eggs', *hay huevos.*

The biggest obstacle for an Englishman learning Spanish, though, is the verb endings. They not only have fourteen verb tenses, but they also use a different verb ending for all singular and plural forms within the same tense. So there are no less than eighty-four verb endings to master for each verb, and it's that complexity that will prevent me from ever being fluent, I'm afraid.

As a result, I'm firmly of the opinion that playing scrabble in Spanish must be a piece of cake, as you can probably put any combination of letters down and there's a good chance it will derive from a conjugated verb ending.

Add to that the general convention for our continental cousins to give every noun a gender, and all of a sudden, as well as remembering the verb ending you have to remember whether or not a chair is masculine or feminine. It's a bloody nightmare.

You'll no doubt recall the popular *Fast Show* with Caroline Aherne playing the Spanish weather girl in front of a map that's full of sunshine symbols, and she repeatedly tells us it's going to be *scorchio*. It's tempting to stick an *o* or an *io* on the end of an English word in a vain attempt at the Spanish equivalent, but it's not as common as you might think. And no, *scorchio* is not a real word.

There are some words I've taken to heart for their quite literal meaning in Spanish. For instance, the word for umbrella is *paraguas – para* (it stops) *aguas* (waters). And the word for a parasol is (funnily enough) *parasol – para* (it stops) *sol* (sun). I'm guessing that last word came from Spanish originally as we don't have much of a need for parasols in Britain. Although they can't hold a candle to the Swahili word I discovered in Kenya for a roundabout ... being a former British colony, they drive on the left and call it a *kiplefti*. Bloody brilliant! And it can't be misinterpreted. What a shining light of simplicity for improving road safety.

At the end of the day, I know that being able to read a menu means I'll never go hungry, but I'm never going to be in the running for president of the Spanish debating society.

But I shall persevere. As Franklin D. Roosevelt once said, 'When you reach the end of your rope, tie a knot in it and hang on'. Although I'm not sure now if he meant hang on in there or give up and put you head inside the knot ... having just done the subjunctive verb tense, I've been sorely tempted to give up because I think they're definitely having a laugh with that one.

13

Local Wildlife

From time to time there would be the occasional exchange of fruit and vegetables with our neighbours on either side. I say 'exchange', but it was mostly one-way traffic to be honest.

Luis did a good line in tomatoes and chilli peppers, and José's prized crops – in our eyes at least – were his pomegranates, which were huge and delicious. Most of José's stuff ended up for sale on the petrol station forecourt. Perhaps I should clarify that, it wasn't us selling them but him, of course. I'm glad we got that cleared up before the rumour mill started.

With one small pomegranate tree on our own plot, I know from bitter experience how tricky they are to grow. I think we were perhaps over-watering ours as they can withstand drought conditions, but each year our fruits would split open before they were ready and then be feasted upon by the bugs. Which is why it was such a treat to be given a few of José's enormous specimens.

We did wonder if there was another secret to his bumper crop, and having read somewhere that Spanish farmers had a habit of crapping under their trees to fertilise the soil and bring on the fruits, I kept my beady eye out for any such nonsense going on next door.

In fact, such is the veracity of the myth about crapping farmers, in some parts of Spain you will find hidden away in the corner of nativity scenes a little figurine crouched down taking a crap. It's called a *caganer*, which is supposed to be a symbol of good luck and represents fertility and the fertilisation of the land. Such is their popularity, what once used to be a simple peasant in the act has been transformed into an amusing political statement, and you can now get a little crapping Boris Johnson or Donald Trump, or even a Britney Spears, who of course rather fittingly had a hit with 'Oops!... I Did It Again'.

Anyway, I digress.

The first time we were treated to some of José's pomegranates was a month or so after moving in, as they are ready from the middle of October. Chris was summoned over to the fence one day for a chat, and I happily left her to it on this occasion. She came back to the terrace complaining about the Andalusian accent, and how they always drop their *s*'s.

'That was a fruitful discussion,' I said, peering lustily at her armful of pomegranates.

'I know,' she said, 'but I was struggling for a while with him there.'

'Why? What were you talking about?'

'Well, at first I wasn't sure. I thought he was talking about coffee. He kept saying *mocha, mocha*. But after a while I worked out he was saying *moscas* but pronouncing the word as *moca*. He was complaining about the flies.'

Having started being plagued by the blighters since the weather had begun to cool down, I could sympathise with him. In the summer it's the mozzies that get you, or rather, while Chris is next to me, they get her instead – probably something to do with how sweet and tasty her blood is, but they don't seem to bother me. The other thing that loves to bite her is what they call 'no see 'ems': little flies so small you don't really see them – a rather accurate name for them, I think.

But the flies were a bloody nuisance to everybody.

Now if you drive through any southern Spanish town in the middle of the day, you'd be forgiven for thinking the place had been abandoned, as there isn't a soul on the streets and all the shutters are down on the rows of townhouses. I thought there might be some illicit lunchtime wife-swapping custom taking place that I hadn't heard of and that at some point we might be invited to join, but no, they keep the shutters down to keep out the heat of the day.

So whereas we were putting our shutters up in the morning and closing them at night, the locals did the opposite. Whilst we were happy to adapt to local customs, Chris and I both agreed that we were going to resist that one as it seemed so unnatural to Northern Europeans like us.

Consequently, once we were up and about, we'd throw open all the blinds and fling open the doors to air the house and let the smells and sounds of the *campo* filter through. And as a result, the flies that we'd trapped indoors overnight went outside to play before returning in the early evening to vie for pole position again on the ceiling light fittings in the living room.

I used to drive Chris mad of an evening seeing how many I could swat before conceding defeat to the last few evasive buggers. It's funny, but when you think you've just killed the last one, another one suddenly appears from nowhere to taunt you.

It got so extreme at one point that I declared out and out war on the *musca domestica*, the Latin name for the common or garden housefly – I can see now where the Spanish derive *mosca* from.

After a little internet research, I settled on the best solution for a house in our situation with open land all around: a special device designed in South Africa called a Red Top Fly Catcher. The one I was looking at was available from the UK and was going to be a chemical-free, non-toxic solution to our problem and, hopefully, the start of a fly-free house. I ordered two and went to the PO Box in town every day for a week until they arrived.

After carefully reading the instructions, I unpacked one, added a little water to the protein solution inside the bag and hung it from the branch of a tree on the far side of the pool, which was more than the requisite fifteen metres from the house. The flies love it so much, apparently, that the protein solution must have the same characteristics as the rotting flesh of a dead zebra being torn apart by hyenas on the plains of the Serengeti – which, having experienced, I can confirm is an accurate description of the smell of this thing.

Sure enough, as I stood a little distance away with my handkerchief over my nose, I observed them enter through the top one by one, make their way excitedly down an ever-tightening funnel to the heady feast they thought awaited them at the end, and then duly get trapped inside. They ultimately drop into the pungent solution and suffocate in what I rather hoped was a slow and lingering death, giving them ample time to reflect on the torment they had caused me up until then. Naturally, their own festering body then added to the enticing aroma, attracting yet more of the blighters to a watery grave.

Too much? Well they are annoying creatures of the highest order.

'What's that awful smell?' Chris asked later, as she stepped onto the terrace with a couple of brews.

'What smell?' I said.

'What do you mean, what smell? Surely you can smell that. Is it that fly trap you've just put up?'

'Probably, but you shouldn't be able to smell it from here. It's right over there on that tree, which is at least twenty-five metres from you.'

'I don't care how far away it is, I can smell it.'

'Well, give it time, eh? It's probably just a gust of wind in the wrong direction. And if not, it'll soon meld into the other *campo* smells, and you won't be able to distinguish it.'

'Are you kidding? It smells like a dead goat.'

'Now come on, don't exaggerate. I'd be surprised if you've ever smelt a dead goat.'

'Well it smells like what I would expect one to smell like, and that's bad enough.'

After convincing her of the relative merits of a bug-free house – and not having to watch me play whack-a-fly every night – she relented and let me keep it up, with only the occasional raised nose in the air when the wind was in the wrong direction.

Sure enough, although not completely fly-free, there certainly appeared to be fewer for me to play tennis with of an evening. And looking at the volume of dead flies rapidly accumulating in the fly catcher, I think it was attracting flies from the whole of the Guadalhorce Valley.

Eventually, after one too many complaints, I conceded that it was time to take down the trap and dispose of it, so one Friday, before the short walk up the road to our Spanish lesson, I took out a bin bag, held it under the trap and cut the thing down from the tree. However, being somewhat unaccustomed to the combined weight of several thousand dead flies, when it hit the bottom of the bin bag, my loose grip on the bag faltered, and it dropped to the floor, whereupon it burst open, splashing dead fly juice onto my flip-flops.

I dashed back inside for a second bag and double-bagged the thing before carrying it up the road with my arm fully extended, where I deposited it in the communal waste bin.

'What's that funny smell?' one of my fellow Spanish students asked, as we took our seats.

'Erm. It's probably my flip-flops,' I coyly admitted. 'It's a bit of dead fly juice from the fly catcher I just took down. I've given them a quick rinse, but it clearly hasn't shifted it.'

'And that smell attracts flies, does it?'

'Yep. By the thousands it seems.'

'It smells like a dead goat.'

Jeepers. How come everyone round here seems to know what a dead goat smells like?

After returning home, I scrubbed at my favourite flip-flops for ages with hot soapy water, but it was to no avail. I had to concede defeat and bin them ... along with the second fly catcher that Chris refused to allow me to put up.

That weekend, the seasonal rains arrived, the first since we'd landed in Spain six weeks earlier. We huddled on the terrace and watched as the sky changed colour, and a distant lightning storm approached from the west. Ultimately, we were forced indoors by the accompanying rapid drop in temperature and an overwhelming desire not to have a billion volts coursing through our bodies.

On the Monday morning, before I headed back to work, and spurred on by the nightly temperature drop, we nipped down to the coast and bought an infrared patio heater to extend our evenings on the terrace in the upcoming cooler months.

That night, as the aircraft wheels touched down at Luton once more, I received a message from Chris proclaiming an evening of encounters with new wildlife. Heading over to the family WhatsApp group for pictures and further information, I was greeted by expletives and images of some strange insect.

Chris had been trying out the patio heater when three of them had ambushed her on the terrace and then scuttled away. They were about two inches long with big meaty bodies; ugly critters to say the least, and it was difficult to determine which end was the front. The girls were debating if they were locusts or not, but we agreed they looked nothing like locusts and must be from a different species.

Whatever they were, next door's cats were having a field day, feasting on them all over the garden.

After further research, it was established that they were mole crickets that lie dormant underground until the rains come, after which they reappear to find a mate.

'I've saved you one of those mole crickets,' Chris said the following lunchtime, while I was trying to eat a prawn sandwich.

'Saved me one?' I said, thinking twice about finishing my lunch or not now. 'You mean you've caught one?'

'Not exactly, there's one in the pool. I'm going to let it drown so you can see it. I'll leave it there till you get back on Thursday.'

'And here was me thinking you loved me.'

'Well, I thought you might like to see one in the flesh. Oh, and I've seen something else new?'

'What?'

'This weird spider.'

'Don't you want me to come home or something?'

Chris was well aware of my spider phobia and delighted in being the big brave one in the household that evicted any that strayed too close.

'What's weird about it?'

'It lives in a hole in the ground.'

'Are you sure you're not confusing it with the mole cricket holes?'

'No. It digs a hole and sits just inside the entrance waiting for an innocent earwig to walk past, and then it leaps out and grabs it.'

I could picture Chris mimicking the actions of a predatory spider on the other end of the line.

'Look, there's nothing innocent about an earwig,' I said, 'and it's welcome to eat as many as it likes, as long as it doesn't think my big toe's an earwig while I'm watering the garden.'

'And it has a bum that looks like a ball of soil.'

'Are you sure that's not just a ball of soil?'

'Er. Could be, I suppose. Maybe that's the lid for the hole then. Anyway, I've got to go. I'm going on an ant hunt now.'

'And here's me thinking I was the one leading the exciting jet-set lifestyle.'

'Jet-set lifestyle? I thought you were in Tesco's car park with a prawn butty.'

'*Touché.*'

When I called Chris a couple of days later whilst waiting to board my flight home, I could tell she was agitated about something.

'What's up?' I asked.

'It's that bloody creature. It's still alive.'

'The mole cricket in the pool?'

'Yes. It's an alien. I was skimming the pool and thought I'd hook it out and leave it on the side, and the bloody thing started crawling up the pole. I had to throw it back in.'

'Don't panic. I'll fish it out myself when I get home.'

'But it's hot and I want a dip in the pool.'

'Well you'll have to confront your fears then and get rid of it.'

'I'll say that to you next time you find a spider in the house, shall I?'

'*Touché,*' I said for the second time that week, pondering if I might have been better learning French instead.

14

New Friends

After waving the taxi driver off at the gate, I headed down the path with a spring in my step. I was getting a kick out of coming home to Spain after working away, much more so than I used to before we emigrated. There was a degree of excitement about living in this beautiful part of the world that I hoped I'd never tire of, although I'd be glad to finally finish working away.

I could see Chris eighty yards away in the orange glow of candlelight on the terrace, waving a warm welcome to me, the returning traveller, like I'd been off to war and back. I know Luton's not got much going for it, but it's not quite a warzone. I just hoped she hadn't saved one of those spiders with a soily bumbag for me.

'Good flight?' she asked, as I dropped my bag on the terrace and embraced her.

'Well, it took off and landed at the right airport with no casualties, so yes, I suppose so. At least I'm avoiding the luggage argument at the gate now I'm flying Business Class.'

'Speedy Boarding working out alright then?'

'Yes. I now get to queue for longer *after* they've checked my boarding pass rather than *before* they've checked it. Luxury. And speaking of luxury, I see the gate's working now.'

I was referring to the large metal gate to our property which up until now we had been sliding open manually after Olivia had promised to get a motor fitted to it when we moved in. The Spaniards love a nice fancy entrance to their property. You'll often drive past half-built villas in the countryside and, without fail, there'll be a huge ornate gateway, even if that's all they've gotten round to building so far. It's like some sort of neighbourly competition of one-upmanship between the locals – I suppose it's their one chance to make a good first impression.

Whilst paying the taxi driver, our fancy gate had opened up behind me as if by magic.

'Yes. All good. In the end, anyway. The engineer came on Tuesday but there was a part missing, so he had to come back on Wednesday. I only just made it out of the house in time to go and meet Kim. We now have a video intercom screen in the lounge and two "clackers" for the gate.'

'Great. And how is your new friend?'

'Still in the pool waiting for you to deal with it.'

'Very funny. I'll deal with the alien in the morning. You know who I meant, your new Facebook shopping buddy.'

'I know. Just teasing. She's really lovely. We got on like a house on fire.'

'And what did you buy from Stradivarius and Zara?'

'How do you know I shopped in there?'

'Joint bank account,' I said, a wry smile on my face.

'Well, next time I'll just draw some cash out and pay with that if you're going to be stalking me online.'

'You know I'm only kidding. Worth remembering though if you get a secret boyfriend and start shopping at Victoria's Secret.'

That last remark might normally have earned me a thick ear, but she ignored it – she must be mellowing in the Spanish sun.

Over a late dinner, Chris filled me in on how her meeting with Kim had gone, the woman she'd befriended on the Facebook expat forum just before we'd left the UK.

'It was so funny,' Chris said. 'Before I set off, I asked her what she was wearing so I would spot her and she said, "Don't worry about spotting me – I'm a six-foot-one-inch blonde in six-inch heels – you can't miss me". And she's right. She's so tall and slim, you can't miss her, especially in Spain where everyone else seems to be a short brunette. We ended up having loads in common and chatted for hours without an awkward silence.'

'Aw, that's good. I'm glad you've found a friend. It's just a shame she lives an hour and a half away.'

'I know. Guess what she drives though?'

'A Lamborghini?'

'No, silly. A Mini. Same as me. Although she's got the soft top Cooper S to my hard top bog-standard Cooper. You didn't want me to buy the S, remember?'

'That's right. I didn't want you to kill yourself, remember? I've seen you going round a racetrack in a Subaru Impreza. You're a nutter.'

'Aw. That was great fun.'

'And *I've* been round a racetrack in a Cooper S, don't forget, so I know how bloody fast and scary they are. I was catching a Lotus Exige in the corners in that thing. So apart from the Mini, and emigrating in the same week, what else do you have in common with Kim? Certainly not your height, as you're only about five foot.'

'Erm. I'm five foot five, thank you very much. And she is incredibly tall, especially in six-inch heels.'

'So what else?'

'Erm … we both studied Spanish at the OU … we're both looking to do some volunteer work out here … Martin is an IT Consultant, like you … we both got married within a month of each other … we're both on our second husbands, although I might be on my third before long.'

'Cheers. Love you too, hun.'

'I said we'd meet up together with her and Martin next time you're both free one weekend.'

'Sounds good. Is Martin a six-footer?'

'Six-two.'

'Wonderful,' I said, as I'm only just edging five foot nine myself on a good day. 'It'll be like two parents taking their kids out for lunch.'

I just hoped they didn't go dwarf-tossing in their spare time.

A couple of weekends passed by, with the small matter of Gary's wedding squeezed in between, and then we agreed to meet up for lunch in El Palo, just to the east of Málaga, a seaside town that was roughly halfway between our respective homes.

On a lovely sunny afternoon, El Palo turned out to be a busy little town, and it was fortunate that Kim had called ahead to book a table as the restaurants along the beachfront were all packed with locals.

Chris and I were the first to arrive, and when Kim and Martin rounded the corner, I didn't need Chris to tell me this was them. Let's just say they're the sort of people you wouldn't want to be stood behind at a pop concert. Kim had heels on again and was towering above Martin.

After introductions and a brief wait for our table, we were seated and got to know each other over lunch. Afterwards, we walked the full length of the promenade, with me chatting to Martin and the girls bringing up the rear. And when we reached the far end, we turned around, swapped partners and walked back again.

It seemed like we were all getting along just fine. Martin was working for a high-profile client in Brussels during the week, which sounded much more appealing than my weekly trips to Luton. During our conversations, we discovered something else we had in common, which was uncanny. In the spring of that year, after Chris and I had run the Edinburgh 10k up and down Arthur's Seat one morning – the first and last official race of that length that the both of us would attempt – Kim had been there watching Martin run the half-marathon event in the afternoon.

Martin was a good few years older than the two of us, but he looked in great shape and clearly loved his running. On the other hand, Chris and I had been just trying to lose a few extra pounds and had only been running for about a year. While I had been jogging round the streets of Copenhagen whilst out there on one of my long-running continental assignments, Chris had been pounding the streets of Bury while being chased by zombies.

Now that shouldn't put you off from visiting Bury, which is a lovely northern market town with a fine line in black puddings, but Chris was using an app called *Zombies Run* that apparently spurs you on to run faster in short bursts by interrupting your running music playlist with the sound of zombies chasing you.

If I had zombies chasing me, I'd be more inclined to follow Simon Pegg's lead in *Shaun of the Dead* and throw some old vinyl records at them ... and like him, I would have been selective, skipping past some of Prince's finest works and instead throwing some of my Mum's old stuff like Shep's Banjo Boys or Shirley Bassey.

Now I generally wasn't predisposed to running. Not that I'm fat or anything, just that in adulthood it's never held that appeal for me. I think I was scarred after a couple of childhood incidents from my short-lived school sporting career. I went to an all-boys grammar school, and the sport of choice there was rugby. However, with me learning to play the trumpet and therefore needing to protect my lips, I'd been excused from rugby and had to run round the local park with all the other lightweights.

After finding that I was a naturally competitive soul and would be one of two boys always out in front, I was entered into my first competitive interschool race. One evening, the sports master took a few of us over to a sports field on the rough side of the city. There I was to be entered into the 1500m race, my favourite distance at the time. As we lined up on the starting line for the standing start, a rangy black lad muscled his way to the front alongside me and gave me a welcoming smile, although it turned out to be the smile of an assassin.

As the starting pistol fired, he shot off, and it was all I could do to keep up with him. As we approached the first bend, the two of us were a good ten yards clear of the field already, and we'd only run the first hundred. We continued on together round the bend and on down the next straight, and as we passed the finish line for the first time, with three more laps to go, we were now well clear of the rest. I'd never run the race at such a pace before and was surely on for a personal best, or I would have been if I'd ever been timed over this exact distance before.

As I struggled on down the next straight, with a gap now opening up between the leader and me, I began to wonder if the lad thought he was in a shorter race. My lungs were screaming for air, and I started to doubt the wisdom of trying to stick with him like this. Then, to my great surprise, as we got to the end of the straight with only a third of the race distance covered, he slowed down and walked off the track, and as I passed him with my arms flailing, he gave me a cheeky grin and waved.

It wasn't long before the pack caught me, and I finished a distant last, if you don't count the lad that pulled out. As I stumbled towards the finishing line, I saw him having a good laugh with the winner. The cheating buggers had only gone and thrown in a ringer from their sprint team to draw in pillocks like me and throw me off my normal pace. Gutted, deflated and my pride hurt, I never spoke to anyone on the journey home.

When I was next coaxed into doing an interschool event, I insisted on running a shorter distance this time, and accepted a place in the 800m event. This event took place in a proper athletics stadium with lots of spectators, and my Mum and Dad had come along to lend their support. It was quite daunting lining up on the curved starting line after my previous humiliation, and it was all elbows and shoves in the back as we jostled for prime position.

This time, when the gun went off, I'd only made it about five yards when some idiot stood on my heel and tripped me up, and I was unceremoniously trampled on by the rest of the pack, with their spiked running shoes turning my body into a colander. As I lay there battered, bruised and bleeding on the track, the Saint John's Ambulance crew had their first casualty of the day. They rushed over and threw me on a stretcher before the lead pack could make it round the first lap and spike me a second time.

And that was the last time I entered a running race, until forty years later when we arrived in Edinburgh. And even then, I only ran the race as moral support for Chris.

Whilst only having lived in Spain for a couple of months, we'd generally avoided what might be described as the expat scene. We'd moved to Spain to become immersed in the culture of the place and didn't want to hang out in the expat bars drinking all day, which would have been very easy to do. There are a lot of Brits on the Costa del Sol, and I imagine we don't have much in common with the majority of them. Like the batty one in our Spanish class, some of them have lived here for twenty or thirty years and barely speak a word of Spanish.

And believe me, some of my fellow countrymen living out here are conmen, or even worse, gangsters. We'd therefore agreed when we moved here that we would need to be careful who we mixed with and be quite selective. After all, friendships are much easier to acquire than dissolve.

Hence, we were delighted to have found a couple of kindred spirits in Kim and Martin who were both here to start an exciting new chapter in their lives together and take full advantage of the rich culture on offer at every turn.

15

Settling In Nicely

Another month was about to begin with me dashing here, there, and everywhere again, but overall, we were settling in nicely.

It was Halloween weekend, and we'd just finished kitting out the third bedroom-cum-study, thanks to a trip to IKEA. We could now sleep six, and I had a desk to work from when I wasn't travelling, although I was still hoping that might be a short-lived requirement. If only I could get this work contract done and dusted, I could start to embrace a more relaxed Spanish lifestyle.

Chris instructed me on the intricacies of cleaning the pool, and it was quite therapeutic to gently tease the vacuum backwards and forwards along the bottom of the pool whilst taking in the fresh air and mountain views. She appeared to enjoy doing that job herself, though, so I wasn't in any rush to usurp her. The temperature was noticeably dropping off at night, which meant so too was the pool temperature, and it wouldn't be long before it'd be too cold to use without a wetsuit.

I'd noticed too that the weeds were getting bigger and bolder, and we'd already been through two sets of gardening gloves pulling them up. And there's a lot to pull up in an acre of land. I was hoping that by pulling them up with brute force, they may not return again, and the workload will gradually decrease, but some of them like to cling on for dear life, and just when you think you're about to rid yourself of another one, it snaps at the base of the stalk and leaves the root in the ground.

The earth here is the weirdest stuff I've ever come across. When it's dry it's as hard as concrete, but when it's wet it's like a swamp, and it sticks to your wellies and steadily climbs up the outside, trying to breach the lip.

Olivia came round again while I was home. I think she was having attachment issues – not with me, the house. It's understandable, I suppose … you spend all your savings building a new house on the land you've inherited, and to recoup your investment you have to rent the place out to a couple of foreign strangers. And a couple of townies at that too.

Apart from turning up to help us eat the fruit off the trees, she usually brought something new to stick in the ground. This week she brought an armful of what looked like dead branches and screwed them into the ground in a rough approximation of a line.

'¿Qué es?' we asked her.

'Uvas,' she said.

Woohoo! We were going to be having our own vineyard, although probably not enough to make wine out of. I was a bit of an amateur home winemaker myself on the quiet, having for years made a rather delicious (and powerful) dried elderberry wine. I also made a sparkling rosé one year from the bucketfuls of fruit off the plum tree in our front garden. But knowing how cheap and plentiful a decent quaffing wine was over here, I'd sold all my demijohns and the rest of the kit before we left.

Looking at the state of these twigs she'd planted afterwards, we weren't convinced they would take. There was no harm in giving it a go, though, so we dutifully watered them in.

Gradually, there were an ever-increasing number of things to water by hand, with the irrigation pipes mostly feeding just the fruit trees. In addition to the plants Olivia was occasionally dropping off unannounced, we were adding to the garden ourselves too. We usually had a mooch round the local garden centre while I was home. Chris was missing her little greenhouse and raised beds back in Bury, and although we still hadn't decided whether or not to plant up some veggies, we were happy to put in the odd shrub ourselves here and there and had plans for prettifying the area surrounding the pool.

Watering the garden was an important task to keep on top of, with it needing doing two or three times a week while the weather was hot. So one of us would spend an hour or so doing that while the other one made a start on dinner. I'd often see Luis out watering too at this time of day, and brief pleasantries would be exchanged through the chain-link fence.

As November began, I had to leave Chris once more and head off on another long stint away from my new adopted country. This time I was going to be away for eleven days. My next two-week stint in Luton was broken up by Gary's Welsh wedding. Apart from Chris falling ill after the first course of the wedding breakfast and subsequently missing the highlight of the day, my best man's speech, the day passed without a hitch and the sun even made a welcome appearance for the wedding photographs.

After the wedding, Chris returned to Spain and I drove back to Luton for a few more days of hard graft – or messing about with computers, as Chris calls it.

When I finally made it back to Spain myself, Chris was in house-cleaning mode, as we were about to receive our second visitors. Our youngest daughter and her husband, Corrinne and Graham, were flying in for a long weekend. And unlike our last visitor, they wouldn't be on a blow-up bed – they would be guinea pigs for our new all-singing, all-dancing, multi-million-pound Danish bed, complete with frame, mattress AND springs.

When they arrived, they loved the place, although they were rather less enamoured with the bed we'd splashed out on. Apparently, it creaked when you moved around under the covers, although what they thought they were doing moving around under the covers I don't know. So despite spending the GDP of a small African nation on buying the thing, I now had to get my toolbox out and make some little adjustments to try and remedy it.

I think the main problem was that the springs were wooden slats attached to a metal frame, which itself then lay inside a wooden bed frame, so the metal frame was rubbing against the wooden frame, and the slats in the upper half of the base could slide over each other to provide what one might call 'adjustable support' for your back. What it did instead was 'creak'. So I damped it down as best I could with masking tape here and there and stuck some rubber under the feet of the bed to stop it sliding on the marble floor, but it was apparently all in vain and made little appreciable difference.

Ah well, you can't win 'em all.

Having guests, and given it was still a novelty, we of course had to get in the pool. This being the middle of November, however, the pool was down to about fourteen degrees, which might sound warm, but it isn't. I was the first one in, and there's only one way to get in a cold pool: to jump in.

'Come on in,' I said, as I broke the surface and gasped, 'it's lovely.'

I think I was trying to convince myself as much as them.

'Bloody hell, it's freezing,' Graham said, swishing a toe across the surface.

'Nah. It's just 'cos you're so hot in the sun. Don't be a wuss and get in.'

'Maybe next time,' he said, 'when you've installed a heater.'

The girls were determined to give it a go, although they preferred the ever-increasing torture of getting in one step at a time. After about five minutes – and a lot of oohs and ahs – they were finally in and swimming.

They swam the length of the pool, all eight metres of it, swam back again and got out. I was determined to put on a brave face, though, and sat on the steps up to my chest in water as we chatted for a while. Never mind *lukewarm*, it didn't even *look* warm.

After about ten minutes, and when my shivering had become hard to control, I conceded defeat and got out. For the rest of the day I struggled to get warm and won't be making that mistake again.

Ever since then, unless I'm going to be straight in and out after working up a sweat in the garden, it has to be twenty-two degrees before I'll get in for a leisurely splash.

So apart from dealing with a noisy bed and getting hyperthermia, we had a lovely weekend. We dined out at some amazing places, like the rather excellent Santiago's Kitchen, regarded by many as the best restaurant in town, a reputation we couldn't dispute after enjoying the warm hospitality of hosts Allen and Natalie, and sampling their exquisite Asian Fusion cuisine. We also took in a few of the local tourist hotspots, like the incredible Mayan Monkey Chocolate Factory in Mijas Pueblo, where we lingered over their extensive range of ice cream flavours.

Sadly, the weekend was over all too quickly and before our visitors left, we asked them to give us a rundown of how we could improve the accommodation for future visitors.

'We're not on *Four in a Bed*, are we?' Graham asked.

'No, we just want some feedback for future guests,' I said. 'So, apart from the creaky bed, have you any suggestions?'

'Yes,' he said, 'you could carpet the place. The marble floor's bloody freezing.'

'It's lovely and cool in the summer months,' I said. 'I'll just get two little squares of carpet for next time you come, and you can strap them to your feet, you wuss.'

'And what about you, Corrinne,' Chris said. 'Anything you picked up on.'

'You could do with a full-length mirror in the bedroom and a waste basket. Other than that, it's really lovely,' she said. 'We've had a fantastic time, and I can't wait to come back.'

So it was off to the airport again, and as Corrinne and Graham headed for their boarding gate, I boarded a different flight for another exciting week in Luton.

While I was away, the cold nights began to force Chris indoors in the evening – it was the middle of November, after all – so she treated herself to a bag of olive wood and lit her first fire in the large woodburning stove in the lounge. You can't beat a good fire to warm the soul on a cold night. We had a similar one in our house in Bury, and there's nothing better than watching the flames lick hungrily up the side of a big log – it beats watching the telly most nights.

I flew home to a nice cosy fire at the end of the week, just in time to welcome our next UK visitors, this time my best mate, Tony, and his girlfriend, Sandra. Thankfully, the sun came out for their arrival, and it was shirtsleeves weather on the terrace. I made a paella, and we sank a good few bottles of red before retiring indoors again to a nice fire in the evening.

For the next couple of days we were back in tourist mode, trying out another few restaurants. It seems we're blessed with a good selection of eateries in Alhaurín, which thankfully includes the rather splendid Fonda El Postillón. This place gives Santiago's Kitchen a run for its money on quality of food and atmosphere. The classical French cuisine is prepared by its chef-patron, Xavier, and his partner, Kairi, looks after the front of house with local waitress, María. In my view, the staff here have no equal in the area, and it's always a delight to dine here. The wine we selected was out of stock in single bottles, so we got through a couple of magnums of the stuff instead – it'd be rude not to.

The following morning, Tony and I were up early to hit the golf course. It was a crisp, clear morning, and before long we were stripping down to shirtsleeves again as we played a leisurely eighteen holes at Lauro Golf, with its generous fairways and views down to the port at Málaga. Tony's a member at his local golf club and plays in the weekly competition, whereas I would describe myself as a social golfer. I don't think I disgraced myself, but I reckoned a few lessons from a pro at some point would make it a more even contest next time, perhaps.

After the golf, we picked up the ladies and ventured down towards the coast at La Cala de Mijas to try out El Jinete for lunch for the first time, as it had been recommended to us by Bruno at our PO Box – and if a Spaniard gives you a restaurant recommendation, you should always take note as they have discerning standards when it comes to food.

Sadly, the weather began to close in, bringing with it some wind and rain, driving us indoors from the large, picturesque terrace while we were enjoying our starters. No matter, the food was delicious and Argentinian chef, Roque, didn't let us down. He was manning the coal-fired grill, and he did a fine job of the lamb chops and other meats that adorned our plates. Definitely somewhere we'll be returning to in the near future, I'm sure.

After a great weekend with close friends, I boarded a flight to the lovely Luton again. Won't be for much longer now, though … or so I thought.

16

The Customer Is Always Wrong!

Now, the Spanish are a very caring and generous nation on the whole. Strangers bid you good morning in the street and they will happily shower you with homegrown produce, as we'd discovered from our neighbours. However, they do possess a dark spirit that is hidden away much of the time. That is until it comes to dealing with customers.

It seems it's not just Spanish government officials that appear to delight in delivering a less than perfect service. And I'm not talking about a general *mañana* attitude … I'm talking about the power struggle that appears to go on when you have a problem with a product or service. It seems in Spain, the customer is most definitely not 'king'.

In the UK, everyone on the high street seems to know their rights, even if some of the store staff don't. And the UK Consumer Rights Act is fairly unequivocal when it comes to the protection of the consumer and the redress available to them when buying products or services of a less than satisfactory quality. There is also no shortage of consumer rights-related television programmes on UK channels, helping you to navigate your way through the high street and spot a cowboy at twenty paces, even if they're not wearing a Stetson and spitting in a bucket

In Spain, particularly for a non-native who is unaware of the regulations, it's not so clear-cut, and as Spain is effectively a federal state in all but name, those regulations can change from one region to the next. Basically, it's a bit of a minefield. And a limited Spanish vocabulary is usually a nail in your coffin because, with the odd exception, a store's customer service staff have a zero patience, nada, zilch, can't be bothered, 'on your way sunshine' approach to customer care, and they often don't speak English.

Our first experience of trying to resolve a problem came about when we decided to buy a television for the lounge, as we hadn't brought one with us from the UK, and up to now we'd been watching stuff on the iPad on the terrace of an evening. Seduced by the promise of unparalleled discounts during 'Black Friday' week in Spain, we headed down to one of the big electrical goods retailers down on the coast one Saturday afternoon.

After comparing the various models, it seemed I could get a 43" Philips 4K Ultra Slim Smart LED TV for about six hundred European pesos. As it was a smart TV, we thought we'd be able to hook it up to the Wi-Fi and get Freeview and YouTube and stuff like that. What I didn't realise at the time was that they don't have Freeview in Spain anyway, but I should at least be able to use my Amazon Prime account to watch some movies, etc.

After returning home and spending half an hour unpacking it and screwing the TV stand to the bottom, I plugged it in, fired it up and entered the Wi-Fi password. At first it seemed to be doing something, but then it just rebooted itself. When it came back on again it did the same thing again … and again … and again – it seemed to have a mind of its own.

After scratching my head for a while – and any other parts of my body that might initiate a brainwave and a solution to the problem – I gave up and spent half an hour packing it all neatly away again into the box.

Off I went on the half-hour trip back down to the coast. Armed with the basic 'it doesn't work' phrases from my Spanish lessons, I hauled the beast of a box back into the shop on my own and awaited my turn at the customer service desk.

'*¡Hola! ¿Qué quiere?*' the man behind the counter asked me.

'*¡Hola!*' I replied. '*La televisión no funciona.* Reboot, reboot. *¡Nada!*'

I thrust the receipt into his hand so he could see I'd only bought it two hours ago.

Now, in the UK, they'd have probably asked you straight away if you want to take another one away or choose a different model, perhaps. In Spain, the guy started getting the thing out of the box and hooking it up to the shop's Wi-Fi, whilst telling me something like the Wi-Fi in the shop wasn't great but he'd have a go.

And would you believe it, it started up first time. He launched a video on YouTube, and it played no problem. You could have knocked me down with a feather.

At this point, it looked like he was going to send me home with it, but I'd already done two trips to the coast today, and I didn't want to do a third. I insisted that I'd tried several times to do what he'd just done myself at home, and I showed him the video I'd recorded on my phone of it rebooting itself.

What he did next was nothing short of bizarre in my view: instead of putting the television back in the box and getting me a completely new replacement boxed TV, he got a replacement, opened it up, took out just the television screen and put it in my box alongside all the other bits which were still in there.

Oh well, I thought, at least I've got a new TV. So I humped it back to the car and drove back round the mountain again. Arriving home, I unboxed it, and Chris was eager to hear how I'd fared with my pidgin Spanish.

'Well I got my point across, but he must have thought I was an idiot as it worked fine in the shop,' I recounted.

'What, they actually got it out and tried it?' she asked, incredulously.

'Yep. He played me a YouTube video on it, no problem. Then he got another telly from another box and put it in my box.'

'How strange.'

Half an hour later, after putting the stand back together and attaching it to this new TV, I was ready to give it a whirl. I entered the Wi-Fi code and waited with bated breath as it connected to the router ... and then it rebooted itself ... and again ... and again!

While I was cursing and wondering how much damage the TV would do to the patio doors if I threw it through them, Chris was googling for some advice.

'It says here that you need a Wi-Fi speed of at least twenty-five megabits per second for a 4K TV,' she announced.

'What? Twenty-five meg just to stream a bit of telly?'

'That's what it says here. What speed do we get with our microwave internet?'

'Well, we pay for twenty meg, and we get about nine or ten at best. We don't even have Freeview, never mind access to 4K TV programs. It won't even load up the menu.'

You'd think Philips wouldn't be stupid enough to build a TV that doesn't even give you the Smart TV menu, regardless of your Wi-Fi speed. I can understand it buffering or just not playing something off YouTube that was in 4K quality, but to just keep bloody rebooting the TV because it thinks your Wi-Fi signal isn't strong enough is ridiculous!

'What're you going to do then?'

'Well, I'm not taking it back again as they'll think I'm an imbecile and won't refund me anyway, probably. We'll just have to keep it and not use the Smart TV bit.'

To compensate, I ended up buying a long HDMI cable with a special connector for my iPad so we could at least watch stuff on a bigger screen when we were stuck inside on winter nights.

Ah well, never mind … I like failure because it's so easy to achieve!

17

Cooking Up a Storm

The weather had turned at the weekend, bringing with it the cold, damp conditions we were more used to in Northern Europe. The clouds had descended into the valley and forced us indoors. To cheer ourselves up, we decided to light the wood burner and make a curry – not on the wood burner, on the kitchen hob ... although we might have had more success on the wood burner.

Coming from the UK, we were used to cooking with gas, and much preferred the instant heat control of a gas hob over an electric hob. Our kitchen in Spain ran solely on electric, and the hob was an induction hob. Apparently, these things don't heat the cooking surface of the hob, they heat the pans instead – what witchcraft is this?!

The first significance of this dawned on us soon after we moved in. You see, the pans we'd brought from home didn't work with induction hobs – you needed special pans whose bases contained ferrous metals, whatever those are. It had been thirty-five years since I'd passed my 'A' level GCSE physics exam and I had no idea what a ferrous metal was. A quick online search later, and I discovered ferrous metals contain a reasonable amount of iron, which means they are magnetic.

And that's the secret: the magnetism of the pan allows the base to heat up rapidly. So before we could even boil an egg, we'd had to go shopping (again!) and buy a new set of pans compatible with an induction hob.

The other thing we soon discovered was that induction hobs – or at least the one we had – are as temperamental as a pop diva. It used to be that pop stars just wanted their own dressing room, but their demands have become ever more outrageous – it's been reported that some of the *riders* they insist on backstage these days include things like a four-pack of brand-new white towels, a specific brand of guacamole, a filled fruit basket, a box of toothpicks, a humidifier, an animal print rug, scented candles … I could continue, but it's starting to sound like I'm trying to remember the contents of the conveyor belt on Bruce Forsyth's *The Generation Game*.

What our induction hob demanded was a constant uninterrupted power supply, especially if you wanted to use more than one ring. Now you might think that's not such an unreasonable demand, but like the Philips TV, if it thought for a moment that you weren't giving it the full and undivided attention of your electricity supply – or in the case of the telly, exclusive access to the Wi-Fi – it just shut down and blurted out an error code, which when you've got three pans on the go as well as the oven, is a tad inconvenient.

Every time the hob decided you were asking too much of it, it simply had a hissy fit, gave up the ghost and flashed its objections at you. After reaching for the manual to find out what the error code meant, we had to turn the thing off and on again at the fuse box, and then run round the house turning off all the lights, the TV, the air con, and anything else that was using the leccy.

Curry night was one of our special treats. We knew there was an Indian restaurant in the town, but we hadn't tried it, and given that the Spaniards don't really 'do' spicy food, we weren't sure if the restaurant would cater especially for the British contingent or water things down a little for the locals. Nevertheless, we weren't reliant on outsourcing the authentic curry experience as we subscribed to the most wonderful spice delivery service from an amazing company in Bristol called The Spicery.

For not much more than a fiver, we could get the most wonderful curry recipe, handed down for generations by someone's great-great-grandma in some remote Asian village, complete with several small bags of mixed spices with just enough of each blend to make a curry for four people, including all the accompanying side dishes. All you had to do – apart from cook the thing – was to go and get all the fresh ingredients. Living in Spain, that's a particularly convenient way of getting our spice hit, as we probably wouldn't be able to source half of the spices that are included in the little sachets.

So then, after rebooting the hob several times, we settled down to a tasty Thai meal that was unusually titled 'jungle curry with son-in-law eggs and nam prik'. Now with a name like that, it sounds more like one of Ant and Dec's bush tucker trials, but believe me when I tell you it was delicious. Rather than eating the boiled gonads of your daughter's unfaithful husband, son-in-law eggs are actually a well-known Thai dish of boiled and deep-fried eggs in tangy tamarind sauce, and nam prik is a traditional Thai spicy chili sauce. What's not to love?

What's also amazing is that when we moved to Spain and informed The Spicery, they were more than happy to continue supplying us at no extra charge. Marvellous customer service. We get one of these packs delivered every month and we've never received the same one twice, although we have intentionally reordered some of our favourites as extra packs.

The rest of the week continued as normal for me, with a Monday afternoon commute to Luton. Winter was definitely setting in as my car was iced over when I left the warmth of the hotel lobby each morning.

Over in Spain, the weather had picked up briefly for the arrival of Andrea, our second eldest. She'd left her husband, Mat, for two days while she paid her Mum a flying midweek visit. So while Andrea and Chris had an enjoyable day down at the beach on Thursday, poor Mat was left juggling a job and two kids under four.

Rather him than me! I love spending time with my grandkids, but when they outnumber you two-to-one, they work as a tag team and mess with your head. The best part about having grandkids, though, is being able to fill them with sweets, whip them into a giddy, sugar-fuelled frenzy and then hand them back to the parents. Call it karma for all those teenage tantrums.

While the girls were down at La Cala beach, they paid a visit to the El Torreón de La Cala, a watchtower facing out to sea. They're a common sight on the Costas, with more than a hundred such towers lining Spain's southern Mediterranean coastline. Some of them were built by the Moors, the rest by the Christians, but both with the same purpose: to look out for invaders from the south. If you want to know who built each one, the ones with square bases were built by the Moors, and the round ones by the Christians. But to add to the confusion, the one at La Cala has a base shaped like a horseshoe, although it was built by the Christians in the eighteenth century.

The main threat to Spain's southern coastline at the time was from Barbary pirate raiding parties coming across from North Africa. They were mostly interested in attacking merchant ships in the Med, but later made land in Spain to enslave some of the natives. The towers had a main door about three metres from the ground to prevent raiders gaining easy access. This style of building fortress watchtowers with a high entrance doorway was later copied by the British, who in the nineteenth century built around a hundred and forty of them, mostly on the south coast of England.

Martello towers, as they were named, became less useful as the size of artillery shells increased, and many are now in a state of disrepair. The tower in La Cala was in good shape, though, and had been turned into a small museum.

It seemed as though Chris's exploration of the local area was continuing apace without me, sadly. And as if to kick a bloke when he's down, the client called me into his office to inform me they were extending the project by another seven weeks! I now had to continue this international travel routine until the middle of February. And more worryingly, I had to break the news to Chris.

Oh, son-in-law-eggs!

18

Christmas Is a Car Crash

Returning home at the beginning of December, I gave Chris the bad news about the contract. I had to explain to her that the project going live over Christmas wasn't a great idea anyway, and on the plus side, it meant we could enjoy our Christmas without the disruption of me working away, so every cloud and all that.

'Come the middle of February, though, that's it,' Chris said, 'you're definitely hanging your boots up.'

'There is talk that the next project for this client might be in Australia,' I said in passing. 'I wouldn't mind seeing a bit more of Oz.'

'Don't even think about it!' she warned.

There's only one boss in my life, and it seems I live with her.

At the weekend, the weather turned even worse, with widespread flooding across Málaga Province, although our town escaped the worst of it.

Málaga had the worst rains since 1989, and there were a few fatalities on the Costa del Sol. Estepona experienced 136 litres of rainfall per square metre in the space of four hours, leading to the death of two people further down the coast.

Many of the rivers burst their banks and the emergency services received over eight hundred callouts for flooding, including eighty-three people who had to be rescued from their properties.

To take our minds off the weather, we decided to put up the Christmas tree, although if Chris had her way, we'd have only been putting it up on Christmas Eve, as she's half German.

You see, even though Chris was Scottish, she was only born there and left for Hong Kong as a baby. Her father was in the British Military Police, hence the overseas postings, and her mother was German. They met in Germany when her mother was due to date a young army chap, but Chris's father wouldn't give him a pass to leave the base, so went along himself, supposedly to explain to the pretty Fräulein why the lad couldn't come. Whether he'd planned it like that or not, I'm not sure, but he took her out on the date himself, and the rest (as they say) is history. Ah!

I, on the other hand, am a huge fan of Christmas, and I'd have the tree up straight after bonfire night if she'd let me.

And what we'd noticed about Spain was that the shops weren't filled with Christmas stuff for months on end in advance of the big day. There's much more of a relaxed, traditional build-up to the Spanish *Navidad* over here. It doesn't seem to be the commercial spectacle it's become in the UK. But give it time – they've already adopted Black Friday, so I expect Christmas will become a longer drawn-out affair in the years to come. I hope it doesn't, however, as no matter how much I enjoy the festive season, it's good that they show some restraint in Spain. They do go to the expense of decorating all the main streets of the town with Christmas lights, which is nice to see.

And no sooner had we put the tree up than my Mum and Dad were over for another visit, this time being able to stay with us in the new villa. They also appeared to have brought the sunshine with them for a few days. Whilst it wasn't warm enough for Dad to strip down to his shorts, he did manage to sit on the terrace most of the weekend and top up his vitamin D levels.

We even lit the barbecue in his honour and made a *bowle*, which is one of their favourite tipples. It's a punch they first experienced during one of their annual summer pilgrimages to the Moselle region of Germany. In fact, they holidayed there so religiously that after about twenty consecutive years, the mayor of Cochem awarded them the freedom of the town. This German punch isn't as good as my sangria, but it's a refreshing drink on a hot sunny day.

My brother used to joke that Dad was a German spy as he loved all things German: the beer, the wine, the sausages. Chris's German mother sadly died quite young, and I never met her. That also meant that my parents never got the chance to meet her, but we know they would have been good friends.

My Dad usually serves bratwurst and *frikadellen* (German burgers made from pork and beef) on his barbecues, but this time we made homemade beefburgers, grilled chicken and corn on the cob with wholegrain mustard potato salad. I did have to track down some German mustard to appease his sensibilities, though.

On the Monday morning, Chris took the old folks back to the airport in the Mini while I got ready to start work for a few hours before I had to leave the country again myself. We're only half an hour from the airport, so when Chris hadn't returned after an hour and a half I started to wonder where she was.

Then the phone rang, and a breathless Chris was on the other end when I answered, so I could tell something was wrong.

'What's up? Where are you?' I asked.

'Erm. I've had a bit of an accident.'

'In the car? Are you alright?'

'Yes, I'm fine,' she said. 'I was joining the motorway, and you know how the slip roads are very short?'

'Yes.'

'Well, the chap in front was queuing to join, and then he moved off, and I looked over my shoulder to see if I could follow him, and then *bang*.'

'What, you hit him?'

'Yes. He'd moved forward and then braked again, but as I was looking over my shoulder, I didn't see him.'

It's a common accident – in fact, I've done it myself in the UK. But in Spain, I expect this type of accident is especially common, as the slip roads for joining the *autovias* (toll-free motorways and A-roads) and *autopistas* (toll motorways) are more often than not extremely short, so you can't get much of a run up. And doing so in a right-hand-drive vehicle makes it even more likely as you don't get the right viewing angle in your left-hand mirror most of the time.

The two-lane A-7 road that runs down the coast from Fuengirola to Estepona is particularly dangerous and a notorious accident blackspot along the entire length. At many of the junctions, the joining traffic has no slip road at all, and the speed limit is, on average, equivalent to fifty miles per hour.

The country roads are equally hazardous as they tend to have a six-foot ditch on either side. As a result, the police don't bother so much with stopping people to breathalyse them as the worst offenders can usually be found upside down in the ditch. I think that's what the 'Old Bill' would call an 'easy collar'.

On this occasion, Chris had been joining a two-lane A-road and driven up the back of a BMW. Thankfully, it was a relatively minor shunt, with nobody injured. The BMW just had a few scratches on the bumper, but Chris's Mini had suffered a bit of front-end damage to the grill.

What complicated matters was that Chris was driving a UK-registered car. She'd only taken out her Spanish car insurance policy five days earlier, but she didn't have the papers with her. So when the chap she'd hit asked to see her insurance details, she didn't have them.

'Can you WhatsApp my insurance documents to me?' she asked. 'The guy has called the police, so I'm a bit worried.'

'OK. Do you want me to come and get you? Is the Mini driveable?'

'No, it's fine, I can drive it. The grill is pushed in, but I can't see any coolant leaks at the moment.'

Chris would know better than me, I suppose, as she's often recounted how happy she used to be with her head under a bonnet as a teenager. Her Dad had shown her how to change the spark plugs and check the oil levels. In fact, most teenagers born in the sixties were not averse to playing about with their early cars – they were much simpler beasts in those days, and you could get easy access to all the moving parts. Personally, I was forever papier-mâchéing over rusty holes in the front wings of my Hillman Avenger.

The police arrived and reviewed Chris's insurance documents on her phone and took pity on her. I'm sure there was at least one motoring offence she was guilty of, such as not having an accident form available or not having all the other insurance documents printed out, but they were happy with what she showed them, and they exchanged details with the other chap.

When she got back, she swore me to secrecy.

'Don't tell your Mum and Dad when they call later,' she insisted.

'Why not?'

'Well, they said they were happy getting a taxi, and now I've had an accident on the way back from dropping them off – your Mum will think it's their fault.'

'You're probably right.'

'What, that it *was* their fault?'

'No, course not. That Mum will blame herself.'

We took the car to a nearby Spanish mechanic with a smattering of English. He popped the bonnet and said the radiator was damaged, and it shouldn't be driven, so we left it with him and walked home. We notified the insurance company and discovered the policy didn't include a courtesy car, but we were back off to Blighty for Christmas so could manage without one till we returned.

19

Seville Christmas Markets

'Can you get Friday off this week?' Chris asked me when I'd settled into my Luton hotel for another few days again.

'Why?'

'There's a coach trip going to Seville for the Christmas markets, and it'd be nice to go. Maybe meet some more people who live round here.'

'Shouldn't be a problem. Book it.'

Friday came and we played truant from Spanish class and went to Seville instead.

We're not what you'd call extroverts, and although we like a good laugh amongst friends, Chris and I were still trying to be a little cautious about who we befriended locally. Observing the small crowds of people waiting to board the bus, I kept an eye out for obvious undesirables, but after giving everyone the once over, I was pleased to note that none of them looked like drug dealers or bank robbers – or certainly not still actively engaged in that practice anyway. Having said that, I'm not certain there is a definitive 'look' for a ne'er-do-well, although you can usually spot them quite easily where I'm from.

Despite none of them looking like the Kray Twins, I was struggling to spot anyone that remotely appeared to be what one might call 'like-minded' … or 'like-aged' for that matter – the 'grey pound' was alive (if not quite kicking) in the Guadalhorce Valley that morning. Apart from the young lad and his missus in their late twenties that had organised the outing, the rest of the group looked like they might have just fallen out of the bingo hall with an empty miniature bottle of sherry in their handbags.

Incidentally, bingo is largely illegal in Spain, and the *Guardia Civil* have been known to raid expat bars up and down the Costas, shutting down these dens of iniquity. You can almost picture groups of pensioners driving round the area of an evening waiting for a WhatsApp to ping in telling them the location of tonight's illicit bingo session and to make their way quickly to some abandoned industrial unit on the outskirts of town.

Maybe that's what this was after all: the journey to Seville was all a ruse to cover up a mobile bingo hall. Eyes down and strap yourselves in for two and a half hours of 'two fat ladies' and 'Maggie's den' as the coach wends its merry way to Seville and back. I think I might have stumbled onto something here, I thought. The young lad was going to perch himself at the front of the coach fondling his balls with one hand and holding a microphone in the other, while his beautiful assistant wandered up and down the aisle selling strips of bingo cards and cut-price dabbers, checking any hopeful shouts of 'HOUSE!' from Mildred and Edna on the back row.

We had a choice to make ... and quick. Do we get on this bus and risk running foul of the law and ending up six to a cell in the nearest maximum-security prison, or do we go straight back home again? Life's one big game of bingo, I surmised, and although ignorance is no defence in the eyes of the law, I coaxed Chris up the steps. We shuffled halfway down the coach, found two seats together and kept our heads down.

We needn't have worried as it happened, as the most nerve-wracking part of the road trip to Seville was how far the driver was going to risk driving before pulling over for a toilet stop for the more bladderly challenged amongst our party. They didn't even break into a rendition of 'Daytrip to Bangor' or 'We're off in a Motor Car'

Three hours and an extended pee break later, we arrived in Seville and parked up on the edge of the city centre. By now, I was in desperate need of some refreshment. The Christmas markets could wait – I needed feeding and watering. I'd whiled away the journey reading TripAdvisor reviews of Seville's restaurants, so depending on which side of town the bus dropped us off, I had it covered.

After making a mental note of where the coach was, we left the blue rinse brigade behind and headed straight into town. Our destination was a rather nice-looking Italian restaurant called La Piamontesa. The place had bags of character as you walked in the door, with some Roman ruins under a plate glass floor in the lobby, and the interior of the restaurant was also very charming, with exposed stone walls.

The place was already buzzing with the usual sounds of animated chatter from the Spanish locals – when you get more than two Spaniards together why does it always sound like they're having an argument? It's like they've never been taught to whisper or talk discreetly … I love it.

But the thing that topped the lot was the wonderful aroma of Italian cooking, a heady mix of garlic, oregano and tomato. And when it came, the food didn't disappoint either – delicious authentic dishes, just like your Italian *nonna* would make … if you had one.

After a leisurely – and suitably wet – lunch, we stumbled out of the doors and into the warming heat of a mid-December Sevillian afternoon. The weather was nothing like we're used to when frequenting the rather splendid Manchester Christmas markets. And after wandering the streets for an hour, the markets couldn't be compared with each other either.

Whereas Manchester has a great mix of vendors peddling both traditional and quirky Christmas gifts alongside a wide selection of European food and drink stalls, the Seville markets were in complete contrast.

The first thing we noticed was that they seemed to group the stalls together based on what they were selling. So the first group we came across were the ones selling nativity scenes and figurines, including the irreverent crapping *caganers*. But there were dozens of these stalls … all identical, and of no real interest to us.

Further up the street, tucked away in another square, were the arts and crafts stalls, selling artisan jewellery, artwork and textile gifts. This was a bit more interesting than the nativity scenes, as at least the stalls had a bit of variety about their wares.

But where were all the food and drink stalls? In Manchester, as well as stalls selling food to take home with you, like salamis, garlics and cheeses, most people are drawn to the markets to eat and drink too, with the bratwurst stalls being one of the most popular. But you can also choose from a vast selection of cuisine that includes French crepes, Dutch pancakes, Belgian waffles, Spanish paella, Italian pizzas and Turkish baklava. Then there are the pop-up bars selling all manner of alcoholic treats.

After the obligatory bratwurst in Manchester, we usually moved on to our favourite stall selling *flammkuchen* – really thin, pizza-like bases topped with cheese and onion – and a delicious, morish, rum-infused *glühwein* called *feuerzangenbowle*, made by setting light to a rum-soaked sugar loaf that drips into the mulled wine.

It's an unparalleled Christmas delight for us usually, but we couldn't find a single food stall or pop-up bar in the whole of Seville. Maybe they were like the nativity stalls, they were all stuck together in one corner of the city that had so far evaded us, but we were at a loss to discover them if that were the case.

As if we were in some kind of early twentieth-century novel featuring the overindulgent Billy Bunter, we 'repaired' to a tapas bar instead to take stock of the situation. Over a couple of *vino tintos*, we surmised that there must be some Spanish bylaw that prohibits the sale of food and drink from temporary pop-up stalls – the proprietors of all the bars in the area must have objected en masse to the Christmas competition and closed down any chance of us punters getting our hands on a cheeky *glühwein* and a spicy sausage. Now that doesn't seem very EU-open-borders-friendly, does it?

Maybe they're overcome with guilt still from the Franco years and have decried anything remotely fascist like a German sausage. Better not tell my Dad, or he'll feel compelled to report them to the *obermeister führer* on his next visit to Cochem!

Ah well, no point worrying about something that's out of our control.

Whilst the markets were a disappointment, the city certainly wasn't. The place was really beautiful, set on the banks of the Guadalquivir River, the only great navigable river in Spain. You can only get as far as Cádiz on it now, but the Romans used to be able to go all the way up to Córdoba, seventy-five miles inland.

And the Plaza de España is jaw-droppingly beautiful – it certainly knocks Manchester's Piccadilly Gardens into a cocked hat, which is sadly a shadow of its former self since the jobsworths at the town hall decided to pave over it ... in fact, one visitor to Manchester has reviewed it with what must be the most damning critique possible when they said, and I quote, 'This has to be the worst place I have ever been to and I am from Coventry!'

And if you've ever been to Coventry, you'll know what they're talking about.

They go on to describe Piccadilly Gardens as having 'gangs of people, pickpockets, drug addicts and men riding around on bikes following people' – which is really bad (and really accurate) ... in fact, it sounds like a scene Tommy Shelby would cast an approving eye over in *Peaky Blinders*.

Seville was definitely too big and too wonderful to see in half a day, or even a long weekend, so we'd definitely have to make an effort to revisit at some point in the future. We hadn't even scratched the surface of this place, which apparently boasted the fourth largest cathedral in the world with its renowned Giralda Bell Tower, and the Moorish Royal Alcázar Palace and Gardens.

We pondered all the sights we should aim to see when we next returned as we emptied a bottle of Ribera with some tapas in bar Maestro Marcelino. This bar in itself is worth the coach trip to Seville. It's a small tapas bar-cum-shop selling wines, hams and cheeses, and has six-hundred-euro Iberian Bellota hams hanging from the ceiling. These come from the prized, black-hoofed pigs that roam the forests eating acorns and are regarded as the best hams in the world.

In fact, where better to enjoy a bit of tapas than the reported birthplace of these small, delicious dishes? Or so the locals claim. It is one of the most hotly disputed facts in Spain, the origin of tapas, but the mainstream view is that they originated in

Andalucía, and probably in Seville. *Tapa* means 'cover' or 'lid', and it's said that a bartender began serving his drinks to his farming clientele with a little plate on top to stop the dust and flies getting in. Then he started putting a little chunk of bread with meat or cheese on the plate, and a tradition was born.

Another popular story is that it was in fact King Alfonso X who started the custom in the thirteenth century. King Alfonso, aka 'The Wise' – a self-dubbed title if ever there was one – was recovering from an illness for which his physician had prescribed he should drink copious amounts of wine. Whilst doing so, he decided to eat small portions of food with each drink to diminish the effects of the alcohol. Upon his miraculous recovery, he proclaimed that all the bartenders of the kingdom should serve a little *tapa* with the drinks to prevent general public inebriation.

If GCSE history had been this exciting when I was at school, I might not have failed it!

As day became night, we wandered the streets a little more, still hopeful of finding a German sausage, before making our way back to the pickup point. After boarding the coach, there were muttered complaints from some of our fellow passengers about their feet hurting, no doubt from the hours romping round the town looking for a bingo hall.

Having spent most of the day sitting in various bars, my bladder came out in sympathy with the majority on board, and I was relieved – quite literally – when the driver was forced to stop when we were no more than an hour out of Seville. In fact, had he not, Mildred and Edna at the back might have had a winning line with 'two fat ladies, eighty-eight', 'in a state, twenty-eight', 'dirty Gertie, number thirty', 'droopy drawers, forty-four' and 'clean the floor, fifty-four'!

20

The Rain in Spain

In the words of the playwright, George Bernard Shaw, in his stage play *Pygmalion* – and perhaps made even more famous in Alan Jay Lerner's more culturally accessible musical, *My Fair Lady* – 'The rain in Spain stays mainly in the plain'.

However, forgive me for reimagining that cockney flower seller Eliza Doolittle might have actually said, 'The rain in Spain falls mainly on Alhaurín El Grande'. Even if it doesn't rhyme.

It's been lashing down all weekend. And it's flooded the pool pump … again!

Now in normal times, there would be no need to discuss the relative merits of Spain's hydrological climate, as we're normally talking drought rather than flood, but we didn't sign up for this much bloody rain.

Alhaurín El Grande is a Moorish name that means 'God's big garden', and lately I think the big fella upstairs has been out watering it and left the tap running. It's playing havoc with our pool pump … and my wellies for that matter.

The fertile earth on which our lovely plot stands has turned into a quagmire with all the rain. As I've alluded to, it's rock hard in the summer months and will put up the sternest fight before yielding, which is probably why you don't tend to see spades being sold in the gardening shops. Instead, they prefer to use a hoe over here, but not the ones you push into the ground and stick your boot on, they use the proper farming hoes that you swing over your shoulder with great force to split the earth. And you can forget using small hand tools in this stuff, it just bends the ends off.

But after a continual downpour, it becomes a big, squelchy, mess. It's quite clearly a clay-based soil. But we have clay-based soils where I'm from, and they're nothing like this stuff.

As I set off down the garden to check the pool pump, the mud started off on the soles off my wellies, and then with each new step it rounded the edges and began creeping further up the sides. By the time I'd covered the twenty yards to the pump housing, I was shin-deep in the stuff.

And it wasn't great news when I lifted the lid.

The big round red thing that contains all the sand – the bit we call the pump, according to Chris – was now half-submerged in filthy water, which was a mystery to me as the lip of the casing for the entire thing was a good few inches above the ground, so the water can't have come in over the lip.

The electric timer was not yet underwater, but it had only escaped a worse fate by a couple of inches itself.

'Has it flooded again?' Chris shouted from the terrace.

'Yep. Bring the mops and buckets,' I sighed.

Thankfully, as this wasn't the first time it had flooded, we'd had the foresight to turn off the fuse when the rains arrived. The first time it flooded was following the heavy rain a couple of weeks earlier. On that occasion, Chris had dropped me at the airport and then decided to get rid of some of the excess water in the pool, and when she opened the cover to the pool pump, she found it flooded to within a whisker of the electrics.

On that first occasion, Olivia had come down to give Chris a hand, and between them, using jugs, mops and buckets, they'd removed about forty buckets of water. The day after, Chris removed ten more, and six the day after that.

After spending a couple of hours cleaning out the box once more, I decided that the source of the water was a conduit that ran from an adjacent small cable box, whose lid allowed rainwater in around the edge. But how to resolve it?

Well, after that first flooding, the pool engineer had apparently been called, and he just squirted some of that self-expanding foam around the conduit in both boxes, but that clearly hadn't worked.

On another occasion, he'd drilled holes in the bottom of the small box, hoping that water would drain into the ground if it filled up again, but typically, when it rained it poured, and so the ground would have probably been at peak water saturation already. I wasn't convinced that would resolve the problem, and it didn't.

It was clearly a design fault in supplying the pool pump with electricity, but who am I to tell that to a Spanish pool pump engineer?

Personally, I couldn't see why the little box was needed at all, as this was clearly the main contributor to the problem. If the cables had just run underground and fed the pool pump timer directly without the need for a hole in the side of the pump box and without this mini reservoir next to it for water to collect in, then the problem would almost certainly not have arisen.

These things are sent to try us, it seemed.

21

Dog Rescue Squad

'Home sweet home,' Chris said, as the gate rolled open.

It felt good to be back. It was the second of January and we'd just returned from a twelve-night trip to the UK. It was great to see everyone, but it was weird not having to host Christmas dinner for all our girls and their families, something we'd done every Christmas for twenty-two years.

But this year we had Christmas dinner with our youngest daughter and her husband's family ... and we bought the turkey and cooked the dinner for them all, so it wasn't that different after all ... just a different family, different house!

I'd also been off work for twelve days, which was a nice break, and I had another nine days off to look forward to before I had to drag my weary mind and body back to Luton. So I was really looking forward to a bit of time off in Spain. Before now, the longest spell I'd had in Spain was only five nights, so this felt like a bit of a treat.

Chris's car hadn't yet been fixed after the accident, so we were in a hire car we'd picked up from the airport. We were a little nervous driving down the long driveway as we parked up outside the villa, not just to see if the pool pump might need emptying again, but that the house and, more importantly, its contents were all still there. Burglary is a very common occurrence in Spain, particularly in the *campo*, despite having bars on all the windows. So too is squatting, in fact.

All the terrace furniture was still there, and inside, the house was just as we'd left it. Plus, there was nobody already in there making a brew and helping themselves to my chocolate digestives. Phew! What a relief.

After a spot of lunch, we were relaxing on the terrace and noticed a small dog wandering round José and Alicia's garden next door. We knew they didn't have a dog, and given we were now in the midst of winter, there wasn't much chance that they would have been down here from the town anyway.

We wandered over to the fence and started calling out to it, but it didn't seem to be responding to our voices. As it drew closer to the fence it was clear it wasn't in the best of health – it was wandering round aimlessly in circles under José's pomegranate trees. It was a cold, grey day, much like the one we'd just left behind in the UK, and the poor little thing was shivering.

I put my wellies on, grabbed an old towel and walked round to go and retrieve it, which should have been straightforward enough as, although José has a gate at the end of his driveway, you can walk round it a few yards further on and into his garden.

On the way, I spotted the neighbour on the other side of José's property. We hadn't met before, but we'd waved from afar a few times as Chris and I had been walking up to the bar at the end of the road.

I already knew the word for 'dog' (*perro*), and being a big band jazz musician, I also knew the word for 'lost', as *perdido* is the title of a famous Duke Ellington song. So I should be able to manage this easily.

'*¡Hola! ¿Qué tal? Soy Drew, tu vecino*,' I shouted confidently, as I met him coming the other way. Well that was the neighbourly introduction out of the way, on my side at least, as I didn't quite catch what he said in reply. Maybe he saw the towel and thought I was just nipping into José's to have a dip in his pool, although given the time of year and the cold spell, it was unlikely.

I soldiered on with the next bit, telling him there's a lost dog in José's garden, and asked him if it was his?

'*Hay un perro en el jardín de José. ¿Es tuyo?*'

108

'*No, no es mio,*' he said. It wasn't his, so I asked if he knew who the owner might be.

'*¿Sabes quién es el dueño?*'

I really was getting good at this, I thought, and I'd had no practice for two weeks.

'*No, lo siento.*'

Well the good news was he understood me, and I understood a bit of what he'd said back. The bad news was the dog's owner was a mystery.

It wasn't his dog, and I knew it didn't belong to the next house down the lane as they had one of those dirty great English Mastiffs that weigh more than I do, and I'm not at my slimmest after hanging up my 10k running shoes.

By the way, those big mastiffs – or *mastíns* as they're called in Spain – are pussy cats really. They have a really deep bark, and if you're nervous around dogs, they'll frighten you, for sure. Every time we walked past this great big thing it would go crazy, barking and following you along the fence until you'd passed his property. We always used to smile and say hello to him, which probably wound him up even more.

Anyway, one day, we were walking past, and he was at it again, giving it the 'big I am' barking, and as we drew level with the driveway the gate was wide open. When he realised this, he just stood there looking at us from the middle of the drive and went completely silent. He realised it wasn't worth chasing us along the second half of the garden now as he knew he'd been rumbled. After that, he only gave a half-hearted *woof* whenever he saw us, and he usually couldn't be bothered getting to his feet either.

I continued down the garden and found the little dog still wandering aimlessly around the pomegranates. I wrapped the towel around him and picked him up. The poor little pooch was indeed in a bad way: lost, cold and alone in a world he could neither see nor hear much of if our assumptions had been right.

I got him back to our terrace where we dried him off properly and tried to give him some ham and water, but he didn't seem interested. We hoped he hadn't lost the will to live as well as his sight and hearing. I couldn't tell you what breed it was, but it was a small hairy dog of seemingly mixed heritage.

While Chris continued to fuss over him and stick a post on Facebook, I walked down to the bar at the end of the lane to see if anyone recognised him from the photos I'd taken. If he were a local dog, I felt the two brothers that ran bar El Bichito might know him (or her perhaps … I don't think we'd got as far as checking the dog's undercarriage).

I drew a blank at the bar – and the dog's doggy pals were clearly not on social media – so we decided to take him up to one of the local vets and see if he was chipped. After a short wait we were ushered in to see the vet. With a mixture of Spanish and the odd English word thrown in – like 'chip', I mean what's the Spanish for chip? … we can't surely use *patata frita* … we're at the vet, not a kebab shop – between us we managed to get our message across.

The vet didn't recognise the dog himself, which was a shame, but like pharmacies and hardware stores, every town in Spain seems to have a disproportionate number of vets to the population size. There are six vets in Alhaurín, along with ten pharmacies and thirteen hardware stores. But this vet's practice was the closest one to home, so it was favourite.

The vet got his scanner out and found a *patata frita*, then keyed it into his system. But there was no match.

We asked the vet if the database was national or international.

'*Solo Andalucía*,' was his reply.

So the database wasn't even a national one, it just covered Andalucía – apparently, the registration system is owned and operated by the Andalusian Council of Colleges of Veterinary. The dog must have been chipped somewhere else in Spain and then brought to Andalucía at a later date.

It was our move. What should we do next?

A thought struck us. Maybe it was a Brit expat's dog, and they hadn't reregistered it after moving here. That was a distinct possibility. After all, half the buggers live under the radar here anyway and just go home for medical treatment – they drive UK cars, probably without tax and insurance and don't pay any tax. Chancers, the lot of 'em!

Our niece, Kim, worked in a UK vet's practice, and their database is national, so we thought it might be worth a punt to give her a call and see if the chip number was registered there with a phone number we could call.

Chris agreed we should ask Kim to check the chip number.

'*¿Qué es el número de la ... patata frita?*' I asked the vet.

And this is where we got a lucky break, because instead of going to his computer screen, which at this point I assumed would still have had the chip number on it, he instead picked up his scanner again and wafted it over the dog once more.

'*¡Ah! Es un número diferente,*' the vet exclaimed.

'A different number?' Chris said, hopefully.

The dog had been chipped twice for some reason, but our luck might just be in now. The vet keyed this new number into his computer and the screen refreshed with a match.

'BINGO!' I almost shouted, before remembering that was illegal.

Without further ado, the vet picked up his phone and called the number on his screen and it was answered immediately. After a brief conversation that we probably understood about thirty percent of, he put the phone down and turned to us with a smile and told us the owner had been found and was on her way there.

We took the dog back into the reception area and waited for the owner. We weren't expecting a reward for finding the dog, but we were looking forward to seeing the joy on the owner's face as we reunited her with her dog.

Within minutes, the door flung open, and in breezed an elderly Spanish woman all of a flap. She whooped with delight when she saw her beloved pet and took it eagerly into her arms.

That was it, I was gone. It was like the climax of an episode of *Long Lost Family*. I was in bits. I love a happy ending.

The relieved owner was incredibly grateful, and I lost count of how many times she said *muchisima gracias*. From what we could glean from the conversation, the dog had gone missing from her garden a few days earlier. It was indeed deaf and blind but had somehow managed to get out of the garden and gone walkabout ... or 'circleabout' from what we'd observed.

We all traipsed into the car park and jumped in our cars. We followed her out of the car park and saw where she turned off the main road, which was a dead end with an urbanisation on it. As the crow flies – or the dog walks – we reckoned the little fella had crossed a main road and ended up down our lane in José's garden, a distance of more than a kilometre, in ever decreasing circles, no doubt.

He was one lucky dog that we found him when we did. And that the vet had found that second chip. And that I knew the Spanish for chip!

22

It's a Jungle Out There

After a fortnight away, and with all the rain that preceded our departure, the garden was definitely in need of some attention. In fact, it was like a bloody jungle out there. Had the poor dog managed to get into our garden, then it might still have been wandering around it, unseen somewhere at the bottom.

Up to now, pulling up weeds by hand hadn't been very successful in diminishing their number and vigour, or indeed their variety.

'Are you struggling, hun?' Chris asked, as I cursed another weed that was getting the better of this twelve-and-a-half-stone townie.

'Yes. The buggers don't want to come up.'

'Keep at it,' she said. 'The only place where success comes before work is in the dictionary.'

'Who said that? Confucius?'

'Vidal Sassoon.'

Nice to see she's reading all the great philosophers.

The ongoing weed suppression battle had defeated more than just this urbanite weakling, it had also involved one of Olivia's relatives who was handy with all things garden related and had been round a couple of times with his pump sprayer and doused the weeds with some chemical concoction only a Spaniard would know about.

I would have done it myself, but you need a licence. In fact, you seem to need a licence to do anything over here – it's the most regulated society I've come across (although I've never been to North Korea). If you want to spray your weeds in the *campo*, to obtain a licence you need to go on a training course … in Spanish – or more probably Andalusian – so that's not going to happen.

If you want to burn your garden waste – an extremely popular pastime in the *campo* – then you need a licence for that, and a special one to burn out of season, from June to the middle of October, which is often referred to as 'wildfire season'.

During that same period, you can't have a barbecue either, unless it's in a tourist establishment, restaurant or authorised camping ground and with the appropriate licence. Or on an urbanisation that's more than four hundred metres from a forest … and 'forest' is a very loose term, which covers orchards and olive groves (like ours) or anywhere with a tree density of x. Are you with me so far?

I'm not sure what x is, but 'if in doubt, don't do it' is the general message. Because if you do decide to do it and you set fire to the *campo*, then you get prosecuted, and you have to pay tens of thousands (or in some cases millions) of euros to cover the cost of the *bomberos* coming round and pouring millions of gallons of water from helicopters over a raging fire covering half the province.

Some French bloke caused a wildfire once by setting light to a wasp's nest. The fire got out of hand and ignited a wooded hillside in Estepona. Forty-two homes were evacuated, and it took 240 firefighters and twenty-two aircraft over three days to put out the blaze, leaving over eight hundred acres of scrub and woodland smouldering.

If you want to retile your bathroom … yep, you need a bloody licence for that too! They're a right bunch of nosy beggars at the town hall.

And when you do apply for a licence to tile the crapper, you have to give a breakdown of the budget so they can slap a tax of between two and six percent on it, depending how they're feeling that morning.

Honestly, only Spain could tax you for having a shit in peace. I thought Franco died years ago and this was some sort of twenty-first century democracy we were living in, but it seems not sometimes.

Anyway, I digress – I'm turning into Mr Angry with all the rules and regulations I'm learning about since we moved to Spain. What was I saying? Oh yes, weeding ... so even when the weeds had been sprayed, I had to wait for them to turn grey and die and still pull them up by hand. My garden waste pile was getting bigger, and I could feel a burn coming on.

And before you ask, yes, we have a licence to burn this time of year, or so Olivia tells me – it must be a licence for the property rather than the person doing it, as I didn't apply for it, I haven't got it and I haven't even seen it. I just hope I'm not expected to invite Olivia round to strike the match every time I want one. It'd be just my luck to light up one wet, windless morning and then the *Guardia* turn up and ask to see my permit.

So that week I was going to do something about the garden, and I needed some mechanical assistance to make life easier. I'd noticed José next door wondering what this idiot of an Englishman was doing every time I pulled a weed up by hand. I'm sure he'd seen me destoning and raking the area around the pool too and wondered what I was expecting to grow there. José doesn't bother with garden aesthetics ... he just gets his son round with a rotovator and ploughs it all up in one morning.

But I'm an Englishmen, and my Dad instilled in me from an early age the importance of maintaining a tidy garden. So we jumped in the car and headed down to the coast to browse one of the big DIY chains for a solution.

When we arrived, I was expecting to browse the big boys' toys in the farm machinery section, but Chris led me straight down to the garden strimmers.

With a garden that was roughly an acre, and with no convenient power points dotted round the garden every ten paces, an electric strimmer like the one I'd left in the UK would be no good without a hundred-metre extension cable. So I started looking at the petrol strimmers and trying to figure out what the differences were.

All the blurb was in Spanish, and it was talking about cc this and two-stroke that, but I was no motorbike mechanic, and I didn't understand all that technical mumbo jumbo, so I was beginning to feel out of my depth and rather inadequate.

'What about this one?' Chris shouted over from the other aisle.

I wandered round to see what she'd found.

'It's a cordless rechargeable electric strimmer,' she said. 'Will that do the job?'

'Brilliant. That's perfect,' I said.

It wouldn't do the whole garden in one go, but I'd need a tea break from time to time so I could recharge it. I started reading the details to make sure it was suitable. It said it would run for about forty minutes on one charge and take two hours to recharge.

So my plan was this: I'd get it home, do a bit, then have a two-hour tea break and a bit of sunbathing on the terrace, and then I'd do another bit before dinner. I could get up with the birds in the morning and get four sessions in and that should be it. Six times forty minutes is four hours. I reckoned I should be able to get round the garden in four hours.

Job done! And it was about a hundred euros, half the price of the average petrol strimmer.

'Let's get one,' I said.

I bought a protective face mask, safety glasses and a thick pair of gloves, and I was looking forward to getting home and getting stuck in.

Arriving back, I unboxed it, checked the charge level and gave it a fifteen-minute boost while I got my wellies and scruffs on and adjusted the head strap on the mask. I was good to go.

I optimistically went to the far end of the garden so I could work my way down towards the house. Hmm. It wasn't quite as easy as I'd anticipated. Some of the weeds were now three foot high and tough around the base. I started experimenting with different ways to chop them down.

Start at the base? If I did that, it just left me with one big weed lying on the ground getting in the way of me chopping the next one down.

Start at the top and work my way down? That seemed better at first as it was shredding the weed into smaller chunks, but getting the last bit cut down was still tough.

After twenty minutes the battery died on me, and it had been three-quarters full when I started. So, realistically, working on the dense weeds, a full battery might last me half an hour at most.

I looked around at the fruits of my labour and reckoned I'd only cut down about six square metres. I started to do the maths ... an acre is just over four thousand square metres ... four thousand divided by six is – I can do that one in my head – 666 ... ooh! six-six-six, the number of the devil ... hope that's not an omen ... but 666 what? Square metres? Hours? Surely not.

Let me start again. You've got a fox, a chicken, a rowing boat, and was there a bag of grain involved somewhere? Oh, I can't remember.

I went and sat on the terrace and scratched my head for a while till I'd figured it out.

If the battery was full, I might have done nine or ten square metres at the rate I was working. Let's say ten, as that divides easier. Take the house footprint off the acre ... so that's a hundred and forty square metres off ... and take the pool off ... that's another forty ... and take the driveway off ... that's about another two hundred ... so I'm left with about three thousand six hundred square metres of weeds.

So let's say I can strim ten square metres on a charge and the charge lasts me half an hour. So, where are we? Three thousand six hundred divided by ten multiplied by half an hour.

'Well,' said Chris. 'How long's it going to take you to get the garden looking nice again?'

'One hundred and eighty,' I said, like a darts commentator.

'Minutes?'

'Erm. No. Hours.'

'What? That's—'

'—seven and a half days. If I don't sleep or eat.'

'Are you sure?'

'Without taking my socks off and counting my toes to double check, yes.'

'Does that include charging time?'

'Oh, shit, no. Half an hour strimming, two hours charging … multiply that by five then. That's thirty-seven and a half days.'

'Well that's no good.'

'I know. And assuming you do let me sleep and eat, then it'll take me about seventy-five days … if I do a twelve-hour day and never go back to work … and then it'll be time to start over again.'

We looked at each other glumly.

'We've rented the Forth bloody Bridge!' I said.

As we were pondering this bombshell, Olivia popped round for the rent money and to help herself to some oranges, which had ripened nicely while we'd been away – we did have fourteen orange trees and we would never be able to eat and juice that many oranges ourselves, so she was more than welcome to fill a few bags whenever she liked.

I had the strimmer charging on the terrace and she asked me what it was. I couldn't remember what the Spanish for strimmer was, even though it will have been written on the box. I knew it didn't resemble the English word, and it didn't exactly trip off the tongue, so I mimed it instead.

'Whoosh, whoosh, *eléctrico*,' I said.

'*¿Eléctrico? No, no. Necesitas gasolina*,' she said.

Yes, I knew I needed a bloody petrol strimmer … now … and yes, I knew I was a bloody idiot for buying a cordless electric one … now … but no need to rub it in, eh?

'*¿Cuánto cuesta?*'

'What's Spanish for a hundred, Chris?' We hadn't done big numbers in Spanish class yet.

'*Cien euros*,' Chris told Olivia.

'*Vamos a la ferretería a comprar una de gasolina. Pagaré la mitad contigo, ¿no?*'

'*Muchas gracias*,' Chris replied.

I looked at Chris for clarification. I didn't catch all of that.

'Olivia says she'll go to the *ferretería* with you to buy a petrol strimmer and she'll go halves with you,' Chris said.

'*Ah, muchas gracias*,' I said to Olivia.

So I jumped in Olivia's car, and we drove round to the local *ferretería* – who funnily enough don't sell ferrets ... they're the Spanish equivalent of your local hardware store – where we bought a two-hundred-euro petrol strimmer and a litre of oil between us. The fella in the shop took me out back, added some two-stroke to it – which I now realise is a petrol and oil mix you make up yourself – and he showed me how it worked. It didn't half go at a fair old lick. I was proper chuffed. This was going to make my life much easier.

When Olivia had gone home, I fired up my new toy and gave it a test drive. It was the bee's knees – or as we prefer to say up north, the dog's bollocks. This was going to make light work of the garden, I thought ... as it happened, it took me sixteen hours over the next three days to do a proper job, but that's a damned sight quicker than seventy-five days with the electric one.

José next door looked on and shook his head.

After I'd tamed the garden, I had to figure out how to get my money back for the useless electric strimmer. I spent an hour cleaning every last trace of weed off it with a bucket of warm, soapy water so it looked like I'd barely had it out. I then dismantled all the parts and repacked them all neatly into the box. Then we drove back down to the coast to get a refund.

It wasn't easy, as apart from the language barrier, the battle-axe on the Customer Service desk wasn't having any of it at first. I tried to explain to her that the point-of-sale bumph had misrepresented the abilities of this piddling toy strimmer and that it wouldn't perform anything like as well as advertised. She told me it was only designed for trimming the borders around tree trunks – which having now used it I'm sure was true – but it wasn't what I wanted it for or what I thought it had suggested it was capable of.

She eventually relented and gave me a credit note. I don't suppose I could grumble in the end. Persistence seems to pay off, then. I'd like to think she took pity on me, but I think she just wanted rid of me as there was an ever-growing queue of people waiting in turn behind me – no doubt returning rechargeable strimmers.

23

A Burning Ambition

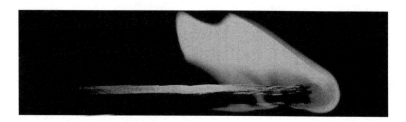

When I was a kid, I was fascinated by fire. I think most kids are. Much like King Louis, I wanted 'to be a man, mancub'. It's something about the hypnotic nature of the dancing flames, and I have memories of building bonfires on waste ground with the other local kids. I also used to collect matchbooks as a hobby.

Incidentally, why is it always boys that collect stuff like this? It's always boys (or men) that go trainspotting. It's always boys (or men) that go to their local airfield and write down plane numbers. I've even been on a few coach trips to Aintree races to watch the Grand National, and as you get close to the racetrack there's a load of anoraks (men again) jotting down details of all the bloody coaches – have you ever heard anything so ridiculous? Nutters.

Anyway, I got rid of the matchbook collection in the end, thankfully. And if, like me, you like seeing a good old fire, there's no better place to see one (or loads of them) than at València's annual *Las Fallas* festival. It's the most marvellous spectacle I've ever seen. The festival runs from the first to the nineteenth of March and is an assault of the senses, both visually and aurally.

In addition to the hundreds of enormous papier-mâché satirical statues on the street corners that are set light to on the last night of the festival, there are the chest-thumping, bone-shaking, daily *mascletas* events – the explosion of thousands of bangers in unison outside the town hall – and incredible firework displays. Not to mention the hordes of young kids running round at all times of the day and night letting off firecrackers that they gleefully toss at your feet as you're strolling the city streets.

There are also the marching bands from each district that accompany flower carriers to the cathedral square where a magnificent floral effigy of the Virgin Mary is constructed over a number of days.

We usually aim to book a hotel on the outskirts of town rather than right in the centre of town, otherwise you won't get any sleep ... in fact, many of the locals leave town for the duration so they can get a decent night's kip.

Imagine my delight, then, that my new life in Spain included the opportunity to build and light fires both in the garden and in the house. The garden fires were garden waste, of course, but in the house, we burnt *leña*, or firewood to you and me. Olive wood seemed to be the most popular wood to burn indoors in Spain, and you could buy it in bags of about twenty-five kilos, or better still, more economical cubic metre sacks. The problem with the larger sacks was that you needed somewhere dry to store it.

Our new villa had nowhere suitable to store a quantity of wood and keep it dry – the shed was only big enough for my golf clubs and some gardening equipment. So if we were going to buy big sacks of olive wood over the winter then I'd need somewhere to store it. What I needed was a wood store.

Now you could buy metal wood stores from the DIY chains, but they were tall and thin and didn't look very stable, so they were probably best suited to standing up against a wall. The only place something like that could work here was up against the side of the villa, and I didn't fancy it being struck by lightning, going up in flames and taking us and the villa with it, so that was out of the question. They also cost a hundred and twenty euros, and I was sure I could build a better one myself out of wood for less money than that, and one that would be squatter and sturdier and could be freestanding next to the garden fence behind the house.

So next time Olivia popped round to stick something in the ground, I asked her where the best place was to buy timber. Before I knew it, I'd been bundled into the car and directed to the local timber merchant. Armed with a pretty decent drawing of what I wanted to build, complete with dimensions, and with a native Andalusian speaker in tow, I was confident I'd get what I was after.

My wood store needed to accommodate a cubic metre of firewood, so the structure I'd drawn was two metres long by half a metre wide and a metre tall, with floor clearance to keep the wood on the bottom dry. I was impressed with my drawing, and I think the guy at the timber merchant was too.

We were soon on the way home with all the wood I needed, cut to my detailed specifications. All I had to do was screw it all together. What I wasn't expecting was how much wood costs in Spain. In the UK, I could have bought all that for about thirty-five pounds. Over here, it had just cost me sixty-five euros.

I then went to the *ferretería* to buy a box of wood screws, a few metres of plastic netting to stop the wood falling out the back of the wood store, a bag of cable ties, and a few metres of plastic sheeting for the top and sides, with enough to make a weighted dropdown plastic flap for the front to rainproof it when we had a downpour.

By the time I'd sourced everything I needed, I'd spent almost ninety euros. But hey, what the heck, my wooden wood store was going to look the business … it was going to be freestanding, rainproof and as sturdy as my nan's old outside loo that even the Germans couldn't demolish … in other words, the dog's bollocks.

It took me a couple of hours to knock up and I was well chuffed with it. I love working with wood – it makes me feel like Tim Allen … no, not the bald funny *Bake Off* host, that's *Tom* Allen … I'm talking about the character called Tim 'The Tool Man' Taylor of 90s' American sitcom *Home Improvement* fame.

I put my wood store up against the fence and mounted it on stones to stop the feet from rotting, then I stood back to admire it.

Chris came out to assess my handiwork.

'You've done a great job there, hun,' she said.

'I know,' I replied, with just a hint of smugness. 'I might enter it for the Turner Prize.'

24

It's Snow Joke

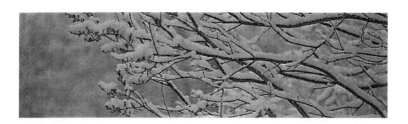

With me resuming my thousand-mile commute to work again, Chris had some respite from the loneliness when her eldest sister, Dee, and her husband, Paul, came over for a few days. It was a rare treat for them – they're normally watching everyone else disappear on holiday, as they run a rather excellent 'if Carlsberg did ...' kennels and cattery in Yorkshire.

While I was freezing my knackers off in the UK, they were sunbathing in my freshly strimmed garden. And while they were admiring blue-sky-framed mountain views and drinking red wine on the terrace, I was looking out over the grey expanse of an industrial estate in Luton, pondering what to have on my Tesco butty for lunch.

Meanwhile, my laptop was on its last legs and the keyboard kept freezing up for no apparent reason, perhaps coming out in sympathy with the weather outside my office window. So I took a detour on the way to Tesco and stopped by Curry's to buy a new laptop that would boot up in under ten minutes and let me type something once in a while.

Despite working with computers every day, getting the laptop configured was a nightmare. It made me wonder how your average member of the public copes with these things. It was for that very reason that when my Dad wanted to get online to book cheap flights to Spain, I flatly refused to help him buy a laptop. I could just envisage the hours of telephone support I'd need to give him afterwards, with him saying things like 'What's a mouse?' and 'What do you mean, turn it off and on again? How's that supposed to fix it?'

Patience is described in the dictionary as 'being able to stay calm and not get annoyed, for example when something takes a long time, or when someone is not doing what you want them to do', and as that would undoubtedly be in very short supply – at both ends of the phone line – there was no way I was helping my septuagenarian father descend into the pit of despair that comes from owning a computer. Instead, I took him to John Lewis and helped him choose a Samsung Galaxy tablet, which would be infinitely more reliable, cheaper and easier to use than anything Bill Gates ever invented.

After overlapping fleetingly with Dee and Paul for one night when I returned to Spain – and being told we'd done the right thing moving here, although I felt a bit of a fraud on that score still – it was back off to Luton again the following week. The light was getting brighter at the end of this contract tunnel, though.

After the plane had skidded to a halt at Britain's fifth busiest – and in my bitter experience, filthiest – airport, I had to scrape snow off my car before I could head for the delights of the Holiday Inn Luton South once more. I flicked on the all-too-familiar kettle and checked how many brews I might be allowed to have based on the number of UHT milk cartons the maid had left when she'd done the changeover this morning. Then I flopped on the bed and called Chris.

'It's snowing here,' I said.

'We might get snow in Spain this week,' she replied.

'Yeah, but not where you are, surely. You're on the Costa del Sol. There were people lying on Torremolinos beach when I flew over it earlier.'

'You never know. Olivia called round to admire your wood store after you'd left, and we were talking about the weather forecast. She thinks we might get snow along the Costas. She said she has a photo on the wall at home of snow on the Sierra de Mijas sixty-three years ago. She's never seen snow in Alhaurín herself.'

'Well, let's hope it's another sixty-three years before she does.'

'She'll be dead then.'

'And so will we be. And if I die not having seen snow on the Sierra de Mijas, I'll die a happy man.'

Two days later it snowed on the Sierra de Mijas.

And halfway down it in Alhaurín El Grande ... and in most of Andalucía ... and even in our garden.

Temperatures across the province plummeted, with most inland parts experiencing daytime temperatures that started with a minus. The Sierra de las Nieves (the 'snowy mountain range') that is visible to our west and gets a smattering on the peaks most years had the biggest snowfall for thirty years, and all road access in and out of Ronda was cut off. They even got the snowploughs out, which I didn't even know they had in Andalucía.

'I need to see photographic evidence, please,' I said to Chris when she rang to tell me the news.

And then a photo arrived of a white mountain and the garden covered in a fine white layer.

'It's exciting, isn't it?' she said.

'Exciting? We've moved there to be rid of stuff that falls out of the sky.'

'Yeah, but I'll be able to tell Olivia that now *I've* got a photo of snow on the mountain too.'

And that's all she was bothered about.

Sure enough, when I arrived home the following evening, the mountain was still white, and the house was freezing if you weren't within six feet of the wood burner.

'Jeepers, it's cold in this house,' I said, as I dumped my case in the bedroom. 'Have you got the air con heating on?'

'Yes.'

'And did you buy an electric blanket?'

'Yes, you nesh bugger. I've put it on full power. Any more questions?'

'Yes. How old do we have to be to claim the UK winter fuel allowance?'

125

25

Caught in the Headlights

When we came to Mijas to find somewhere to live, we had a look at the price of secondhand cars and were quite shocked at how expensive they were. It seems that, compared to the UK, there is a very buoyant used car market in Spain, with prices holding up unnaturally high. I don't know why, given most Spanish cars I've seen so far have at least one badly dented panel.

Maybe the lack of rain (and snow) meant they didn't rust like they did in the UK.

Having seen how much we'd need to pay to buy left-hand drive cars of a similar quality to those we already had, we decided to import our own cars. There was the cost of changing the headlamps over and the import duty to pay, but even with those costs factored in, it seemed the best option.

Also, with Chris's Mini and my Lexus being twelve and ten years old – and having longer and more distinguished service histories than your average squaddie – we felt it was 'better the devil you know'.

And so it was that we found the deadline fast approaching for when we had to have Chris's car converted to Spanish plates. Prior to receiving its new plates, this would first involve the car passing its ITV, the Spanish *Inspección Técnica de Vehiculos* – or MOT to you and me. And before it could do that, we had to replace the headlamps with left-hand drive ones.

After first trying (unsuccessfully) to find any at our local scrap yard, I found myself trawling the internet for some.

Eventually, I tracked down a pair of new ones for a not inconsiderable – although much cheaper than my Lexus ones I was to discover later – 368 euros, being sold by a reputable German auto parts company via the German eBay site.

Fifteen days later, and with only twenty-six days until the Mini had to ace its ITV, I collected the headlamps from our PO Box and took them, with the car, to the Spanish mechanic that had repaired Chris's car after its little contretemps with a BMW last month.

An hour and a half later the mechanic called me. There was a problem.

'You give me left lights,' he said.

'Yes, that's right,' I said. 'I've given you left-hand drive lights.'

'No. You give me two left lights.'

'What?'

'Two lights the same. Both for left side.'

Bugger.

I walked back up to the repair shop and brought back the car, which now sported one European left-hand headlamp and one UK right-hand headlamp with the deflector still stuck on it.

I quickly contacted the seller with the photographic evidence. It didn't seem possible. Inside the box I'd received were two smaller individual boxes, one of them liveried in black lettering with a sticker that described its contents as being a left-hand lamp for an 04-06 plate Mini and an image of a Mini with a big arrow pointing to the left headlamp position, the other liveried in red lettering with a sticker proclaiming the contents to be a right-hand lamp with a corresponding image pointing to the right headlamp.

I had to explain to the German seller that the right lamp was not right at all – in fact, it was very wrong, it was a left one … in a right box, but not THE right box.

I asked them if they wanted me to send the extra left lamp back in the right box, i.e. the one marked for left so they could sell it on again in the correct box, or to send it back in the wrong box, i.e. the right box.

I think they understood me, even if I was confused myself.

I was to return it in the right box – the wrong one – so they could send it back to their supplier. Sadly, it was Saturday afternoon and the Spanish post office, Correos, didn't even open in the afternoon on a weekday, never mind at the weekend.

Now the Spanish are known for a lot of things – good weather, fine wine, picture-postcard white villages (and pretty brunettes) – to name but a few, but they're not really known for their efficiency … it was the Germans who were known worldwide as being Teutonically efficient … until, that is, they sent me a left-hand headlamp in a right-hand box!

And now the clock was ticking down rapidly to the ITV date.

On Monday morning, I ventured into our local Correos office with my parcel duly labelled up for Germany and replete with my homemade, informative (yet cheerful), capitalised, red-texted, multi-lingual, 'Don't dare lose or bloody kick this fragile parcel unless you want the gates of Hades to open up on you' stickers.

As I walked into the cramped, busy little office, there appeared to be no queuing system in place. Some people were standing, some were sitting, some people were shouting pleasantries to the person next to them … and then there was me.

As I looked around the space, somewhat bewildered, someone in the far corner shouted in my general direction.

'*Soy el último,*' he said.

I looked behind me, but there was nobody there. Was he talking to me? Who knows?

A moment later, the door at my back swung open, and I stepped aside to make way for a tiny old woman, who stepped into the middle of the room. She looked around her, letting on to some people, then she turned back to me.'

'*¿Eres el último?*' she asked.

The woman next to me stepped in and ended my obvious confusion, confirming to the old *señora* that yes, I was indeed the last person in the queue before her.

And that must be how it works: you walk in, stand (or sit) wherever you like, and when the next person comes in, so they know you were the last person in before them, you shout '*Soy el último'* at them in a rather charming old-school, sociable, Spanish queueing system kind of way.

Now that I wasn't the last in the queue, my job was done – I no longer had to shout my position in the queue at anyone. So I kept my beady eye on the bloke in the corner, and after he'd gone up to the desk, I went up next.

The queueing system seemed to work beautifully, like a carefully choreographed Torvill-and-Dean-inspired, Ravel's-Boléro-fashioned, "it's a six from the Russian judge!", 1980s' puff-sleeved ice dance. I was just thankful that my Bambiesque hesitant stumble onto the ice in Alhaurín's Correos office wasn't witnessed by 150 million people live on TV.

I stepped out into the sunshine and went for a sit down and a stiff drink at the nearest café bar. It didn't bother me that the little hand hadn't reached the number ten yet … it had just cost me an eye-watering thirty-six euros to send a smallish box by recorded delivery to Germany. Did it have its own plane or something?

Six days later, and with less then three weeks now until the ITV date, I checked on the progress of my return on the Correos website. It had left Spain after two days passing between several sets of bored Iberian hands but hadn't yet reached its intended destination – I guessed it was probably currently strapped to a donkey somewhere in the Massif Central.

I pinged the supplier to make sure they weren't waiting for the donkey to arrive before they shipped the replacement. They weren't. They'd received the replacement from their own supplier but had had the foresight to check the contents before shipping it onto me. In doing so, they'd discovered the right-hand-labelled box contained another left-hand headlamp.

Was there a Mini somewhere in Bavaria driving round with two right-hand headlamps? Very probably.

This brought to mind a story from one of the core textbooks for my Marketing degree that told of an East German glut of left-hand (or strictly speaking, left-foot) shoes. In a stunning example of everything that's wrong with communism, some bright spark behind the Berlin Wall had decided that it was more efficient if a factory only made one half of a pair of shoes, with another factory making the other shoe; that way, the tooling could all be the same in each factory and the process more efficient. When the factory making the right-hand/foot shoe closed down, they forgot to tell the other factory, and production of the left-hand/foot shoe continued unabated for quite some time. Top marks for ingenuity there, Helmut – you couldn't make it up, could you?!

A further three days passed before the correct headlamp was despatched forthwith, the donkey hopefully having been fed and watered on the finest bratwurst and glühwein money could buy before it was turned around, pointed in the general direction of Spain, and given whatever humane encouragement it needed to make haste.

The lightly laden *burro* made reasonable time, all in all, traversing the Pyrenees once more and delivering the headlamp to me eight days later, beating the ITV deadline by a sphincter-relaxing nine days. The headlamp was duly attached and the little Mini was ready for its big test day.

Not yet knowing the system and lacking the language skills to get through the big day unscathed, we decided to employ the services of Bruno at the PO Box. He booked the test date for us and then met us down at the test centre.

In the UK, you take your car to a garage that, among other things, is authorised to carry out the MOT test. In Spain, they either don't trust car mechanics to do a proper honest job of it, or it's some kind of public employment scheme, because you have to take your car to one of only a handful of government-owned test centres. In Málaga Province, there are eight of them … covering an area of 2,821 sq. miles, i.e. one every 352 sq. miles … and seven of those are on the coast.

We took ours to one on the outskirts of Málaga city. It was utter carnage down there. The place was a right dump – although we've since been using a brand new one on Mijas Costa that's very swish. It was busier than the turkey aisle in Aldi on Christmas Eve, and some old boy came close to taking the entire right side of the Mini off while he was manoeuvring out of a parking space. If I hadn't been in the driver's seat pressing the horn, he would have done.

After going into the office, presenting the requisite documents and paying for the test, you then wait in your car in the car park until your registration number comes up on a digital display telling you which entrance door to head to.

And that's the other difference with the test in Spain. In the UK, you just give the mechanic the keys, and he puts the car on a ramp and carries out all the tests while you get a brew in a grease-laden side office. In Spain, you stay in your car and drive it along a line of test equipment yourself.

Bruno sat beside me as my translator and off we went to our nominated entrance. After lifting the bonnet to check the Vehicle Identification Number matched the car's paperwork and noting the mileage, the mechanic whipped out a tape measure.

'What's he doing?' I asked Bruno.

'He's measuring the car.'

'Why, to see if it's really a Hummer instead of a Mini?'

'Eh? No, he's checking the ground clearance and the height of the car to see if it's been modified since you bought it.'

They apparently do that the first time through. After that, he checked the exhaust emissions and headlamp alignment. I felt a bead of sweat slide past my right eye as I had no idea if the mechanic had fitted the lights correctly or not. I needn't have worried.

Then he checked the other lights and indicators, the seatbelts, window mechanisms, windscreen washer and wipers and the horn. You then drive forward to the wheel-spinning thingies while he checks your brakes. And finally, it's forward once more over the inspection pit. He clips a walkie-talkie onto your window and gets under the car shouting instructions to you to waggle the steering wheel while he checks the shock absorbers, suspension, tyre wear and underside of the car. All very nerve-wracking the first time through.

You then wait while he tells you if the car has passed or not. The Mini got full marks and was rewarded with a little ITV sticker to go on the windscreen. And the price for this little exercise? Not much change out of a hundred and fifty euros. However, that was only because it was the car's first ITV in

Spain, as after that it's around thirty euros, or about half the price of a UK one.

We dropped Bruno off and celebrated with a *menú del día* at El Bichito, which incidentally costs a remarkable seven euros for olives, bread, a starter, main course, dessert and a drink. Why do we live in Spain again?

26

Agent Orange

One of the lovely things about living in Spain, even in the winter when it's as cold as the tip of a polar bear's todger inside the villa, is that you can sit on the terrace in the morning sunshine and have your breakfast. We're not big on breakfast normally, but it's made a pleasant change to have some toasted bread with olive oil, salt and freshly grated Spanish tomatoes every now and again.

You can't beat a Spanish tomato – they're just so full of flavour and so fresh, unlike the ones you get in the UK that have been picked too early and ripened in the back of a lorry for a week.

You also can't beat a freshly squeezed Spanish orange juice, especially if the orange was on the tree five minutes earlier.

Oranges are one of the world's most popular fruits, and nowhere more so than in Spain, where you're never more than five yards away from an orange tree, even in town, where they line the streets and plazas – although the town oranges are marmaladers, so don't try eating them.

A typical large Spanish orange delivers around one hundred calories, and although it's mainly made up of water and carbohydrates, they're a great source of vitamin C. But when I've been juicing the oranges off the trees that line our back fence, I've noticed that there's a wide variety of flavours amongst them, some of which are nicer than the others. And I have to avoid the acidic ones if I can.

You see, since my mad, beer-addled, disco-dancing, teenage university years I've had a problem with acid reflux. I used to call it my lager throat, as at that time I had no idea what it was … I just knew that if I'd been out on the lash, then chances were, I'd get heartburn, although why they call it that when mine is at the top of my throat and nowhere near my heart I don't know. Maybe everyone gets it differently, and mine is just remarkably high up my oesophagus. I've no idea.

It was Chris who diagnosed me in the end. We were having a cheeky little weekend break up in Galloway in the southwest corner of Scotland, and we'd been out for dinner and a few drinks. We were the only guests in a small B&B in a quiet little backwater, and we'd gone off to bed as soon as we'd got in. In the middle of the night, I felt sick and headed for the bathroom down the corridor – no en suite in this place. Well, I didn't quite make it as far as the bathroom, and I projectile vomited about twelve square yards of floor and wall. It was like a scene out of *The Exorcist*.

Poor Chris spent the next few hours cleaning it all up with whatever products she could find under the bathroom sink, to the point where, come morning, you couldn't really tell what had happened. I really don't know how she managed it. It was a miracle. She's a miracle! And given this was before Aggie and Kim could be found dispensing their household cleaning tips on *How Clean Is Your House?*, how did she know what to do?

A short while before this trip, I'd been to the hospital to see a specialist at Ear, Nose and Throat, and he was suggesting operating on my throat. That sounded a bit drastic, especially as I played the trumpet, and he couldn't give me any guarantees that the operation wouldn't affect my ability to play. So I said I'd live with it, thanks.

Anyway, after my remarkably authentic impression of Linda Blair at the guesthouse, Chris told me that it was her considered (and learned) opinion as a hospital sister on a surgical ward that my problem lay not in my gullet but in my stomach, and that she reckoned I had a hiatus hernia.

And would you believe it, she was right – my flabber was truly gasted!

Chris recommended one of the surgeons at her hospital, and I had surgery to repair it. This was done at a time when keyhole surgery was still a bit risky, so I let him open me up with a butcher's knife so he could have a good rummage around inside me. Afterwards, I was fine for about twenty years until it went again. I also had a six-inch vertical scar above my belly button, but the reward was worth the minor detriment to my beach body, and I now tell the grandkids I was attacked by a shark.

As a result of my continued gastronomical troubles, which included a less successful repeat operation recently, I now found myself trying to figure out how acidic or sweet the oranges were on our fourteen trees. There was only one thing for it: a taste test.

Up the garden I went with a marker pen and a plastic bag, and I carefully selected the juiciest looking orange off each tree, marking each one in turn with a number from one to fourteen. Trust me, you'd do the same if you suffered for your diet like I do.

I then juiced them all by hand, one at a time, and poured the contents into fourteen glasses on the kitchen worktop.

'Chris?' I shouted when I was ready.

'What?'

'Can I borrow you for a minute?'

She came into the kitchen and looked at me, nonplussed.

'What are you doing?' she asked.

'We're having a taste test. One orange off each tree.'

'Why?'

'I want to see which ones are best for juicing.'

'You're a complete idiot.'

'No, I'm not … I'm missing a few bits so I can't be a *complete* idiot. Anyway, it's an important scientific experiment; one that may prevent the onset of heartburn and cut down my dependence on Gaviscon.'

So we both worked our way along the row, tasting each one in turn. I gave Chris a pad and a pen and asked her to record our tasting notes.

'Here's tree number one,' I said, sloshing the contents of my glass around to aerate it. 'This is the tree at the top of the garden. What do you reckon to that?'

'Hmm. It's a bit sweet for me, that one.'

I tried it myself and loved it. Chris wrote '1. Sweet' on the pad.

'Now try number two,' I said.

'Ooh. I like that one. Nice and tart.'

I tried it. Not to my taste.

'Heartburn in a glass,' I said.

She wrote down '2. Tart'

We both agreed that number three had a strange woody aftertaste, so she made a note. The process continued until we'd tried all fourteen. Reviewing Chris's notes afterwards, our oranges varied across the scale from sweet to tart, with one even having the unusual characteristic of tasting synthetic – maybe that's where next door's cats did their business ... either way, we wouldn't be eating them.

The upshot was, Chris preferred the tarter ones, although she'd taken a real aversion to number seven, and she'd drawn a sad face after number fourteen.

'There,' I said. 'That was worth doing, right? So we'll avoid eating three, six, seven, thirteen and fourteen, juice eight to eleven, you can eat two and twelve, I'll eat one, four and five, and if we run out of good juicers, we can mix two with one, four or five.'

'You're a complete idiot,' she said again, and she went back to doing whatever she'd been doing.

27

You Can Call Me Chef Paco

'Wow! That looks like a great paella, Drew.'

'You can call me Chef Paco,' I replied.

I've always liked the name Paco. I've a couple of old Spanish clients called Paco. It's a familiar term for someone christened Francisco, a bit like John being changed to Jack. In fact, Francisco can be shortened to Frank, Paco, Cisco, Pancho, or even Chico.

We had a couple of friends visiting, and I'd done one of my seafood paellas again – or rather two paellas, as I always had to make Chris a separate one without the shellfish. Our friends had come over for some winter sunshine and were holidaying in Benalmádena, down on the coast. We'd been down to collect them and bring them back to our place for a spot of lunch. Chris and I thought there was a chill in the air, so we had jeans and hoodies on. We therefore laughed when we picked up our guests at Benalmádena marina, who were both in shorts and flip-flops.

'Spot the tourists,' I'd said to Chris when they came round the corner.

Like me, my mate Andy was a trumpeter, but unlike me he was a bloody good one. And a great lad, to boot. He was ex-army, so salt of the earth in my view, as I have a lot of time for our service personnel. After leaving the army he'd joined the police force and, since serving Queen and country for the requisite number of years, had just taken early retirement.

His wife, Ali, was also a copper, and a right good laugh. Being fans of the Spanish lifestyle themselves, they fully understood why we'd emigrated, and were a bit jealous of us, they said.

'Have you come over here to escape the rationing?' I asked them.

'What rationing?'

'I saw on the news that you've hardly any veg left in the UK – the supermarket shelves are empty according to the newspapers.'

'I bought spuds and carrots at the weekend,' Ali said.

'I think it's the stuff you import from Spain you're short of … avocados, tomatoes, lettuces, courgettes, that sort of thing. Morrisons are limiting customers to two lettuces.'

'I don't think I've ever bought two lettuces in one visit anyway,' she laughed.

'What's caused that, then,' Andy said.

'Something to do with all the sodding rain we had over Christmas up and down the Costas. It's played havoc with the growing season.'

'Have you got shortages here, then?'

'No. Full shelves here. The wholesalers are making sure the Spanish market has enough stock before they export anything to you lot. You might want to dump your clothes and fill your cases with avocados before you fly home.'

'I don't know about avocados, but I'll have a bag of your oranges,' Andy said.

'You're more than welcome. Do you like them sweet or tart?' I asked.

'Oh, don't go down that road again,' Chris laughed. 'And while you're at it, go and pick a lemon for the paella.'

The food was great – even if I do say so myself – and I had a load of extra mussels to go round too. Next door's cats had smelt the shellfish and had come wandering over, looking for leftovers. They got to share a plateful of prawn heads and shells, which they wolfed down.

After everyone had been fed and watered, they spent the rest of the afternoon licking each other – the cats, that is. We then dropped our guests back down on the coast.

While they were with us, Andy had asked me if I'd been practising my trumpet, and I had to admit that I hadn't really. And I felt a bit guilty about that. I'd been playing for over forty years, mostly in big bands, as I loved my jazz music. As teenagers, four friends and I had gone into Manchester in the run up to Christmas and set up outside the Marks and Spencer store to do a bit of busking. Thankfully that day, the IRA didn't try and blow it up, something they achieved fifteen years later in 1996 with a one-and-a-half-tonne bomb that was bigger than anything to hit Britain since Hitler carpet bombed London with doodlebugs.

I'd done some jazz arrangements of popular Christmas carols, and we made a killing. We earned about five pounds an hour each over the space of a few hours, which was good money in the early eighties. We had such a fun time that we went back every week until Christmas. At one point, the store manager came out and asked to speak to the leader. I thought we were in trouble for making a racket, or perhaps plagiarism … we had a handmade sign in the tuba case that bore the name 'The *St Michael* jazz band' – I'd nicked one of M&S's brand names and even used the same font.

He hadn't come out to complain. In fact, he wanted us to go and play for half an hour while his staff ate their Christmas lunch. He paid us and fed us afterwards.

The landlord of one of the oldest pubs in Manchester, The Shakespeare, also booked us. Although the pub was only built in 1923, some of it dates back to the seventeenth century and was brought from Chester to Manchester. The pub's supposed to be haunted by the ghost of the chef who hung himself in there at some point in the past. I'm not sure what he made of our busking, but I hope it cheered him up a bit. We did half an hour in there, sent the hat round afterwards and then tucked into a free lunch again.

But the weirdest gig we got from our busking experience was playing Manchester's infamous nightclub, The Haçienda, on

139

New Year's Eve. I wouldn't say the punters were exactly 'mad for it' that night as we wandered round the place playing jazzy carols, but we probably weren't the worst band to ever play there. In fact, given the amount of drugs knocking round town in the eighties, some of the space cadets that witnessed our performance might have just put it down to the drugs messing with their heads.

Anyway, after Andy had sown a seed about getting back to playing my trumpet, I had a look round on Facebook for any local musos that might need a trumpeter. A local expat drummer called Richie agreed to meet me in a bar in Alhaurín the following weekend, and there was a chap on the coast who ran a big band, but it was out of season, so they weren't back playing again yet.

I only had two weeks left to work, and I was starting to get demob happy. I had one more week to do in Luton while the project went live, and then I could offer support from Málaga for the final week of my contract. I left Luton and drove my car up to Manchester one last time. I had dinner with friends then took Mum and Dad to watch my old big band playing. It was great to see and hear the band play again, and it was another reminder of what I'd left behind in the UK. But hopefully I could find someone to play with in Spain soon.

The other big news was that we had tenants moving into our old house – at last! I didn't know why it had taken so long, but they sounded like a nice, respectable young family that planned to be in the area for some time. With my contract ending, the extra income would come in handy.

The following morning, I left my car at Manchester airport and flew back to Spain. On Sunday night, I took Chris into town with me while I went to meet up with the drummer. We'd agreed to meet up at a place called Nuevo Y Sur, a lively little bar we hadn't been in yet that was run by a young Dutch lad. When we got there, there were a couple of Spanish guys setting up with microphones and guitars, so we found a table in the corner and got some drinks in.

The drummer was a no-show – something to do with a family emergency, which was a shame, and we never did meet up again afterwards – but we had a great night all the same. The two guitarists, Tim and Jay, were talented musicians with great voices, and they performed around Málaga as The Gypsy Bros. They were incredibly good (and incredibly good-looking). For two guys, they had a huge sound, and before long, we were singing along to all our favourite Gipsy Kings tracks. Apart from great music, the bar was buzzing, inside and out, and the food was delicious. Suffice to say, we left the car and got a taxi home.

'Now that's why we moved to Spain,' I said, as I flopped on the bed fully clothed and passed out.

28

Floody Marvellous

The following day, in honour of my final working week – and to remind me what I'd be missing by leaving the UK – it rained heavily in Alhaurín all morning.

Just before lunch, during a brief respite, I went down to check on the pool pump, and it was half full of water again. So I jumped in the car and went round to the *ferretería* and bought a portable electric pump and twenty metres of hose.

With the saturated ground around the pump box adding to the problem, I thought it best to pump the water halfway down the garden, hence the long hose. Using the electric pump allowed me to clear the pump box of all but the last few inches of water, but I still needed a mop and bucket for the last dregs.

So in the absence of a permanent solution to the flooding problem, I resigned myself to the idea of having to pump the water out every time we had really heavy rainfall, which thankfully on the Costa del Sol, with at least three hundred days of sunshine, shouldn't be that often – although in our first five months it had flooded three times already.

With the weather not being great, I used the office we'd set up in the third bedroom to continue working and supporting my client. As it was a bit chilly, I closed the door and put the air con on heating mode and the room was soon quite toasty. The go-live had gone well and there were very few issues for me to deal with – it was like the last day of school when the teacher said you could wear what you wanted and bring a toy in!

On the Thursday, I flew over to Manchester on my own for the night. Our eldest granddaughters, twins Grace and Lucy, were celebrating their fourteenth birthday soon and I was flying them back to Spain with me the following day as a birthday treat.

I knew all about bringing up stroppy teenage girls, and it wasn't a time I often looked back fondly on. The twins were mostly no trouble – although their mother might beg to differ. However, they did appear to suffer from the same affliction as most teenage girls in that they leave a tangle of clothes, hair and make-up strewn around the place – it's as if someone has been dragging an overflowing wheelie bin behind them.

After the earlier rain, the weather had brightened up, and it was blue sky central by the time we landed on the Friday night – or it would have been if it wasn't midnight when we landed.

Unfortunately, with it being the middle of February, having a dip in the pool was out of the question for the girls as it was barely ten degrees. So we went and spent the day sightseeing in Málaga instead. They're both keen and skilled young artists, so we took them to visit CAC Málaga, the city's Contemporary Art Museum. The American artist, Mark Ryden, who has a particularly thought-provoking style, had an exhibition there.

His work is described as Pop Surrealism, being a blend of pop culture and surrealism, but using techniques handed down by the old masters. There's an unnatural and brooding element to his work as he mixes cherubic girls with mysterious figures, and as a result, I would describe it as downright creepy. I loved it, personally, and I think the girls did too. Chris a bit less so, I reckon. It was much more interesting, I felt, than works by Málaga's most famous son ... what? ... no, not Antonio Banderas ... Pablo Picasso.

Then it was off to Mijas Pueblo on the way back to visit the Mayan Monkey ice cream parlour. We went in and made our own chocolate bars in the little on-site chocolate factory, which was a fun experience and excellent value for money.

It was a weekend full of our favourite trips out, including Sunday lunch on the large terrace down at El Jinete. And to round the weekend off, we took them into Alhaurín on Sunday night to listen to The Gypsy Bros in Nuevo Y Sur again, although this time I behaved myself and only had the one beer.

On Monday morning, I was up bright and early ... not that I had any work to do ... I was retired! Until I could find a job in Spain, of course – I had to keep Chris in the lifestyle to which she was fast becoming accustomed.

No, I was up early because we were all on the eleven o'clock EasyJet flight to Manchester. It was time to take the girls home and go and collect my car from the airport for the last time. The Lexus was finally going to be starting its own *New Life in the Sun*.

29

Taking the Wine Route

Ten days later, after driving through the Channel Tunnel – and after making a few detours on the way down through France to load up the car with essential supplies (i.e. bottles of Pomerol from some of Bordeaux's finest wine estates) – we finally found ourselves hurtling down the rather monotonous and longer-than-you-think A63 past Biarritz and onwards to the distant Pyrenees that separate the Iberian Peninsula from the rest of Europe. Approaching the final French toll barrier, Chris suddenly perked up in the passenger seat.

'Are we at the border?' she asked.

'Just about.'

'Have you got the CD in?'

'Yes. It's ready to play.'

'And can I press the button?'

'Yes. You can press the button.' God, it was like having the kids in tow again.

And as we crossed the river Bidasoa and drove into Spain, Chris pressed 'Play', and the sound of Spanish guitar music filled the car as the Gipsy Kings opened up with '*Djobi, Djoba*'.

This was a long-standing tradition of ours. Whenever we crossed the border from France into Spain with the kids, we always put the Gipsy Kings on, and the kids used to clap their hands and sing along – to the few mispronounced words they knew. They loved it, and so did we, to be honest. It usually meant we were only about an hour away from Estartit, and the excitement was usually palpable.

It was much the same again, as we were only two hours from our next stopping off point, the rather wonderful bodega of Eguren Ugarte in the foothills of the Cantabrian mountains, just outside Laguardia in La Rioja. There's no chance of accidentally driving past this place thanks to the unique architectural feature that sits atop the hotel: a large round tower containing a revolving private dining room – sadly, the 'private' bit relates to the family and not the hotel guests, so we didn't get to see the inside of it.

What we did see the inside of was the wine cellar. Descending in the glass lift, our view of the reception was replaced by row upon row of oak barrels in a long, domed room built into the rock. It was like something out of a James Bond film.

The lift descended further until it reached our hotel floor. All the rooms in the hotel looked out over the bodega's 130 hectares of vines, and with this being La Rioja, they were tempranillo vines. Tempranillo comes from the Spanish word *temprano*, which means 'early', as the tempranillo grape is an early-ripening variety that thrives in the higher altitude and cooler climes of La Rioja. And nowhere in the world does it perform better than here, producing wines that have structure, depth and outstanding ageing properties.

Whilst writing about aged wines, I was minded to recall the rather expensive bottle of 1964 Faustino I Gran Reserva that I bought for my best mate, Tony, on his fiftieth birthday. And when I've looked it up, according to the people that know about these things, the best time to drink it is between 2018 and 2022. Well, I reckon the best time to drink it is when I'm there, so I'll have to remind him of that next time I see him.

Come to think of it, how do these experts know that a specific bottle of wine is best drunk when it's somewhere between fifty-four and fifty-eight years old? Has the same bloke been drinking a bottle of it every year since 1964 and saying, 'No, it's not quite ready yet – give it another year, maybe'? If so, can I get a job doing that?

It's safe to say that most great Spanish wines are produced on or around the vast central *meseta* – or plain – that lies north of Madrid, and the winegrowing regions of Ribera del Duero and La Rioja are testament to that fact. Spain devotes around one million hectares of land to wine production, which is more than any other country in the world. As I ponder that for a moment, I can almost hear Chris saying for the umpteenth time since we arrived here last September, 'Remind me again why we moved to Spain'.

With the northern plains being over two thousand feet above sea level, the vines get a good deal of sunlight without the scorching heat, and temperatures at night don't tend to fall too low during the growing season.

But despite having more acreage devoted to wine production than any other country, the wine yield in Spain is particularly low. The yield in France, for example, is three time larger than Spain's, which can be explained in part by Spain's incredibly old vines and the often-challenging growing conditions. But while the yield suffers, the quality certainly doesn't, with those older vines producing wine that really packs a punch.

We'd booked to stay at this rather spectacular bodega for two nights, and included with our hotel stay was a cellar tour and wine tasting, which we'd prebooked for that afternoon. In the meantime, we relaxed for a couple of hours on our terrace.

The wine tour was a real treat. We were taken through wine caves that had been hewn from the mountainside in 1870 by the bodega's founder, Anastasio Eguren. Winding through them, we were intrigued to see that dotted here and there amongst the barrels were individual cases of wine locked away behind small gates in cutaway sections of the rock wall. These, we were informed, were the private wine repositories of the bodega's many clients, who for a few hundred euros each year can store their Eguren Ugarte wines down here. They are then permitted to bring their friends, family or business associates along at any time to enjoy their wines in these unique surroundings around a table in one of the cosy seating areas. How cool is that?

After visiting the caves, which extend for two kilometres under the hillside, and after learning about the family and the wine production, we returned to the airy shop for the wine tasting part. Here we were treated to a good selection of reds and whites, and unusually for us being red wine drinkers, we were quite taken by the monovarietal white tempranillo. A single-grape white Rioja is quite a rarity, apparently, and we thought it would be a particularly welcome drink in the summer months, so along with a case and a half of red, we added half a case of the white too.

At this rate, with the wine we'd collected on our travels south, and now the two cases of Rioja we'd 'invested in', I wondered if I should inflate the tyres on my Lexus a bit more to cope with the extra weight.

After a brief relax and freshen up, we took the James Bond lift back up to the restaurant where we were booked in for a five-course dinner complete with wine pairings. And guess how much that cost? A mere thirty euros each. Our relocation to Spain vindicated again right there. Unbelievable value.

Like the guest rooms, the restaurant looked out over the vineyards and surrounding countryside, although the sun had long disappeared over the horizon now. Apart from one other couple that had already begun eating dinner, we were the only ones in the restaurant. The chef was on top form and the food was delicious. You also had a choice of the Eguren Ugarte wines to go with your main. We were being spoiled rotten.

When our dessert plates had been cleared away, we took our glasses over to the comfy seating area to relax. The waiter then very kindly offered to leave the remainder of the bottle he'd just opened for us. I think you know me well enough now to know that I'm nothing if not polite, so of course we accepted – it'd be rude not to.

'I like it here,' Chris said.

'Me too.'

'Can we come back some time? Maybe at harvest time so I can see all the vines full.'

'I wouldn't mind coming back in the summer because that's when the wine battle takes place.'

'Wine battle?'

'Yeah. It's like the tomato festival in La Tomatina, but instead of throwing tomatoes, they throw red wine at each other.'

'But you hate getting messy.'

'I don't want to get covered in tomatoes, but I think I'd make an exception if someone was throwing red wine at me.'

'And where do they hold that?'

I explained to Chris that battle takes place at dawn, halfway up a mountain outside Haro. The party starts in the town the day before and runs through the night, and then they bus you up the mountain in the morning for the wine fight.

'Well, I'm up for that. It sounds madder than *Las Fallas*.'

The following day, after a late breakfast, we headed out in the car. It was a short drive to Briones and the impressive Vivanco Museum of Wine Culture. Opened in 2004, the museum gives tours of the vast premises, half of which are underground where the winery is based.

The museum consists of several halls that are home to a collection of ancient machinery used in viticulture, along with artworks and a section housing an impressive three and a half thousand corkscrews from around the world, some dating back to the eighteenth century. It's an eye-opening collection, particularly the ones with a very obvious fertility reference, although it's by no means the largest collection of such barware; that record is held by the Museum of Romanian Records, which has an incredible thirty thousand corkscrews ... although I think three and a half thousand is more than enough to satisfy anyone's curiosity.

The winemaking area was a really special place to visit too. I particularly liked the modern-looking oak vats that resembled huge beehives. After spending a couple of hours taking the tour and browsing the museum pieces, there was only one thing left for us to do: taste the wine, of course.

We retired to the café afterwards for a spot of lunch before returning to our hotel. Dinner was another five courses with wine, although the chef had created a different menu for us. We were the only ones dining, so we had the 'full and undivided attention' of our waiter again, if you get my drift.

'It's a hard life,' Chris sighed, as we finished the last bottle of the day.

The next morning we had a long drive ahead. Our destination was the quaint, ancient town of Chinchón, that lies less than thirty miles south of Madrid.

Given that our road trip was a journey of discovery, I'd wanted to drive over the mountains due south of us, going via Soria and then down past Madrid, but we'd had snow overnight and were due some more later, and although we were well below the snowline at the hotel, you could see it on top of the mountains I was aiming for. My original preferred scenic route peaked at around 5,600 feet above sea level, and as we learnt from bitter experience in the Lake District one winter, a rear-wheel drive Lexus is no match for an icy mountain road.

We therefore decided to take the more sensible route that took us west and past Burgos, the provincial capital of the Castile and León autonomous community and home to the tomb of the eleventh century military commander, Charlton Heston – or rather, Rodrigo Díaz de Vivar, known to his mates as El Cid. The mercenary's last remains are reportedly held inside a chapel in the French Gothic Cathedral of St. Mary, and Burgos is one of the major stopping-off points for pilgrims walking the Camino de Santiago.

It was rather fitting to be passing the pilgrim trail as you could say we were on our own pilgrimage: the Camino de Málaga, with a boot full of wine.

We stayed on the ring road and hurtled south towards Madrid, Europe's highest capital city, lying 2,188 feet above sea level. Four and a half hours, two hundred and fifty miles and a pee break later, we arrived at the Parador hotel in Chinchón.

Los Paradores are a chain of luxury hotels in Spain, and our new friends Kim and Martin had been extolling their virtues to us. They are a state-run enterprise – yeah, I know, you wouldn't dream of staying in a hotel run by the British Government, but stick with me on this one. These Parador hotels are usually located in restored historic buildings throughout the country and are known for their stunning locations, quality rooms and high service standards … oh, and as we were to soon learn, excellent breakfasts.

There are two in Málaga, although one of those is a golf hotel, but the other one is a fine old building overlooking the marina and the fortifications of the seven-hundred-year-old Gibalfaro Castle.

Given our early taste of Spanish bureaucracy, you'd think we wouldn't have much faith in the state running a hotel chain, but we'd been told they do a rather incredible job. Kim and Martin's particular favourite was in Salamanca, which was only about ten miles from the gorgeous Hacienda Zorita Wine Hotel & Spa that we'd stayed at on our first road trip, so that was even more of an excuse to explore that region more in the years to come.

But tonight, we'd be staying at the one in Chinchón. A former Augustinian monastery, the hotel has a beautiful courtyard garden, and the wide, sweeping balcony that overlooks it leads to the generously-proportioned bedrooms. On arrival, we were given a voucher for a complementary drink in the bar, so as we were ready for something to eat, we stopped by the bar and ordered a sharing plate to accompany our free wine. Then it was off up the road to see the town. And what a town.

Walking into the central square, the Plaza Mayor, was like stepping back in time. Rather than being square, it's circular in shape, and it's surrounded on all sides by a series of three-storey terraced buildings that accommodate two hundred and thirty wooden balconies. We stopped and looked around in wonder.

If he hadn't died in 1999, I wouldn't have been surprised to see Oliver Reed ride into town with the rest of *The Three Musketeers*. Alright, smarty pants, I know that film was set in Paris, but I wouldn't raise an eyebrow if you'd told me it was filmed on location in Chinchón. This place just evoked those happy childhood memories of being enthralled by the swashbuckling adventures of D'Artagnan and his mates – although as a prepubescent ten year-old boy, I was obviously quite taken by Raquel Welch's character too.

We grabbed a table at one of the many café bars and ordered a bottle so we could do a spot of people watching for an hour or so.

'¡Salut!' Chris said, raising a *copa* of the red stuff.

151

'All for one and one for all,' I replied heartily.

'Careful what you're saying … the waiter might think you want to buy everyone a drink.'

We browsed the restaurant menus and booked a table for dinner later, then we went back to get changed. After dark, the square was even more magical lit up, and we dined like musketeers … and drank like Oliver Reed.

I've since discovered why Chinchón looked a little familiar to me … it wasn't a backdrop for *The Three Musketeers* but instead was used to film the bullfight scene in the David Niven movie, *Around the World in 80 Days*. How marvellous! (Although bullfighting isn't a sport we agree with.)

In the morning, we had a bit of a lie-in before popping downstairs for a leisurely breakfast. We were amazed by the selection of food on offer, from hot bacon and eggs to all manner of charcuterie, cheeses, breads, fruit and cakes. Had I not been driving I would have had a Buck's Fizz, but instead I opted for coffee, apple juice and a continental cold plate selection. Oh, and a cheeky donut to put a lid on it all.

We checked out and headed off to our next destination, the town of Almagro. But on the way, I wanted to make a detour and take in the ancient walled city of Toledo, an hour to our southwest.

30

Almost Home

Halfway to Toledo, we approached the town of Aranjuez, a favourite haunt of King Philip II, a.k.a. Philip the Prudent – although the name is a bit of an oxymoron seeing as he sent the Spanish Armada to invade England in 1588, and most of the fleet sunk in bad weather in the English Channel ... the Spanish even fired 100,000 cannonballs without seriously damaging a single English ship ... good shooting, guys!

Seeing the signpost for the town, I became quite animated – which, with that donut still sitting heavily in my stomach, was to be applauded. I asked Chris to have a look on my iPod for an album by Jim Hall called *Concierto*.

'Found it,' she said.

'Right. Plug the iPod into the stereo and play "Concierto de Aranjuez", please.'

'Why?'

'Because we're about to drive through Aranjuez. Don't you think that's serendipitous?'

'If you say so, but I bet you can't spell it.'

I couldn't, but for the next nineteen minutes and nineteen seconds – eleven minutes longer than it took us to drive right through the pretty, neatly laid out UNESCO World Heritage Site of Aranjuez – I was in my happy place, listening to the dulcet tones of Chet Baker's trumpet over Jim Hall's classical guitar ... although Chris was less enamoured with it. Ah well, there's nowt as queer as folk, is there?

Toledo old town sits atop a hill above the plains of Castilla-La Mancha, surrounded on three sides by the river Tagus, although as you approach it from the east as we did, the topography isn't immediately apparent. We parked up in the main car park under the city walls and took the modern route into town: up the myriad covered escalators that magically transported you from the underground parking to the town's streets above. So magical was this piece of pedestrian transportation that it won the award for World's Best Escalator project in 2003. Who even knew such a thing existed?

Castilla-La Mancha is where the author Cervantes based the travels – or more typically, the travails – of an elderly, eccentric chap called Don Quixote, who donned a suit of armour, tooled up and headed off into the countryside where he picked a fight with a bunch of windmills. He'd no doubt been overindulging on the Rioja like us recently.

The tradesfolk of Toledo clearly had a soft spot for the silly old fool, as every other shop in the main square seemed to be selling armour or medieval swords and daggers. If Chris had designs on doing me in for the insurance money, here would have been a good place to do it. Thankfully, the only thing she bought was a scarf – maybe she was planning a less messy strangulation instead.

Believe it or not, there were times when people of differing religious persuasions all got along perfectly well in Europe, and nowhere more so than in Spain. Toledo was the seat of the Visigothic kingdom after the fall of the Roman Empire and was referred to as the 'City of the Three Cultures', thanks to the relatively harmonious coexistence here of the Christians, Muslims and Jews.

We would have liked a bit longer to take in the tourist sites, but we'd only really stopped off for a bit of a mooch round and a coffee. I wouldn't have minded visiting the army museum in the old royal palace, the Alcazar, which crowns the city at its highest point and dominates the landscape, but not today.

It must be said that, from what we saw of it at least, an awful lot of Castilla-La Mancha appeared to be rather flat and featureless plains. It's no wonder Don Quixote was a chorizo sandwich short of a picnic when he encountered the windmills, especially if he'd done the trip at the height of summer. But on we drove until we reached Almagro, and our final overnight stay before arriving back in Alhaurín the following afternoon.

The town of Almagro is another hidden historical jewel and is designated as a conservation area. The characteristic local clay used in the buildings around the Plaza Mayor has a red ochre (or *almagre*) tint to it, which gave its name to the original Arab castle that once stood here, the *Almagrib*. Like the Parador we'd just left, the one in Almagro was a converted monastery, this one dating back to the sixteenth century. Although not a brown-hooded smock or bald head in sight, this place appeared to be a bit more monastic than the last; it was so quiet, I felt guilty walking down the corridor with my shoes tip-tapping along the marble floor. Thankfully, there was nothing monastic about our room, although the door looked to be original.

One of the things I think is really great about the old buildings in towns and cities throughout Spain, and something they seem proud to preserve, is the doors. Some of them have lasted hundreds of years. I love a good door, me.

As it was early March, and still a bit *frio*, we couldn't avail ourselves of the outdoor pool facilities, so we wandered into town to see if Almagro's red-ochred Plaza Mayor could hold a candle to the wooden balconies of Chinchón – although holding a candle to a six-hundred-year-old wooden balcony might not be the smartest thing to do.

After such a hearty breakfast in Chinchón, we weren't too bothered about having a big lunch, so went in search of a bit of tapas. Walking the short distance into the centre of town, the heavens looked like they might open up on us soon, and despite most places being seemingly closed, we found a little bar that had a couple of tall tables and bar stools outside under the galleried outer walkways of the square, although we weren't entirely sure this place was open either. This being more of a tourist destination, there probably wasn't a huge amount of passing trade on a wet Sunday afternoon in early March.

I peered through the glazed door and saw an old man and his family sitting around a small table in the little bar having their lunch. I shoved open the door and they all turned around.

'*¿Está abierto?*' I enquired, with more than a degree of hope in my voice.

'*Sí, Sí,*' the old boy said and jumped to his feet. '*¿Qué quiere?*'

'*Dos copas de vino tinto, por favor.*'

The old boy scuttled off behind the bar and I joined Chris outside, just as the first drops of rain landed in the square.

'Are you *por favor*-ing again?' she asked.

'I was. It costs nothing to be polite. Why?'

'Do you know what the Spanish call us Brits?'

'Is it derogatory?'

'No, not really. They call us the *por favor*s. Have you not noticed the Spanish rarely say *por favor* when asking for something? It's not that they're rude – although it might seem so to us – but it's just their way.'

'A bit like *oiga* then,' I said.

'Yes. I could never shout *oiga* at a waiter – it sounds too much like "oi!"'

'Is that what it means, "oi!"?'

'No. It means "excuse me", but I'm still never saying it.'

The old boy hurried out with a tray and planted two large glasses of red on our table, plus a small plate with two complimentary tapas.

'*Gracias,*' we said in unison – I wonder if the Spanish also called us the *grassy arses* sometimes!

The wine was half decent and the little morsel of fried pork loin on a piece of bread was really succulent.

'Tasty that. I could eat another ten of those,' I said.

We watched the rain get steadily heavier, and as a cold breeze blew through the arches, we pulled our coats a little tighter around us. We seemed to be the only fools out here as the entire area was deserted. Soon, with our glasses emptied, I waved at the owner and swished my hand round in a circular motion, the universal symbol for saying 'we'll have the same again'.

'So what's Almagro famous for?' Chris asked.

'It's home to the oldest open-air theatre in Spain. Just off this square somewhere. It's called the Corral de Comedias and dates back to the early seventeenth century.'

'Impressive. A four-hundred-year-old comedy club.'

'Erm. I think *comedia* in this instance probably refers to a "play", as I can't imagine a Spanish Chubby Brown playing Almagro in the sixteen hundreds, can you?'

The owner appeared and asked if we liked the pork. We told him it was delicious, and he beamed from ear to ear as if we'd just delivered his first-born. He proceeded to tell us in an animated fashion that it was *his* pork – which I assume meant he'd had a hand in the entire process from farm to fork – and off he went.

'We've made him happy,' Chris said.

'We have. It's probably the busiest he's been all year.'

A minute later and he's out again carrying two more large reds and another two mini pork butties. By the time we'd finished our drinks, the rain had cleared, and the sun was poking fingers through the clouds. We got the bill, left the man a big tip – and probably got an invite to his first-born's wedding – and then we meandered arm in arm back to the hotel to avail ourselves of the complementary wine.

We'd already sampled a Parador breakfast this morning in Chinchón, and that evening we'd be sampling a Parador dinner. The restaurant only had two other diners in, which was a shame, as the food was great, as you might expect. I was definitely warming to the Parador chain.

'How much a night is it here?' Chris asked.

'Ninety-nine euros for bed and breakfast. And Chinchón was a hundred and forty.'

'The rooms at Chinchón were bigger and the place was prettier with a lot more going on in the square, so I suppose that justifies the price difference.'

'It's also a Sunday night, so maybe it's more expensive on Fridays and Saturdays. I just think it's lovely staying in these beautiful old buildings.'

'Me too. Much more soul and history to them than the big hotel chains.'

'Right then, shall we go and say our prayers before bed, or do you want to do a bit of Gregorian chanting instead?'

'You daft sod!'

And with that, we went to bed and watched *Top Gear* whilst sharing a bottle of Saint-Estèphe out of the boot – how decadent!

After another hearty breakfast – minus the donut this time – we set off on the last leg of our journey. This time, except for a quick trolley dash round Aldi for some essentials, we headed straight for Alhaurín.

Seven days and eighteen hundred miles after leaving Bury, we arrived at the villa with six hundred euros of wine in the boot. The sun was out, and it was in the mid-twenties. Even the pool thermomcter read twenty degrees.

'Here we are: home sweet home,' Chris said.

'Yep. And no work in the morning,' I replied gleefully.

'You can clean the pool tomorrow then.'

31

I Beg Your Padrón!

It felt weird sitting on the terrace the next morning with my coffee. It was a weekday, and I had no work to do. Unless I was able to find a job somewhere, I was effectively retired ... at fifty-three. It was also exactly six months to the day since we disembarked that Brittany Ferry in Santander. At the time, I'd expected to be working for only another seven weeks, but twenty-six weeks later, there I was at last ... putting my feet up.

So this was it ... this is what we'd planned for: to live in the Spanish sunshine and take it easier while we had our health ... day one of my retirement. There was no going back. With our house rented out, we had no home to go to, so we needed to complete the formal process of making our move to Spain permanent. Since January that year we would be classed as Spanish tax residents.

We had our NIE numbers already, but there were now a few more hoops to jump through. We needed to apply for Spanish residency, and we should ideally complete that before Theresa May invoked Article 50 and kickstarted Brexit.

Before we could obtain residency, though, we had to go and get a *Certificado de Empadronamiento* from the town hall – or *padrón* for short. This was needed to prove to the authorities that we were officially registered as living in or owning property in the town and was a prerequisite for obtaining residency. It also meant that the town hall received sufficient funding from the central government to cover the facilities needed for the local population.

The town of Alhaurín El Grande has a population of around twenty-four thousand people, of which about five thousand are foreigners. Judging by the accents I'd heard around town, I'd say that most of the foreigners were British or Dutch, with the odd Moroccan thrown in. The Scandinavians had a bit more cash to splash so they tended to live down on the coast.

One of the town's most celebrated former residents was a British writer called Gerald Brenan who died there in 1987. He spent the vast majority of his life living in Málaga Province, with his later years spent up here in Alhaurín. His most famous work was an account of the Spanish Civil War called *The Spanish Labyrinth*, which was critical of Franco's reign and therefore banned until the dictator died in 1975. One of the main streets in the town is named after him, and I've walked past his house a few times.

We parked up in the old town and headed off to the town hall with our paperwork.

'*¡Hola! Buenos días.*'

'*¡Hola!*'

'*Buenos.*'

Walking through the narrow streets, we exchanged greetings with the old locals who were standing around having a chinwag with their neighbours.

'Do you think they'll name a street here after me one day?' I asked Chris.

'Why would they do that?'

'Because I've decided … I'm going to be a writer.'

'Course you are, sweetheart,' she said, rolling her eyes.

The town hall is a rather grand, typically Spanish looking two-storey building in the centre of the old town, sitting majestically alongside one of Alhaurín's three churches, the neo-Gothic Ermita de Santa Vera Cruz, the hermitage of the Catholic brotherhood known locally as *los verdes* (the greens), although nothing to do with saving the planet. Around holy days and festivals, the locals in the old town drape coloured banners from their upstairs windows, and the people in this part of town display green banners.

We entered the town hall and waited in a short line to be seen at the desk. Not wishing to be caught out, we had everything we thought we might need in original and photocopied form. When it was our turn, we both stepped forward confidently, and Chris, our self-appointed official keeper of documents, pulled out the photocopies of our NIE certificates and a photocopy of our rental agreement on Olivia's property – she was only going to let the woman touch the originals if the photocopies wouldn't suffice … no point taking unnecessary risks. Chris explained that we wished to register on the *padrón* and get certificates.

'*Pasaportes,*' the woman requested.

Chris whipped out photocopies of our passports.

'*Originales,*' the woman demanded.

Chris reluctantly handed over our original passports.

She started tapping away on the keyboard, and her computer screen was angled so I could see what she was doing. It looked like she was simply editing a Word document from an old nineties' version of Office 95 or something. Remarkable. She took photocopies of our documents and returned them to us and then asked for ten euros.

We gave her a tenner and waited expectantly for our certificates. After a brief moment, she realised we were still there and looked up.

'*Mañana,*' she said. '*Vuelven mañana.*'

'Oh! We have to collect them tomorrow,' Chris informed me.

We stepped outside into the sunshine, somewhat deflated that we had to come back again in the morning.

'Why can't they just print them now?' I said. 'Or does the mayor blackball you if he doesn't like your passport photo?'

'I've no idea. Just the way they do things here, I suppose.'

'I bet the Spanish don't have to wait a day,' I grumbled.

The following morning, we parked in the same spot, and I felt like Bill Murray in *Groundhog Day* as we exchanged greetings with the same people as yesterday.

'I bet they've been out here chinwagging all night,' I said.

161

As we entered the town hall for a second time in two days, we bumped into Bruno from the PO Box coming the other way.

'Hi, Bruno,' I said. 'What are you doing here?'

'I'm getting a *padrón* certificate for a client.'

'Us too. We came yesterday to register but had to come back today to collect them.'

'Yes,' he said. 'Me too. It's normal.'

Bruno breezed out the door.

'Feeling guilty now?' Chris asked.

We went inside and queued for a short while again before we were called forward. Chris explained why we were there, and the woman rifled through her papers. Our certificates were clipped to yesterday's photocopies. She separated them and handed them over. I was giving them a once over as we turned around to leave.

'Bugger,' I said.

'What?'

'They've got my names the wrong way round.'

I turned back to the desk.

'*Lo siento. Mis nombres no son correctos.*'

I showed her my certificate and she compared it to our other papers, and then declared that it was correct: the *padrón* had to match my NIE certificate. So thanks to the Fuengirola copper getting my names the wrong way round, I was now registered incorrectly with the town hall too.

'Come on,' Chris said. 'Felipe told you last time that it didn't really matter, so let's go.'

I didn't have the stomach or the language skills to take my protestations further, so I traipsed out a bit disconsolate.

* * *

On the third day, God created dry land, plants and trees. On our third day, we just took out private health insurance.

This was another prerequisite for residency. Unless you were working and paying into the Social Security system, you needed private medical insurance. As with anything in Spain, there's always a range of opinions available online. As Clint Eastwood once said, 'Opinions are like areseholes, everybody's got one', and most argumentative, keyboard know-alls seem to have more

162

than one of them. In this case, the debate was regarding what degree of cover was needed to pass the residency test. Some of the cheaper policies meant you had to pay extra for treatment, and others were more comprehensive, and the Facebook Army couldn't agree on which would be accepted. And as we were soon to find out, the only opinion that mattered was the one the policeman had on the morning he was dealing with your application. I say 'morning' because it seems you can't get anything official done in Spain after 2pm, and a Spanish morning runs until 2pm, when the two-hour lunch break kicks in, or in the case of civil servants, the working day ends.

At the end of the day, we decided not to take any chances so went for fully comprehensive cover and chose a policy offered through our bank.

The process was made easier once more by the lovely bank clerk who'd opened the account for us the previous year. Her English was still much better than our Spanish might ever be, and by going via the bank, we got a small rebate on our contributions at the end of the year – not to be sniffed at ... although can you believe that you have to pay tax on the rebate?! ... it's money you've paid them and they're giving you a bit back, but oh no, sir, that's 'income'. We had our contents insurance with the bank for those same reasons, so having the bank set everything up for us again made life a bit easier.

Having done that, and got the evidence, we then called to see Felipe at the PO Box to get him to make appointments at the police station for our residency applications. Felipe used to send Bruno down to the police station to handle NIE and residency applications, and while he was there, he'd block book some future appointments that he could use for his clients.

'The earliest date we have is the thirtieth of March,' Felipe said, looking down his handwritten list.

'Oh, do you have anything sooner?' I asked. 'The UK is invoking Article fifty on the twenty-ninth. I'm wondering if the police might be awkward if we turn up after that date.'

'Don't worry,' he said. 'Everything will be fine.'

I had to applaud his optimism.

'Do you have private health insurance?'

'Yes, we've done that this morning.'

'Do you have *padrón* certificates?'

'Yes,' I replied.

'Are they less then three months old?'

'Yes. We got them yesterday.'

'Do you have jobs or a pension or something?'

'Chris gets a pension, but I'm not working at the moment.'

'OK. We can use Chris's pension letter for her application, but it needs to be officially translated into Spanish by a *gestor*.'

'And me?'

'You will need to pay for a certificate from the bank to say you have more than six thousand euros in your account.'

Great. More costs. And we've only just come out of the flipping bank.

'Does it matter if it's a joint account?' I asked.

'No, it should be fine if Chris is using her pension. Otherwise, you'd need twelve thousand in the bank.'

I agreed to email him a copy of Chris's pension award so he could get it translated for us, and we went home.

'Do you think they'll let us stay?' I asked Chris, as we walked back to the car.

'Yeah, I'm sure they will. You worry too much.'

For the second time today, I was in awe of someone's optimism.

32

Party Time

After lunch we threw some clothes in a bag and drove east along the coast to Algarrobo. When we got there, we headed inland for another half hour on a ten-mile trip up a hairy mountain pass, climbing four hundred metres in the process. It sounds high, but I've been up to the observation platform on level 148 of the Burj Khalifa, and that's a lot higher – Mrs Slocombe would have got out on floor 106 for Árchez and 'telephones, gents' ready-made suits, shirts, socks, ties, hats, underwear and shoes … going up'.

We were going to help Kim celebrate her fiftieth birthday and she'd invited us to stay overnight at their villa.

We were following her directions to the tiny village of Árchez, and Chris was gripping the door handle all the way up the windy, blind-bended, not much wider than two cars, road – she's not terribly good with heights … she doesn't even like looking out of the window of a hotel room three floors up. The population of Árchez wasn't quite four men, one woman and two dogs, as I'd suggested earlier, but it wasn't much bigger – I've seen more guests at an Indian wedding, put it that way. The villa was a picture-perfect, single-storey white villa perched on a sticky-out bit of the mountain, just below the road.

When Chris had prised her fingers from the door handle, we got out to be greeted by our hosts and not one but two dogs. Toby, their fifteen-year-old labrador was slower to his feet and much less boisterous than the young podenco they'd found abandoned. The podenco – or Pod as he'd since been christened

– was a gorgeous yet very inquisitive little fella, and also a bit of an escape artist. On one afternoon walk to the pub, they'd left Pod on a long chain in their garden, as he had a habit of getting out. As they were enjoying their afternoon tipple, a podenco went wandering past dragging a chain behind him. It took a moment for the penny to drop that it was Pod, but how he'd managed to unshackle the chain and do a runner remains a mystery.

Podencos are a Mediterranean breed of warren hound that are used for hunting rabbits. They're beautiful but powerful dogs of medium height with upright ears. Sadly, the Spanish hunters don't tend to treat them very well. They'll take a pack out hunting, and if they feel one is not up to scratch, they will often just abandon it at the side of the road – and that's if the dog's lucky. The more malicious hunters will kill or main them instead, either by hanging them from a tree, breaking their back, shooting them or stoning them to death. Now if we could just get them to stop doing that, and implore the other minority of Spaniards to stop stabbing bulls for fun as well, then the world would be a much nicer place – having said that, the British aren't much better when they let their hounds tear foxes to shreds.

Pod was one of the lucky ones, having simply been abandoned. But he now had a doting Mum and Dad and an older stepbrother for company, although he was probably still smarting from having his bits chopped off the day before – I mean, wouldn't we all?

'Did you find us alright,' Martin asked.

'Just the one missed turn for the village,' I said.

'I'm not looking forward to the drive back down,' Chris said.

'Are you not good with heights?' Kim asked.

'No. And going down we'll be even closer to the edge.'

Poor thing. She needed a stiff drink. Thankfully, that was something that wasn't in short supply at the villa.

Kim was delighted with the birthday wine, a bottle of her favourite Saint-Estèphe and a bottle of that nice white Rioja we'd acquired on our trip.

'Aw, thanks. Did you get the Saint-Estèphe from the vineyard on your way through France?' she asked.

'No, Majestic Wines in Manchester. It would have been too much of a detour,' I laughed.

'But we did get the Rioja from La Rioja,' Chris added.

Kim was a confirmed Francophile. In terms of fluency, Kim's language proficiency (after English) was French and then Spanish, and Martin's was French and then German. Leaving Belgium the previous year, it was almost a toss-up whether they'd settle in southern France instead of the even warmer climes of Spain's Costa del Sol.

Martin reappeared from the house with a chilled bottle of champers and nibbles to get us in the party spirit. Kim's birthday bash was being held at a local bar, so we were just getting a bit of a head start on the other guests. There were only a couple of bars in Árchez, so instead we'd be getting a taxi up to the expat stronghold of Cómpeta, another ten-minute, harum-scarum drive away. The party venue was one of their favourite restaurants, El Pilón, and as a second bottle of champers was opened, it was clear the plan was to hit the dance floor 'boogying', our inhibitions suitably and alcoholically assuaged.

We had exclusive use of the restaurant's upstairs room, and the party was a riot of unabashed British revelry, with the dance floor taking a pounding all night. Kim knew the Spanish owner, Dani, from when she used to holiday in Cómpeta as a teenager, and he did her proud with the plentiful supply of tasty Spanish food.

I'm not sure how much we had to drink, but it was a slow start to the morning the following day. A lie-in was called for, and then I took a long hot shower before emerging for a lazy breakfast on the south-facing terrace. My head was still thumping like a subwoofer at an Iron Maiden concert, and my mouth was as dry as a camel's nostril, so I might have been better seeking out a bit of shade. As Pod came to sit next to me on one of the comfy chairs, I consoled myself with the thought that it could have been worse … I could have just had my balls chopped off like Pod.

Chris looked ready to continue partying – she has a much greater alcohol threshold than me, having once seen off a challenge from an ex-serviceman in a Guinness drinking contest

– so I'm glad it was me driving down the mountain later, although only after I'd downed two coffees, an OJ and two cups of tea.

We had an uneventful drive back to Alhaurín, thankfully, with Chris grabbing a mobile siesta once we were back at sea level. On arriving home, I discovered that Iron Maiden had decided to do a third encore, so I donned a pair of trunks and jumped in the pool to give my body another sensation to worry about: cold water.

'How is it?' Chris asked from the warmth of the terrace.

'Bloody freezing.'

'Is that your first dip of the year?'

'Yes, and it'll be my last for at least another month.'

'Wuss!'

'And I'm never drinking again,' I declared.

Chris just rolled her eyes.

33

How Much?!

In this world, nothing can be said to be certain, except death and taxes. So said Benjamin Franklin, and never has a truer word been spoken ... especially in Spain, it seems.

I had to go to the PO Box and pay Felipe to handle the importation of Chris's little Mini Cooper. We knew this was a cost we had to grin and bear if we wanted to continue driving our own cars over here, where we knew the full service history of the vehicles, and in Chris's case, had grown extremely attached to the car. It would be another few weeks before the new plates were issued, but in the meantime, we had to dig deep and cough up. All the same, I wasn't looking forward to the bill.

Have a guess how much?

'That will be ... nine hundred and seventy-four,' Felipe said with a straight face, as he read the number off the bottom of the invoice.

'What? Pesetas?' I said.

'No. Euros. There is a lot of paperwork and legal things to do,' he countered.

'Have you added it up right?' I said hopefully.

Felipe just laughed and handed me a copy of the invoice.

It was all here, laid out in black and white, but that didn't make it any more palatable. Nigh on a bloody grand to import a car, and a small and quite old one at that. I know ... you can't believe it can you? ... neither can I ... it's already OUR car, we're not buying it again, although it felt like it. We'd had this car from new for twelve years. It's done 78,000 miles and had one careful (sic) lady owner. It's worth about six thousand pounds tops in the UK – less here, of course, with the steering wheel on the wrong side.

The funniest part of the invoice was the eighteen euros for an exemption certificate from the tax office ... exempt from what exactly, as it looks like we'd paid every goddam tax and admin fee you could dream up? And don't forget, it's already cost us about seven hundred euros to buy new headlamps, get them fitted and then put the car through its first ITV. So a total of around one thousand seven hundred euros to import a twelve-year-old Mini.

It got worse soon afterwards when I had to import the Lexus. Most of the individual elements were the same as for the Mini, but with a few exceptions. First of all, the Emission Tax came in at wallet-draining 945 euros. And the road tax of 120 euros was twice the price of the Mini, although that was still only about one-third of what I was paying in the UK.

All told, if I added in the cost of changing the headlamps in the UK, it had set me back more than two and a half thousand euros. For a ten-year-old Lexus with 107,000 miles under its cam belt that was worth less than eight thousand pounds.

Quite staggering.

And when you're getting fifteen percent less euros to the pound than we did a year earlier, that hurts.

Life in Spain was supposed to be cheaper than living in the UK, so these big bills were doing nothing to support our carefully nurtured plans. We had to eke out our money as long as we could now, although I was still hopeful of finding a job. I was quite picky about what I wanted to do, though. I suppose I would have liked to continue working in IT or marketing, as that's what I was used to, so long as the job was a local, nine-to-five, Monday-to-Friday job, and I could be home in time for dinner.

I didn't want to get a job working behind a bar as that would impinge too much on my evening social life, which was a particular joy, what with the great selection of bars and restaurants in the town. It was even lovely to relax with a homemade dinner on the terrace and watch the twinkling lights of the town on the hillside.

Most other jobs, though, would be ruled out by the language barrier, unless I could find an international company with premises in Málaga that used English as their company language. I wasn't even interested in earning a big fat salary, I just wanted to make a meaningful contribution in a happy working environment and earn enough to cover day-to-day living costs.

At that moment, however, getting another job was furthest from my mind. Chris had already enjoyed six months without working, and I wanted to spend the next six months doing just the same: absolutely nothing. We were sure to have a busload of visitors from now until autumn and it would be a shame not to be around to enjoy this little corner of paradise with them.

And speaking of which, we needed to prepare for our third set of staying guests of the new year that were due shortly. So it was off to the garden centre first. As the weather was warming up, the plants needed more watering, and we were a bit short of hosepipes. So far, we'd been dragging one hosepipe round the entire garden, hooking it up at the various water taps. So we invested in two more long hosepipes and variable rose attachments for them. That should speed up the watering routine, especially if we both did a bit.

We also bought a small almond tree to replace something that hadn't survived the winter, and two hardy house plants to go on the terrace, which we later discovered were Devil's Ivy and the bringer of bad luck ... and God knows, we could do with no more of that.

Next up was more garden furniture. We needed sunloungers for round the pool, so got four of those, along with four nice (for nice read pricey) cushions for them and a couple of small tables for drinks. Finally, we finished this frenzied retail activity by buying some more big candles for the terrace lanterns – don't forget, it's all about the ambience, especially when the terrace lights weren't dimmable and were bright enough to attract the odd passenger jet en route to Málaga.

And relax!

'You need to water the garden,' I was informed after I'd just sat down.

'OK,'

'And don't blast the plants.'

'OK.'

Chris and I appeared to have different techniques for watering the garden. If a particular plant needed a lot of water, rather than stand there for twice as long, surely it made more sense to set the rose to the most powerful setting, right? Get more water flow? I might not have studied horticulture at college, but I had an 'A' level in physics, don't forget.

With the hosepipe on full, the water was gushing forth pretty *rápidamente*, and I'd have the garden watered in no time.

'Oi!' Chris shouted from the terrace, a pan in her hand. I didn't know if she was planning on using it to make dinner or to beat me with … and I thought she said she didn't like that word anyway.

'What?'

'Stop blasting the plants!'

'Sorry.'

That was me told.

34

When Did We Agree to Open a B&B?

After a fortnight with no proper male company, I was looking forward to Rick arriving at the end of the week ... we could both get shouted at then.

Rick was the husband of Karen, with whom Chris had worked for years on the wards at North Manchester General Hospital. Karen was Chris's best mate, and Rick was fine company for me too. We both liked a drink, a nice meal and a good laugh. It's what makes the world go round in my view. Rick had retired a couple of years earlier and they'd recently bought an apartment on the Mar Menor for extended holidays. They were planning on staying with us for a few days before heading up there.

They landed at Málaga on the Saturday morning, and no sooner had we given them a tour of the villa – and the now customary 'If it didn't come out of you, it doesn't go down the loo!' warning – than Rick was lying prostrate on a sunlounger with a beer in his hand. He was a master at switching to holiday mode – he could unwind faster than the anchor chain of an aircraft carrier going flat out. And there's a lot to be said for that.

Later on, we tarted ourselves up a bit and enjoyed the culinary delights of Santiago's Kitchen ... and then I collapsed into bed with the satisfaction of a man who had the good fortune to put a tenner on Foinavon at 100/1 in the 1967 Grand National and now counts himself as one of life's winners. Not that I had done, of course, as I was only three at the time, but you get my point.

The following evening, we found ourselves back in town listening to the captivating Spanish guitar sounds and passionate voices of The Gypsy Bros. And judging by my blurry photos of the night, the girls were up dancing, and we all had a skinful.

On the walk back to the taxi rank, Rick and I were accosted by the aromas emerging from the Turkish Kebab House. It's the law, you know … you can't pass a kebab shop on the way to the taxi rank without giving them your custom.

Armed with a couple of donner kebabs, we made it home and unwrapped these marvels of the Ottoman Empire. We plated them – we're not bloody animals, you know – and plonked ourselves on the couch. I remember the girls going to bed, and I vaguely remember Rick giving me a nudge at some point to wake me up and tell me he was taking himself off. I woke a while later with a half-eaten kebab in my lap and decided to call it a night too.

The following morning, at breakfast, Chris wanted to know why the fridge had been taken over by the remnants of two kebabs. Us boys looked sheepishly at each other over the rims of our coffee cups.

The weekend was soon over, and we dropped our guests off at the airport car hire so they could take off up the coast. With an open invitation taken as read, we promised to come and visit them at some point … when they'd finished redecorating, of course – I had enough to be getting on with in the garden.

The following weekend was Mother's Day in the UK, and I'd been chivvying up our four girls to make sure they didn't forget. If they hadn't already posted cards etc. then they were likely to arrive too late. One daughter, though, had decided that only delivery by hand would do, and I was sworn to secrecy.

When we got home from dropping Karen and Rick at the airport, I was pleased to see Chris wasting no time in putting a wash on and doing the bedding. She'd have become immediately suspicious of a man who doesn't know how to work a washing machine if he suddenly took a keen interest in changeover times and the cleanliness of the bedding. After all, we weren't running a B&B … or were we?

On the Saturday morning, as I brought Chris a coffee in bed, she got a video call from our youngest, Corrinne. She and Graham were sipping drinks in an airport departure lounge.

'Ooh!' Chris said, 'Where are you two going?'

'To come and see you for Mother's Day.'

'What?!'

'Surprise!'

'Aw. How wonderful.'

A tear escaped an eye – not mine.

After the call I had to admit knowing all about it.

'You know I don't like surprises,' Chris said.

'Nothing I could do. I had to sign the official secrets act.'

'We'd better get up,' she screeched.

'Don't panic. You've got three hours. Even you can get ready in that time.'

'How long are they staying for?'

'Till Monday. Why?'

'Well, your Mum and Dad arrive on Wednesday.'

'I know. You'll have to wash the bedding again,' I laughed.

After collecting our guests, we went from the airport straight to La Cala where they have a big market on Saturday mornings. Graham and I followed the girls round trying not to look bored. It was a lovely sunny day with just a few clouds drifting aimlessly in a sea of blue, so we dropped the shopping in the car (clothes probably) and walked down to the seafront for lunch on the beach.

Back at the villa, Corrinne was pleased to see that we'd heeded her recommendations from her first visit. We now had a full-length mirror stuck to the bedroom wall and a waste bin for the detritus that the fairer sex seems to accumulate and then discard. Graham was less impressed that we hadn't carpeted the place and refused to wear the slipper socks we'd bought for him. Talk about ungrateful. Well, he was only thirty-one, I suppose, and would have looked quite ridiculous in them. Corrinne loved hers, though.

Saturday night out for dinner was followed by the now obligatory Sunday lunch at El Jinete, but not before Graham and I had played eighteen holes at Lauro Golf. If was a fine, bright morning with clear views down to Málaga port. Graham had brought an old set of clubs over and agreed to leave them with me so that I always had a spare set for future visitors. My golf didn't seem to be improving much, although I do remember hitting a peach of a shot over the lake and onto the green on the last hole – otherwise, the scorecard looked like Stevie Wonder had been playing Ray Charles.

Sunday night saw us back up in Alhaurín again for some fusion tapas and Spanish guitar music at Nuevo Y Sur. Unlike the bars down on the coast where there is a constant stream of looky-looky men (and women too these days) plying their fake designer goods or African jewellery, up here in Alhaurín there is just the one looky-looky man. However, some Spanish old boy has also gotten in on the act, touting single roses for a euro to the evening revellers. Graham was suckered in and bought the girls one each during an interlude in the musical entertainment. It was no great surprise to me when Chris unwrapped hers when we got home, and the head fell off. Ah well, you get what you pay for.

With our second visitors of the month safely despatched to the airport on Monday, the washing machine went back on ready for the next guests. Two days later, Mum and Dad landed for their third visit in little more than six months. They'd been up since 3am for the early flight as Dad likes to get his money's worth from his holidays – and to maximise his sun-bathing time. As a result, we thought the best thing to do was to fill them up with food and wine and let them have a siesta. So we walked up the lane to El Bichito for their wallet-friendly, seven-euro *menú del día*.

Afterwards, we walked back and laid Dad out on a sunlounger slathered in factor thirty with his hat on. Mum was positioned in a reclining chair in the shade of the terrace. Then we left the two of them there for two hours while we did our chores.

I was on garden duty again. I'd finally bought some grass seed two days earlier and had sprinkled that on the lovingly prepared, weed-free soil on two sides of the pool, so that needed watering in. The grass seed we'd chosen was a strong, drought-resistant, trample-proof type called Gobi grass. If it could grow in the Gobi Desert then it would do for me, I thought.

The rest of the garden was also due a dousing. We still had plenty of oranges on the trees, although next season's blossom was already in full glorious show. We also had the first crop of the fig season ripe and ready to eat. Figs are unusual in that they give you two crops each year, one in the spring from last year's growth (which is apparently called the breba crop) and another better-quality crop from the new growth at the end of summer (which is just called a fig, as far as I can tell).

Every day's a school day, eh?

The other fruit ripening at the moment in our garden is the loquat, or Japanese plum (known locally as *níspero*), a fruit I hadn't even heard of before arriving in Spain. They're related to apples, peaches and pears, apparently, and taste like a kind of cross between an apricot and a citrus fruit, giving them a sweet and tangy flavour. Like most of the fruit in our garden, I just saw them as free food. There might be no such thing as a free lunch, but it seems there is such a thing as a free breakfast, and I happily wolfed them down with some Greek yoghurt each morning.

We had a lovely week with the old folks in tow. I can't say we did very much other than lounge around eating and drinking. Mum turned seventy-nine last week, while Dad just turned a nice shade of brown. They were both in rather good shape for their age – save for Mum having a troublesome hip, despite having it replaced a couple of years ago – but we obviously wouldn't be taking them paintballing or bull running.

Dad's tan was courtesy of his week-long tanning session, which started when the sun came up over the eucalyptus trees at one end of the garden and lasted until it went down again at the other end of the garden. He'd lie on a sunlounger all morning and afternoon, and then around teatime, he'd take a chair round to the side of the house to catch the last of the sun's rays while reading his book.

He wasn't much trouble, as guests go, although he was told off a few times by 'Sister Chris' for not wearing his hat in the sun and not drinking enough water.

'We don't want a repeat of Gozo,' Chris kept carping at him.

My folks had joined us on holiday eighteen months earlier, and he'd succumbed to sunstroke one day after failing to heed Chris's prophetic warnings.

Apart from his minor insubordination, Dad was fun to have around – although Mum might beg to differ after fifty-six years of being married to him.

My parents have been lucky enough to have lived to enjoy their retirement, unlike Chris's parents who both died in their sixties, thus being robbed of the pleasures of a long and happy retirement together, a key driving force for our own early retirement.

Mum particularly seemed to enjoy our now habitual Sunday night out in the Dutch bar. After being on the rosé all night she decided to have a Baileys before we left, and the fishbowl glass she was given must have contained more than half a pint of the stuff. When we got back to the villa she was still up for a nightcap and so I opened the bottle of Baileys we'd bought in especially for her.

'Ooh, you've not opened that bottle of Baileys you bought me yet,' she commented the next morning, as I was laying the table on the terrace for breakfast – although I don't think she was intimating she wanted one with her toast and jam.

'What're you talking about? You had one when we got back last night,' I said.

'No, I didn't,' she insisted.

Then Chris walked out with a basket of toast, and Mum beseeched her to put the record straight.

'Chris, I didn't have a Baileys when we got back last night, did I?'

'Course you did. Don't you remember?' And we all laughed at her.

She's not a big drinker, my Mum, but she was refused entry to a taxi in London once for having had one over the eight, but let's not go there.

After breakfast, I walked up into town to go and retrieve my car. Dad likes a walk, so he came with me to buy a Daily Mail. It's a fairly strenuous walk as it's all uphill. We'd left the car outside the Dutch bar, which was a mile and a half away and a climb of more than a hundred metres, so we stopped a few times to let him 'take in the scenery'. On the edge of town is quite a rundown street where some of the impoverished population live. The council should tidy it up a bit really, even if it was probably the residents that had dumped the toilet and the other furniture in the street.

I'd warned Dad beforehand that we were about to pass through the 'favela'.

'It is a bit rough round here, isn't it?' he said, as we walked on by. 'Are they Gypsies?'

'Yes, or *gitanos* as we say over here. Remember that time you fell for the old "we've got a bit of tarmac left over if you want us to do your driveway" scam?'

'Yes, I do. Thieving buggers. They made a right mess. I won't fall for that again.'

'I know you won't. You live in a block of apartments now, so you don't own a driveway.'

When we reached the town, we stopped for a coffee to get our breath back after the uphill slog.

'Are you enjoying being retired?' Dad asked, as we watched the morning Spanish hustle and bustle play out around us.

'It's only been a month,' I said. 'Anyway, I haven't really retired, I've just changed bosses, from the one who hired me to the one who married me.'

'Very true,' he agreed, so there must be some truth in it.

35

Another Roll of the Dice

I'm not what you'd call a gambling man, but in the words of the Indian Test Cricketer, Navjot Singh Sidhu, 'One who doesn't throw the dice can never expect to score a six'. Today, we were rolling the dice of life as we headed down to Fuengirola police station with Bruno to apply for Spanish residency status.

We left Mum and Dad at the villa and headed out with a veritable treasure trove of identification papers and two photocopies of everything. Bruno was confident there wouldn't be a problem, even though Theresa May went through with her threat of invoking Article 50 the day before. Dad was hoping that meant his passport was immediately invalid and he'd be able to stay in Spain after the end of the week, but he'd be lucky.

Fuengirola police station was as we remembered from last time: a bewildering cacophony of noisy Spaniards with all the hustle and bustle of a Mexican border town. At the appropriate time, Bruno ushered us over to a gruff, weather-beaten policeman at one of the desks, no doubt working here after being demoted for some police procedural misdemeanour in a quieter part of the country – he certainly didn't look pleased to be here and grunted when we sat down opposite him.

I know we wouldn't have stood a chance without Bruno with us, especially if things turned a little ugly. I honestly felt like I was here under duress at the behest of a hastily served European Arrest Warrant issued by Interpol.

Bruno handed over my paperwork to the policeman who started looking through it carefully, no doubt eager to spot something he didn't like, and periodically raising his lifeless, squinting, distrustful eyes to scrutinise me as he shuffled through the papers a second and third time.

'Can you ask him if he'll put my names the right way round this time?' I asked Bruno.

After a brief exchange with the man who literally held my life in his hands, it was a no. The residency had to match my NIE document which had been issued incorrectly in the first place from this very building only five months earlier. Although I felt now wasn't the time to remind him of that.

He picked up the certificate from the bank that said our account had a little more than six thousand euros deposited in it.

'*¿Esta es una cuenta conjunta?*' he asked me.

I searched Bruno's face for a translation.

'He wants to know if it's a joint account.'

'Yes,' I said, 'but Chris is applying with her pension.'

Bruno relayed the information. Another grunt from our inquisitor, and he began tapping away at his computer for a little while, an action interspersed with more scrutiny of my paperwork and suspicious glances over the top of his glasses. I wouldn't have been surprised if he'd have stopped halfway through the process while he went outside for a *cigarillo*.

Eventually, he did wander off – maybe he was going for a fag after all – but he soon returned carrying a small, green, credit-card-sized piece of paper. He slipped it inside a little plastic wallet and handed it to Bruno, along with a verbal instruction in his most unintelligible Andalusian drawl.

'You're not to laminate this,' Bruno said. 'And you need to carry it with you at all times.'

I thanked him and breathed a sigh of relief. To be honest, I'd have squealed like a pig or done the highland fling if that's what the policeman wanted of me. And miracle of miracles, we didn't have to come back in a week to collect anything – it had all been done while I waited. It just shows that they *can* do things there and then if they get their fingers out.

181

I checked over my precious pass to an untroubled new life in the sun, and sure enough, I was henceforth to be forever known in Spain as the man with his names the wrong way round. It wasn't all over just yet as Chris was up next, so I now had to wait to find out if I'd be living out my days in Spain with Chris alongside me for company, or if they'd slap irons on her, lead her off to the cells and start the deportation process. I hoped not, as we'd already got something in for lunch.

A friend called Ian we met a few months later told us of his experience of coming down to obtain residency more than twenty years earlier. As a police officer, he'd been able to retire early on a comfortable pension, and when the policeman was scrutinising his translated pension statement, he was making all sorts of disgruntled utterances to Ian's translator.

'What's he saying?' Ian enquired, more than a little peeved with the dirty looks he'd been receiving.

'It's nothing,' the translator assured him.

'Tell me. I want to know,' Ian insisted.

'Well, he says you have an incredibly good pension. More money than he earns in his job.'

'Well, tell him it's my bloody money and I earned it. And I didn't earn it sitting behind a bloody desk pushing papers – I was out nicking criminals.'

I'm assuming the translator didn't translate that word for word as his residency was approved. I don't think offering his Spanish counterpart outside for a shuffle in the dirt was the wisest of moves, but I can see why Ian wasn't happy with the guy's jealous disdain. Let's see if Chris's much more miserly pension statement for a life of service to the NHS would elicit a similar response today.

After a few moments, it was clear there was a problem. But it wasn't the fact a woman of Chris's tender years and undoubtable beauty – all natural by the way – was able to be pensioned off so early that was the problem, it was that the document we had from the NHS pensions provider was more than three months old.

'But it's a pension,' Chris protested. 'It's for life. They can't take it away from me.'

'He's saying it must be less than three months old.'

'Well, it's the only paperwork I've got. And it says there, in black and white, that I am to receive that amount per year.'

A brief exchange was had once more with Señor Plod, but he wasn't having it. He'd won. He was denying Chris's residency on a technicality. He'd found the one thing he wasn't happy with – and one tenuous thing was all he needed. He looked across at me, and I swear the fella was smirking under that poor excuse for a Tom Selleck moustache.

It looked like the Devil's Ivy on the terrace was already working its hoodoo.

We stepped out into the sunshine in a zombie-like state – not bewitched exactly, but certainly bothered and bewildered.

'It's no problem,' Bruno said. 'We'll try again next week. I have a spare appointment. You just need to get a bank certificate.'

'Does that mean we need to put another six thousand in the joint account?' Chris asked.

'No. It's fine. Just get a new certificate issued in your name.'

We drove back up the mountain in a more sombre mood than we'd driven down it that morning, dropped Bruno off and went straight to the bank. Four days later, Chris headed off with Bruno for another roll of the dice, while I stayed home with Mum and Dad in a kind of sun-worshipping, beer-sipping show of solidarity.

Chris took a seat in the waiting area with Bruno and could see the same policeman was on duty behind the clear glass screen that separated the offenders – sorry, applicants – from the disgraced former officers.

'Fingers crossed we don't get the same policeman,' she said.

Looking at the manned desks, she had a one in three chance that morning, apparently. She kissed the dice for luck and rolled it … it fell off the table – they were called through to see the same guy. She sat there nervously as he went through the same paper-shuffling, eye-rolling, grunting routine. But he must have had a couple of brandies with his *churros* for breakfast because, remarkably, he didn't recognise her from the week before, and nor did he query the bank certificate, despite the account clearly being in joint names.

When she returned home, she leaped out of the mini waving her little green sunshine permit around with a broad smile on her face. And all was right with the world once more.

The following day we were up bright and early to take Mum and Dad to the airport. As we said our goodbyes in the car park, Dad wanted to know when they could come back again.

'You're banned in the summer months,' Chris said.

'Why?'

'Because you won't do as you're told and wear your hat or drink enough water.'

'I wish you'd told me that before I left a glowing review in your guest book,' he joked.

36

Passion, Penitence and Pointy Hats

Easter week was now upon us, and we'd been told it was a big deal in Spain. Whereas UK kids are looking forward to an Easter Egg Hunt, Spanish kids are putting the finishing touches to their costumes and polishing their instruments for the Easter parades.

Holy Week in Spain is a sight to behold, with the huge processions that take place in Málaga city a particular draw. Antonio Banderas is a native of Málaga, and regardless of where in the world he might be filming, he makes a concerted effort to return home for Easter to often lend a hand in carrying one of the enormous floats with statues of Jesus and the Virgin Mary that literally weigh a tonne or more.

Banderas has shares in a few tapas bars and restaurants that trade under the name El Pimpi, all of which can be found nestled together in a small square facing the historic ruins of the Roman theatre at the foot of the Alcazaba fortress that predates Christ. Inside the old bar you'll find lots of photos of film stars posing with him. He is a much-loved son of the city as you might imagine.

Unlike most of the other Spanish fiestas that have little or no religious significance, Holy Week – or *Semana Santa* – is taken very seriously in this majority Catholic nation. The final days of the life of Christ are known in Christianity as 'the Passion', and the paintings often seen adorning the walls of churches the world over show the 'Stations of the Cross', or the last days of his life from his condemnation by Pontius Pilate to his entombment.

Whether or not you are a practicing Catholic, you cannot fail to be moved by the emotional reenactment of those scenes by each town's different brotherhoods (*hermandads*) in the distinctive colours of their church.

We'd been informed that we should go into town in the late afternoon on the Thursday before Easter to witness Alhaurín El Grande's procession. When we arrived, there were lots of people in various uniforms and outfits making their way to their local churches to amass there in their respective marching bands and processionary troupes beforehand. We found a suitable vantage point at one of the crossroads and waited for it all to unfold. People had brought chairs out of their houses and were lining the streets as far as the eye could see.

The procession featured lots of marching bands from around the town – who would have thought this many people played musical instruments in a town of this size? – and you heard them before you saw them. When the procession rounded the corner at the top of the narrow street we were facing, the first group of marchers we saw were those wearing the long head-to-toe gowns and distinctive pointy hats, and they were carrying a large cross, or tall silver torches and staffs.

The pointy hats, particularly those worn by the adults, are pointed hoods with an integral full-face covering and eye holes. Despite their misappropriation by the far right in America, the significance of the hoods is twofold: the hiding of the face is because the wearer is ashamed of the weight of their sins in the presence of Christ, and the hats are pointing up towards heaven. I imagine the lead marchers, known locally as *capirotes* (hoodies), probably held high offices within their particular church.

Whilst now associated with Easter, the hooded garb dates back to the Middle Ages and, dare I say it, the time of the Spanish Inquisition. '*Nobody expects the Spanish Inquisition,*' I hear you cry, but it was a horrifying period in Spain's rich history that was responsible for the expulsion of the Moors and the execution on a whim of anyone reported for blasphemy. Those found guilty of the charge were often burned alive wearing a pointed hood, a visible sign they were sinners.

Behind this lead group came a group wearing army uniforms and bearing rifles. As they periodically paused their marching, these men faced each other and demonstrated their rifle twirling and tossing skills. They were accompanied close behind by a marching band in similar olive uniforms.

Next came some hooded penitent flagbearers carrying the scenes from the Stations of the Cross. These in turn were followed by men in Roman soldier costumes with one character portraying Jesus as he was roped and dragged through the streets. Even for a lapsed Catholic like myself, it was a very moving spectacle.

Another troupe of mixed-sex soldiers followed in a more colourful uniform with rifles and tailcoats. These too were accompanied behind by a marching band that treated the crowds to a rousing tune. After these came a group of young boys, no more than seven or eight years old, dressed in little army uniforms and showing off their own rifle-tossing skills.

And then came the most moving part, for me at least. A large float was carried down the street by a group of at least fifty men. The float was a large silver affair, decorated with flowers, candles and a canopy, under which stood a large statue of the Virgin Mary. As they marched to a slow, solemn tune played by the band that followed, the men all swayed from side to side in perfect unison. It really was a very poignant sight, particularly when they passed us by, the music growing louder as the band drew nearer.

It was all quite emotionally draining, and the pride displayed by those involved, especially the kids, was clear to see. If this were the kind of spectacle that a relatively small town like ours could put on, we really must go and see the Málaga processions.

As we walked away, we vowed that this was something Mum and Dad must witness at some point, and it was a shame they'd left a week earlier.

'You should join one of those bands,' Chris said.

'I may do. I quite liked that army uniform on the first band. I think I'd look good in olive.'

Chris rolled her eyes, something I'm noticing her do more often these days.

'Come on,' I said. 'Let's go for some tapas and a *cerveza.*'

37

Call That a Lawn?

A month after scattering seed to the wind, we had a big patch of grass alongside the pool. I was pacing around it slowly, scrutinising the blades. This Gobi Desert stuff seemed to be a blend of two types, one a more broad-leafed and tough-looking grass, the other a more delicate, slower-growing type. Chris came out with a towel and her swimming costume on.

'What do you think of my lawn?' I asked.

'Call that a lawn?'

'I know. It's not quite what I was expecting. I was hoping it'd be like that Grama grass they had in Estartit.'

Grama grass, or Buffalo grass as it's also known, is quite common in Spain. I'd read that you couldn't grow it from seed, though, and had to buy plugs of it instead. That sounded too complicated for a man of my limited horticultural background, so I'd gone for this Gobi seed mix instead.

'Anyway, it's not your lawn. I spent days getting stones out of that while you were galivanting round the UK.'

'I was hardly galivanting. I was working in the back end of nowhere. Alright then, what do you think of *our* lawn?'

Chris stepped down from the terrace and padded around.

'Well, you couldn't play bowls on it,' she said.

'Well, I don't want to play bowls on it. I just want to be able to walk from the pool to the terrace without getting muddy and walking dirt back into the pool.'

Since putting it down I'd discovered they use Gobi grass on Mediterranean golf courses – only for the rough, though, but I felt I needed to defend myself.

'They use this on golf courses, apparently,' I said.

'Well, you're not playing golf on it, either.'

That's what she thought. I could work on my approach play around the greens by chipping some balls into the pool ... but only when she wasn't there, of course.

'It needs cutting too,' she added.

'I know. I'll go and buy a lawnmower tomorrow.'

'And it's a bit patchy.'

Jeepers, she's a harsh critic.

'Alright, Monty Don. I know. I'll throw some more seed down after I've mown it.'

'You're not getting a Flymo, are you? You'll get grass in the pool.'

'No. I'm not a fool. I'll get a push-along one with a collection box.'

'It doesn't feel too bad underfoot,' she said, dropping her towel on the edge of the pool and taking the first tentative steps into the water.

'I don't know about underfoot, you'll end up under the lawn if you're not careful,' I muttered under my breath.

'Did you say something?'

'I said, there's still a few stones poking up through the lawn, so you'll have to be careful.'

The following day, we returned from one of our regular jaunts down to the coast and its more extensive retail opportunities with a small lawnmower and a long extension cable to reach the far end. I should have left Chris at home, though, as we also came home with a load of cushions for the terrace furniture.

After a quick ten-minute cut, the lawn looked a lot better, and I began to feel my efforts had not been wasted. José was out in his garden next door smacking his fruit trees with a stick to disturb the tree rats – although I'd yet to see one – and his matriarchal black cat was doing its impression of a dog again by following him around. Perhaps she was hoping for a rat-flavoured meal to drop from the skies. I'd like to think he was casting lascivious glances at my freshly trimmed lawn, but he was probably thinking, 'What's the English pillock doing now?'

As I pondered that thought, I wondered what the correct Spanish for that might be, now that my *español* was improving … '*¿Qué hace el pillock Inglés ahora?*', I decided.

After lunch, I had to go and get a new tyre for the Lexus as it was booked in for its first ITV. It's a requirement in Spain that the tyres on the same axle match each other, and one of them didn't. As it turned out, the tread was worn on another one, so I had to put two new tyres on the rear axle. They were less than half the price I'd been paying at Lexus, so I wasn't too upset.

There were no dramas down at the ITV centre and the car passed all the required tests. After a celebratory lunch out, we then packed the cases for a trip back to the UK to visit family.

When we returned a week later, we had Spanish squatters … don't worry, it was nothing serious … the ants had moved in. They seemed to have attacked on two fronts, one tribe from the terrace doors and another from the front door. They could walk right under the front door, but the battalion attacking from the terrace had been particularly ingenious – they'd climbed to the top of the *persianas*, through the pull chord mechanism, then abseiled down the chord to the floor. Both groups had then made a beeline for the kitchen and were fighting over the contents when we arrived. We must remember to spray around the doorways next time we go away. That'll teach us … another lesson learned.

Out came the Dyson to suck the pesky things up, which made me ponder another of life's imponderables: Can ants survive in a vacuum cleaner? Who knows? And I wasn't going to waste my time looking. It would just have to get filed alongside life's other great mysteries, like why do they never give you enough pancakes with your crispy duck?

But my own curiosity got the better of me. They can't apparently … survive … the ants … if the impact of the high-powered suction doesn't kill them, they suffocate – nice!

The next morning, I was sitting on the loo, thinking how lucky I was to be living in Spain, and an ant walked across my eyeline. It went up the wall, and before it disappeared behind the plug socket, it stopped to look at me, and I swear blind it winked.

'I'll deal with you later,' I vowed.

I had more important things to do today: I had a lawn to mow, plants to water and a fiesta to attend. There was another religious festival going on today. This one was called *La Fiesta de las Cruces*, the festival of the crosses. The festival takes place every year on the third of May and is a local public holiday – although that makes no difference to me, as every day's a holiday right now.

As we walked into town later on, there was a distinct aroma of rosemary as we approached the old town. A key part of this festival involves the men of the Alhaurín brotherhoods heading out into the mountains in the morning to collect rosemary to spread on the ground. And judging by the amount on the street, they must have picked a truckload of the stuff. I reckon they probably just tell the wives that's what they're doing, then go and sit in a bar all day until the truck arrives with the rosemary they ordered. That's what I'd do anyway.

It was another evening of costumes, marching bands, rifle tossing and pageantry. Most enjoyable, although we left unsure as to what the whole thing was about. So I did a bit of digging, and here is a precis:

Once upon a time, there was a Roman Emperor called Constantine who led his army into battle for a bit of fisticuffs with some rough-looking pagan types. Constantine, concerned his men were outnumbered and that he wasn't going to survive the battle, got tanked up on red wine the night before and had a weird dream about a big cross hanging from the sky with a prophetic inscription that told him he was going to be victorious. So he got his chippies to knock up a quick cross which they would parade before them into battle. And would you believe it, he won!

After exaggerating his victory when he returned to Rome, he was given a Christian baptism and told to venture forth and build some churches – they probably just wanted rid of the braggart. Anyway, he sent his Mum, Saint Helena, off to Jerusalem to find the cross upon which Jesus was crucified. She ascended Mount

Calvary and found three hidden bloody logs, but she didn't know which was Jesus's. So she went round touching some sick (and dead) people to see which one had healing powers. The log that cured the sick (and revived the dead) was considered the real deal, and the veneration of the True Cross is celebrated with today's fiesta.

And that's the gist of it, or as much sense as I can make of it. I've no idea where the rosemary comes in, but it's a good excuse for a *fiesta* – not that Spaniards need an excuse for a knees-up.

That night, we were sitting on our terrace at midnight enjoying the clear skies and were treated to a firework display somewhere over the town. Again, I've no idea if it had anything to do with the festival, or if someone had a big birthday to celebrate, but it was lovely to watch all the same.

38

Feria Time

As May wore on, we had more guests: Chris's two sisters, Dee and Sue, had come over for a week of rest and relaxation. We were at the start of another busy period of visitors to the villa, but we wouldn't have it any other way. Dee had already been over with her husband, but it was Sue's first visit. She's a nervous flyer and it might be some time before we see her again, so it was nice to have her. After losing her husband, Ron, a couple of years ago, she'd had a tough time of it. Spending some quality time with her two sisters should do her the world of good.

'Do you like it here, Sue?' I asked her.

'It's lovely, but it's too hot.'

'Too hot? It's only May. You should see it in July.'

'No, I couldn't come if it was any hotter than this.'

That night we went out for dinner. We're trying to get Sue to eat a bit more, as she often skips meals. You get big portions in Spain, and she seemed to be enjoying her food for once.

'Shall we skip dessert and go across the road for an ice cream?' I suggested.

There was an ice cream parlour across the street, and even though it was almost eleven o'clock at night, the place was still open and doing a brisk trade. I love that about Spain: the ice cream parlours have the same opening hours as the kebab shop.

'Ooh, I'd love an ice cream,' Sue said.

She's a sucker for a Mr Whippy, thankfully, and we were determined to fatten her up a bit before she went home. The

194

following morning, I walked into town on my own to pick up the car again. After working up a sweat, I had to stop off for sustenance, so I treated myself to a *café con leche* and a plate of *churros* with chocolate sauce – my guilty little pleasure.

When our guests left at the end of the week, we had another quick changeover – or rather, Chris did – as we prepared for our next guests. Kim and Martin had found a dog-sitter and wanted to come and visit us. There was another *fiesta* in town, and this one was the biggest of the year so far.

Most towns in Spain have a big area of land set aside for the annual *feria*. A travelling fair arrives the week before to set up all the rides and food stalls, and Alhaurín El Grande was no different. They make a real big thing of it, and our *feria* takes place in the runup to and throughout the last weekend in May.

These huge celebrations had to be approved by the sitting monarch originally, and the first such *feria* permitted in our town was by Royal Decree from Queen Isabel II in 1853. She decreed the Mayor of Alhaurín was to permit a market to take place inside the walls of the town, with a place outside the walls reserved for the cattle, down by the river Fahala. That first festival began with a bullfight in the centre of town – now no longer featured, thankfully – followed by a musical procession led by an image of Jesus. Day two would see a mass being said, followed by another musical procession and a further bullfight. In the evening there would be a grand firework display. And on the third and final day, another bullfight preceded the transferal of the image of Jesus to its resting place in the hermitage of San Sebastián in the centre of the town.

Some forty years later, the festivities had expanded into a five-day celebration, where the town's patron saint, Our Lady of Grace, was now most prominent. To this day, the *feria* still spans five days, from Wednesday through to Sunday, and includes performances of song and dance throughout the town squares and in the main festival tent. Pop-up bars are set up around the town, and huge paellas are cooked to feed the hungry masses. Many people dress up in traditional Spanish costume for the dancing, while the younger ones look forward to the travelling fair the most.

One of the first activities each year nowadays is the inauguration of a festival queen and her 'Mister' – I don't know why he's not called a king, but it must be a huge honour for the young couple. The principal *caseta* is a huge tent at the bottom of the fairground where the main bands and dancers perform. It has long trestle tables catering for hundreds of people, but we had no idea how you secured a seat, or even if it was a ticketed event.

When Kim and Martin arrived in the late afternoon, we sat and had pre-dinner drinks on the terrace. Chris and I were already dressed and ready for dinner. Kim was her usual glamorous self – all legs, hair and make-up – and Martin was looking forward to not having the dogs sleeping with him for once.

'What time's the taxi coming?' Kim asked, as the sun began to lower in the sky.

'In about fifteen minutes,' I said.

'What? I need to get ready,' she protested.

'I thought you were already ready. You look lovely.'

With that, Kim dashed off inside and presented herself back on the terrace fifteen minutes later in a change of outfit and freshly made up.

'See,' I said to Martin, 'they *can* get ready in fifteen minutes when they have to.'

The town was buzzing as we passed through it on the way to our dinner reservation at Restaurante La Alegria ('the happy one'), the place we'd eaten the week before with Chris's sisters. Afterwards, we wandered down to the fairground to see what all the fuss was about. It was a hive of activity. All the kids were having the time of their lives, and the stallholders were making a killing. The atmosphere was a heady mix of fried food smells, twinkling bright lights, lively music and normal Spanish discourse (i.e. shouting). Chris and Martin were not really into fairground rides, so it was down to Kim and me to try a few out, all with the obligatory screaming of course.

As our guests prepared to leave after a late breakfast the following morning, we asked for their impressions of the villa, and if there was anything we could do to make our guests more comfortable in future.

'I struggled with the mirror in the bedroom,' Kim said. 'I could only see myself from the breasts down.'

When we'd installed the mirror, we'd stuck it on the wall at a height that suited the more diminutive proportions of our family; not, it seems, the appropriate height for a six-foot-one-inch blonde in killer heels.

'Does it not work if you stand further back?' I enquired.

'No,' she laughed. 'My eyes are the same height no matter how far back I stand.'

Technically, she was right, or course, but I'm sure perspective comes into play the further back you go, but with her eyeline above the mirror and the bedroom only being five metres deep, she had a point. So we vowed to raise the mirror in time for their next visit and bade them both a safe journey home up the scary mountain pass.

We had a lazy afternoon round the pool before venturing back into town the following afternoon to see what daytime activities were taking place during the *feria*. We went to the old town where they'd set up a stage, and a flamenco band was playing. Some of the old dears in the crowd had made a real effort and were dressed up to the nines in their flamenco gear, stomping around the square like someone thirty years younger. We looked on in admiration at their stamina while we sank a few beers and a plate of paella.

Next day, Chris was back on washing duty again as we had more visitors arriving in a couple of days. Sue's daughter Kim and her husband James were coming over for a few days.

'Make yourself useful,' she said, handing me a scrubbing brush. 'See if you can get the grime off the water line in the pool'.

So I poured myself a beer, donned a pair of trunks and jumped in ... the pool, not the beer, of course. It's a tough job, but someone has to do it.

We enjoyed a relaxing few days with our niece and her husband, although before they left, Chris got the scrubbers out again and pressganged the three of us to form a pool cleaning party. Our TripAdvisor rating is going to plummet if she carries on like this.

On the way home from dropping them at the airport, the back end of one of the exhausts on the Lexus fell off. I managed to tie it up with some string I had in the boot, and we hobbled home. Strictly speaking, you're supposed to call out the *grúa* (tow truck) in Spain as you can't do your own roadside repairs. All they do, though, is come and tow you to a garage, and it didn't need a tow, it just needed a little ingenuity.

The following day was a Saturday, and I wasn't sure where to go to get it fixed. I tried one of the local garages that the batty woman from Spanish had suggested, but they were closed. I knew there was a national tyre and exhaust chain down on the coast that was probably open, so I drove down there. The cheeky buggers wanted fifteen euros off me before they'd even put the car on the ramp. After waiting an hour for my turn on the ramp, they told me it needed a replacement exhaust, which was blindingly obvious. They would have to source one from Lexus in Málaga and said they'd call me back with a price and availability, so I left them and headed home again.

When they rang me later on with the bad news, it was even worse than I'd feared – I wasn't going to get much change out of a grand, which was ridiculous. Most of the cost was the parts, but even so … I was starting to wish I had a Spanish-built Seat rather than a Lexus.

On Monday morning I went to the postbox to collect the mail and asked Felipe where he took his car for repairs. He sent me to a mechanic in the centre of town.

'Ask for Paco,' he said. 'Tell him I sent you.'

Paco turned out to be a lovely fella and a great mechanic. He put the car on the ramp straight away for me, and we both ducked underneath to see what the damage was. There was a mismatch in our language abilities, as Paco had no English, and given he was gabbling away at me in Andalusian, I may as well not have had any Spanish myself. I got the gist of what he was saying, though. I left it with him and went off to find a café. When I returned ninety minutes later, he'd had the exhaust off, welded it and put it back on again, all for sixty euros. Paco is now my new best friend.

39

In a State of Alarm

DON'T PANIC

We had another invasion of ankle-biters to deal with – but don't panic, it wasn't the ants this time ... some of the grandkids were coming over, and I was charged with child-proofing the pool. So I bought a load of netting and some fence posts from the DIY shop.

Our second eldest daughter, Andrea, was coming to stay in a few days' time with her husband, Mat. They'd timed their visit to coincide with a friend's wedding at the Marbella Beach Club, a rather gorgeous, swanky hotel on the coast. Their two rug rats, Jessica aged three and Caleb aged one, would be with them, but were *persona non gratae* for the wedding, so Nana and Grandad would be on babysitting duty that night. Naturally, at that age, they couldn't swim yet, and we needed to keep them safe. The dangers of an open pool were brought into stark reality little more than a week earlier with the tragic death of a toddler in a private pool on the Costa Blanca, and we didn't want to take any chances.

With that in mind, four weeks earlier, I'd done lots of research on pool alarms. After much deliberation – which Chris will tell you is an annoying personal trait of mine – I chose to buy the most appropriate alarm from Amazon in Spain. The Poolside KidSafe Mark II (name changed to avoid a lawsuit) was a battery-powered device that sat on the side of the pool with a sensor that extended below the waterline and gave off a high-pitched alarm if a ripple was detected on the water surface.

That should do the job nicely, and at a hundred and seventy euros, you'd expect it to. The seller was a French company, but the name and model of the unit advertised led me to believe it was made by a US company with a good reputation for build quality and reliability.

Delivery from France took ten days in the end, and I wondered if they were using the same donkey that had delivered the Mini headlamps from Germany.

Upon opening the box it was clear that what I'd ordered was not what I was staring at. Since being advertised as a Poolside KidSafe Mark II it had somehow morphed into what the (ripped) box described as a Poolside ChildKiller JB1 (name changed to avoid another lawsuit). The instructions were in Chinese, and the device looked very poorly made, with soldered connections that a one-armed chimpanzee could have made a better job of. This was quite clearly a cheap Chinese knock-off of the original. I was livid.

I immediately made a refund claim through Amazon and the vendor then called me to apologise and to see if I'd keep the device for a discount. Absolutely not, I said. You can't put a discount on the price of your grandchildren's lives.

I then spent days deliberating over alternative solutions, none of which I was entirely happy with, so with two weeks until the nippers were due to arrive, I bought an authentic Poolside KidSafe Mark II from a US distributor for one hundred and ninety dollars and paid a premium of seventy dollars for international FedEx delivery to ensure it arrived on time.

One week later, the distributor still hadn't shipped it out to me, so I complained to them about the express delivery charge when they couldn't even express ship it in the first. I was becoming the equivalent of a chess Grandmaster in the art of complaining.

Two days before our guests arrived, I still couldn't get an answer from the US supplier, but I received an email from someone at FedEx. They had a parcel for me in Madrid and wanted to know my full name and NIE number.

After sending the information, I was informed that the combination of my name and NIE number was not registered with the tax office. I replied, telling them that the tax office was happy to deprive me of a couple of grand for importing my own car last month, so why should it be a problem for them now?

I sent them copies of my NIE certificate and my tax office registration. They replied to tell me that I was in fact registered with the tax office but that I had to 'activate' my NIE number there because it's not recognised by the Customs office.

For pity's sake, all I was doing was importing a pool alarm from the States. How hard should it be?

It was time to involve Felipe at the PO Box, as he might know what they're talking about. Felipe said my number was registered with the tax office and that activation with Customs was something they'd never heard of before. The phone number I had for the person at FedEx wouldn't work, so I emailed them to see if they'd call me back while I waited at Felipe's office. Twenty minutes later, the little hand on the clock clicked over to lunchtime, and Felipe was off for his *menú del día*, so I went home again.

I called another number when I'd calmed down a bit and spoke to someone else at FedEx who said they'd entered my number in the Customs system and that I should now expect to receive an email from them saying how much import duty I had to pay and how to pay it.

I passed this information onto my original contact at FedEx, then received a reply email stating the information was incorrect and that I needed to go to the tax office to activate my NIE, or alternatively supply details of another valid Spanish citizen who can pay the taxes on my behalf. Given that half the population are probably working in the black economy, I couldn't see how that was going to work, so I didn't waste my time pursuing it. I was also quite sure that if I bowled up at the tax office and asked them to activate my NIE with Customs, they wouldn't have a bloody clue what I was talking about. I think FedEx thought I was running some kind of multimillion-pound import and export business.

I emailed back in the most pleading of terms, pointing out that this parcel could save the life of a child (or two) and that I was bewildered how a first world country like Spain couldn't make IT systems talk to each other.

The next morning, before we set off for the airport to collect our visitors, Felipe was back at his desk, suitably refreshed after an afternoon off. He mailed to say he'd call FedEx to find out what was going on. A couple of hours later, he was able to confirm that the confusion arose because my names are the wrong way around at the tax office.

Well, bugger me! Haven't I been trying to tell everyone that for eight months?

And would you believe it, the simple trick of using my name as it appears on my NIE certificate allowed Customs to recognise me and they released my parcel. And all it took in the end was thirty emails, a few unanswered phone calls and seventy-two euros in import duties.

But was that the end of this epic tale of misfortune? Oh no, not on your nelly … it wasn't over until the fat lady sings, and she was still in the dressing room warming up.

It seems the Yanks couldn't make stuff much better than the Chinese. My new US-sourced Poolside KidSafe Mark II only had one joint on it, in the crook of a right-angle, and three of the four 'glued' edges were no longer adhered to each other.

I immediately sent photos and a complaint via email to the US distributor, pointing out the delays, poor service and costly delivery import charges for a product that had been poorly made and insufficiently packaged for international delivery – in fact, it hadn't been packaged at all … instead of putting the product in an outer shipping carton, all they'd done was stick a few labels on the outside and throw it at the courier.

After six days of unanswered emails, I sent another email with a copy to the manufacturer stating that if the matter wasn't resolved within twenty-four hours, I would arrange a chargeback via my credit card company and, perhaps more damaging to them both, publicise the poor service and build quality as widely as I could on social media. I'd ramped up the threat to DEFCON 1 and peeled back the trigger guard on the nuclear button.

That seemed to do the trick – the power of social media, eh? … or the threat of it, at least. I received an almost immediate response from the manufacturer to their credit. They'd called the distributor and hauled them over the coals to sort out my complaint without further delay. I was contacted by the distributor and asked if I wanted a replacement or a full refund. As I had no desire to make the Spanish Tax authorities believe I was indeed a kingpin in the import/export business, I declined to return the item and requested a full refund. I'd actually repaired the device myself with gaffer tape and had deployed it successfully for the last few days.

It was then that the distributor realised they'd only ever applied a pending charge to my credit card and had never actually billed me for the product or shipping costs. They cancelled the charge, and that was that. I could have seen that as fortuitous, but I chose to instead view it as further evidence of mismanagement by an incompetent and poorly run US distributor.

And in true US fashion, when I thanked the distributor's respondent, 'Britney' – who didn't once include her job title or telephone number in her four emails – her closing remark to me was 'Have a great day!' – unbelievable.

And … breathe.

It was great to see the grandkids splashing around in the pool. I'm not sure who had more fun, them or us. On the day of the wedding, I drove the adults down to the coast then came back to help Chris corral the nippers round the garden. When you've got two of them, you usually find that one runs off one way and the other runs the other way. It's just what kids do, consciously or otherwise.

'I'm taking Jessica to the toilet,' Chris said. 'Don't take your eyes off Caleb for a minute.'

'Why? Am I likely to find him round the back of the couch ripping the legs off a spider?'

'No, you're more likely to find him trying to climb over the fence into the pool.'

And she was probably right. The thing you can't have is always the most attractive thing when you're that age. They were well-behaved at bedtime, and Mummy and Daddy had a wonderful time without them no doubt.

Come the end of the holiday, everyone had had a smashing time, nobody went home sunburnt, and thanks to the temporary fence I erected around the pool in conjunction with the repaired Poolside KidSafe Mark II, I'm pleased to be able to report that Jessica and Caleb didn't fall in the pool. In fact, Jessica even learned to jump in and swim without her armbands on ... and Daddy thrashed Grandad on the golf course. Grrr!

40

I Need a Holiday

We waved our daughter and her family off at the airport, did a quick headcount to make sure they'd not left one of the kids with us, then drove home. The journey back wasn't without incident, however, as I ran over a snake. I'll say that again in case you missed it: I ran over a snake. I'll be honest … that's not something I ever thought I'd have to worry about avoiding. It was an accident, pure and simple.

We'd taken both cars to the airport as we wouldn't all fit in mine. Chris was following behind me in the Mini, and I was trailing a car in front of me by a few car lengths. We were about a mile or so from home on the quiet back road that cuts into the bottom of town when we came over the brow of a hill. The car in front of me made a sudden movement into the middle of the road and back to avoid what looked like part of a tyre. There was an oncoming car which meant I wasn't able to swerve, so I ran straight over this piece of rubber. Only it wasn't a piece of rubber, it was a snake, warming itself on the tarmac.

Chris said she saw my front wheel go over it and the snake reared up briefly in what I can only assume was a mixture of surprise, fright and not inconsiderable pain. I then ran over it again with the rear wheel, which I rather hope killed it stone dead, as I wouldn't like to think it suffered for long. I still thought I'd run over a bit of rubber until Chris told me.

Anyway, can't be helped, and I'd provided breakfast for the local griffon vultures.

We arrived home with some repair jobs to attend to after our guests had departed: a broken bed and a ripped cover for a child car seat we'd borrowed off a generous stranger on Facebook.

Oops! Kids, eh? Who'd 'ave 'em? I'm glad we had our kids when we were younger, because I don't think I'd cope well with being an older Dad.

Chris got her needle and thread out and stitched a new piece onto the car seat from a length of waterproof fabric cut from one of my hiking gaiters, and the owner was happy with the repair (and the bottle of wine).

That afternoon, my kebab-eating buddy, Rick, got in touch to invite us up to stay at their place in Murcia. He'd finished his current bout of decorating and the place was ready for visitors. We jumped at the chance because I was ready for a holiday. And it would be nice to see another part of Spain and just relax for a couple of nights with good friends again.

So the following week we set off in the Lexus and headed for San Javier Airport in Murcia, five hours and 285 miles away. Karen and Rick were flying in early evening, and we said we'd pick them up.

The drive up was uneventful, if rather boring. We chose to take the coast road as, although it was slightly longer than the inland route round Granada, we thought it would be more scenic. However, from somewhere just before Motril until you get way past Almería, the countryside is blighted by polytunnels. This part of Spain is what you might call the veggie basket of Europe. It's a major production centre for a lot of the vegetables that find their way onto the dinner plates of the British, but I wish they hadn't chosen to spoil more than a hundred miles of rugged coastline in the process.

We arrived in San Javier in plenty of time so went and found a bar on the beach at Los Alcázares. Owned by the Spanish Air Force, San Javier Airport was a dual-use airport serving both the local military academy and the European budget carriers. It was a tiny airport in commercial terms with an enviable location handy for the tourists on the edge of the Mar Menor, and it normally handled more than a million visitors a year.

I'd flown from here once before on business several years ago but was otherwise unfamiliar with the region.

Rick's flight landed on schedule, and they were out to meet us before the engines had stopped spinning, one of the benefits I suppose of a small airport.

'You didn't have to pick us up,' Rick said. 'We could have walked to the apartment. It's less than two and a half miles away.'

'You wouldn't have dragged your cases that far, would you?'

'No, we'd have got a taxi. But you get my point. It's only down the road.'

And down the road it was, literally. We drove in a straight line for about a mile and a half, over the roundabout, and a bit further on, and we were there. A crow couldn't have found a shorter route. Very convenient. Well, it was until soon afterwards when they moved all commercial flights to a new airport twenty-five miles away. They definitely won't be walking from that one.

The apartment was a two-bed place on the second floor in a quiet block, a few streets back from the shoreline, and the town was called Santiago de la Ribera. This charming old fishing village was a lovely low-key tourist spot these days, with a few miles of beach bordering the calm waters of the Mar Menor, an inland sea protected from the Mediterranean by a strip of land called La Manga, which is where the England national football squad sometimes came for winter training.

After dumping our cases and having the obligatory holiday arrival beer on the balcony, we headed into town for dinner. We were only two hundred and fifty metres from the promenade and had a relaxing stroll down towards the centre. It was still only mid June, so we weren't into peak season just yet, and as such, we found it a very pleasant place to while away a couple of days. We dined on fish and seafood with not a kebab in sight. Rick and I vowed to save that delight for another visit, though.

The Mar Menor (the 'minor sea') was like a big warm bathtub, with shallow waters and gently sloping shorelines that were ideal for bathing ... that is if you ignore the pollution. According to reports in the Spanish press, the area had just been stripped of its Blue Flag status thanks to pollutants entering the water. There were reports it was close to ecological collapse. I'm not sure where the restaurants got their fish from, but perhaps a lamb kebab might have been the safer option after all.

The waters of the Mar Menor are only seven metres at the deepest point, and I'm fairly sure they don't have any great white sharks in the water. In fact, Spain has only ever recorded eight deaths from shark attacks, the last of which was over a hundred years ago, so you should be alright. Having said that, the last non-fatal shark attack in Spain was only last year, and it was just up the coast from here near Alicante. On that occasion, a blue shark was the culprit.

La Manga is a thirteen-mile sandbar that almost cuts off the sea of the Mar Menor completely from the Mediterranean, apart from a small section at the northern tip that allows boats in and out. The land is only a hundred metres wide as its narrowest part, yet they've still managed to pack it with apartments and hotels. The sandbar and the shallow passage into the Mar Menor are probably enough to deter the larger sharks, so if you're planning a pleasure cruise, unlike Chief Brody in *Jaws*, you shouldn't need a bigger boat.

On our only full day there, we had a long stroll up the prom to San Pedro Del Pinatar. Whilst there, we had a look at the therapeutic mud baths on one side of a sticky-out bit of promenade. Europe was in the grip of a heatwave, and nowhere more so than in southern Spain where the mercury on the Mar Menor was nudging thirty-seven degrees, so you can imagine what kind of stench the sulphur-rich mud was giving off. We smelt it before we saw it.

The tourist bumph described the mud as having 'a high percentage of cations, calcium, magnesium, potassium and fluoride, as well as anions, chloride and sulphate in levels which are well over the expected ones, even for waters of this salinity level'. I don't know about you, but apart from having an aversion to getting muddy, I didn't like the sound of the water composition, so we gave it a swerve and went for lunch instead.

If, like me, you like your seafood, you've got to try *pulpo gallega*, which was widely available along the beachfront. It's a deliciously simple dish of octopus, olive oil, paprika and salt, and it originates from Galicia, on the northwest tip of Spain where it meets the Atlantic Ocean. Galicia seems to be to Spain what Scotland is to Britain, the northernmost part of the mainland with a Celtic heritage, a rocky coastline and shit weather – it barely gets above twenty degrees all summer. They even play the bloody bagpipes up there, which might be why the Moors were put off invading the place. The food's good though, if the *pulpo gallega* is anything to go by.

The following day, after the briefest of visits, it was time to move on. Our hosts had more visitors arriving and had to get the bedding washed – we knew how they felt, or rather Chris did. This time we went via Granada to avoid the polytunnel hell of Almería. On the way, we went past – or rather under – the historic town of Lorca. The motorway burrows through the rocky hillside, under the medieval fortress of Lorca castle.

From there we headed inland to skirt around the northern side of the Sierra Nevada mountains, the highest point on continental Spain at just under three and a half thousand metres, which is more than two and a half times higher than the UK's highest mountain, Ben Nevis. As you drive through this stretch on the way to the city of Granada, the provincial capital, you pass the town of Guadix, and you start to see some of the cave houses built into the sides of the mountains. These houses are hand-carved from the rock and claim to maintain a pleasant year-round temperature, which sounds hard to believe when the Sierra Nevada is Spain's primary ski resort. Cave houses are so popular in Guadix that half the town live underground like Spanish Wombles and are thus more than worthy of the troglodyte name.

We stopped just past Granada as we were getting peckish, and you can't usually go wrong stopping at one of the restaurants on the motorway service areas. The food is usually of a high quality and very reasonably priced, unlike the overprocessed rubbish you mostly find at British service stations. And the coffee is always good too, which is another fantastic thing about Spain. A bad cup of coffee in Spain is almost as rare as an appearance in the knockout stages of a major tournament for the Scotland national football team – which at the time of writing, incidentally, stands at a big fat zero.

If you pay more than one euro fifty for a coffee in Spain, and you're not sitting in the main square of a major city or in the most scenic part of a tourist hotspot, you're being ripped off. In Alhaurín El Grande, I can buy a coffee and a bacon butty and get change from three euros.

We were back at the villa an hour and a half later, and I was glad to be out of the car. A couple of days afterwards we were off to the airport again, but instead of picking someone up, we were flying out ourselves this time. We were off to the UK again to visit family, just so all the grandkids didn't forget what we looked like ... and so Chris could get her hair done and stock up on her preferred brand of e-cigs.

When we came back a week later, we had some hangers-on, as Corrinne and Graham flew back with us for the weekend. It was their third trip in a year – I think they were having a competition with Mum and Dad. They might have now matched them on visits, but the old folks were winning hands down on length of stay. Either way, they were a most welcome distraction from having to weed the garden.

41

Seville in the Summer

When the young 'uns left we had a twenty-four-hour changeover again. My footie mates, Neil and Darryl, were coming over to check us out. I met Neil when he was a client of mine, and a demanding one at that. You couldn't slack on Neil's watch. Not that I ever did, of course. Neil's retired, like me – it still feels weird saying that at the moment, although technically I'd say I'm just unemployed and not eligible for the Spanish dole. He hit burnout in the same industry as me, so I know how he feels – it can take its toll. Darryl is Neil's next-door neighbour, and we go to the football together, or we did till I broke up the triumvirate by emigrating.

Darryl said he's got eleven weeks off work – now there's a slacker if I ever I saw one. He's a public servant, so technically, I pay his wages, and I don't remember approving his holiday request. Anyway, they wanted to come over for a few days – I think they must have been pining for me.

'Yay. We're putting the band back together,' Neil had said a couple of weeks earlier when the idea was first mooted.

Who did he think he was? John Belushi? I could tell he was excited.

'We wouldn't mind seeing Granada or Seville while we're there,' Darryl said.

'Good stuff. To give you an idea, Seville is thirty-nine degrees today, Granada thirty-five, with both close to forty all next week. It's hot, hot, hot!'

'Bloody hell,' my fair-skinned friend replied. 'I was suffering yesterday when it was twenty-eight here.'

'Love the heat,' Neil countered smugly.

'So which city would you rather visit when you're here?'

'I'd like to see both,' Neil said.

'Jesus. You're only here for three full days. Granada is two hours and a hundred miles to the northeast of me, and Seville is two and a half hours and a hundred and twenty miles to the northwest. Fitting both of them in will be a bit of a slog. Maybe save one for another time, eh?'

'Well I didn't actually mean see them *both* in three days, I meant I'd like to see them both at some point, although people I know rave about Seville.'

'Seville it is then.'

After a bit of my customary detailed research, I determined that the best place to hang out at night looked to be in the *barrio* (district) of Triana, on the west side of the city. It's sandwiched between the main Guadalquivir river and an offshoot that cuts back on itself, surrounding the area with its waters. And, more importantly, Triana is packed with tapas bars and restaurants. I found a lovely Airbnb for two nights that would only cost us two hundred and ten pounds.

'Five-bed apartment, one double, two twins, two nights, seventy quid each. How does that sound?' I messaged them.

'Great!!! xx,' Darryl sent back.

'You can keep your kisses or you're not coming.'

'Thank God we've got a bedroom each,' Neil added.

When we'd visited the UK recently, I'd popped in for a brew to see the boys. Neil had his sun cream ready, and Darryl had packed a hat. On the morning of their visit to Spain, I went to pick them up from the airport on my own.

'See you soon,' I'd messaged earlier. 'I'll be straight ahead of you as you enter the arrivals area. Don't be tempted to follow the crowds by turning right as you'll end up outside the terminal.'

'Can you hold up a sign?' Neil asked.

'You should recognise me – you only saw me last week.'

We went from the airport straight to La Cala as I had to call by the opticians to pick up my new reading glasses. My eyes were getting worse – occupational hazard when you work in IT, I'm afraid. Then we wandered down to a beach bar for a beer and to get the lads in the holiday mood. The beach was busier than usual as we were just getting into the start of the main holiday season, and with the mercury still rising, the beer was a welcome refreshment.

'It's nice 'ere innit?' Neil said.

'Who do you think you are, Lorraine Chase? I should have ordered you a Campari.'

He was impersonating women now as well as the Blues Brothers. Back at the villa, the lads got a quick tour round while Chris laid out lunch on the terrace.

'Right, one of you can have the double bedroom, and the other can have the office with a trundle bed that pulls out into a double … or you can share the double bed if you like?'

'I don't want Darryl getting the wrong idea,' Neil said, 'so a separate room for me, but I don't mind which.'

'The office is cooler. It's north facing so doesn't get direct sunlight, it's smaller and the air con works better in there.'

'I'll have that then,' Darryl jumped in.

'By the way, in the morning, as we only have one bathroom, Neil is going last in the shower,' I said.

'Why's that?' he protested.

'I've shared a room with you before. You take bloody ages, and you nick all the hot water.'

'I can't help being meticulous with my personal hygiene.'

'Well, you can scrub your balls clean for as long as you like after the rest of us have been in.'

The following morning we set off for Seville, leaving Chris to her own devices. She'd much rather lounge by the pool with a book than listen to us three putting the world to rights for the next few days. We took the scenic route up past Ardales and Teba before joining the main A-92 *autovia* into Seville. After a brief coffee stop to take in fluids on such a hot day, we arrived in Seville to find the traffic as busy as I'd seen it so far in Spain. Thankfully, the apartment came with underground parking, so we didn't have to drive round looking for somewhere to park.

We'd chosen a great place to stay, in both accommodation terms and location. The apartment was huge and really clean, and there was no squabbling over bedrooms – the lads graciously offered me the double en-suite, and I equally graciously accepted. We did a quick shop for essential breakfast fodder at the local minimarket – although we ended buying enough for a party of eight – and then it was off out to explore the city.

We passed through the main hub of the Triana district, which was a hive of activity, crossed the river and headed for our lunch stop. I'd booked us in at that nice Italian Chris and I had frequented at Christmas. It was as good as I remembered it to be, and we filled our bellies with pizza, pasta and wine. Then it was off to roam the city centre for a few hours.

Seville is one hell of a city: fantastic architecture, loads of great bars, and quite spread out if you want to take it all in. We wandered round like the tourists we were, stopping for liquid refreshment every now and then, and planning which of the key sights we wanted to visit the following day. After covering about four miles on foot, we found ourselves back in the apartment making a shortlist of the best tapas bars in the area.

First stop on tonight's tapas crawl was one of those unassuming places that are a hit with the locals, Bar Casa Ruperto, also dubbed Las Codornices. The word *codorniz*, the singular of *cordonices*, featured on the menu stuck to the wall outside the kitchen window where you went to place your order. I hadn't come across that word in Spanish class before, so I had to google it. I assumed it was Spanish for those little fried birds that were flying out of the kitchen – which thinking about it, is an unfortunate turn of phrase, especially given Neil was a pescatarian.

'It means quail,' I read out.

'Count me in,' Darryl said.

So he and I ordered a quail each, which came whole, gutted and fried, presented to you with their legs in the air on a slice of white bread. Ruperto had been serving his speciality quail out of his kitchen window for more than thirty years at the rate of about two hundred a day, and he was a master. Neil had a plate of

Roquefort cheese and olives, which were the only things I could be sure he'd eat off the menu.

Despite living in Spain for a while, there were still lots of things on the menu that I've no idea what they are as they're names of local delicacies. It's a bit like a Spaniard wondering what things like toad in the hole or Cullen skink are – they won't find a direct translation in a foreign language dictionary.

Then it was round the corner to Gastrobar Al-Andalus, which had a more extensive list of things Neil could enjoy. I had eggs stuffed with salmon, cheese and caviar, and that was soon followed by a visit to one of the lauded Las Golondrinas bars where the grilled mushrooms with *alioli* are heavenly.

We were three bars in and already starting to feel quite 'happy', so we decided to stretch our legs a bit more before our next pitstop. We ambled east and closer towards the river where we eventually stopped off in Plazuela de Santa María, a lovely little square with tables served from Bar Bistec. The Rodriquez family had apparently been serving the local *trianeros* (as the natives of Triana are proud to be known) for more than a century, which tells you they're doing something right. The speciality here was *pechuga de paloma en salsa* (breast of dove in sauce). Not being a fan of George Baker's 1975 novelty hit *Una Paloma Blanca*, I opted for the octopus and shared a plate of spicy *patatas bravas* with the boys.

After that, replete with food, we ordered one more round of drinks. Then, feeling done in from today's efforts, we wandered slowly back to the apartment and a well-earned night's rest.

Our second day in Seville was going to be tough on the feet if we were going to pack everything in that we planned to see, so we filled ourselves up with a variety of breakfast items, juice and coffee before heading out. It was going to be *scorchio* (sic) again, so Neil slapped his factor thirty on, Darryl donned his sunhat and off we went.

First up was a trip to the Cathedral of Saint Mary of the See, the city's impressive Gothic cathedral. At the time of its completion in the sixteenth century, Seville Cathedral became the largest one in the world. It began life in the twelfth century as a grand mosque, but fifty years after its inauguration, Seville fell to the Christian armies of Ferdinand III. It was thereafter used as the city's cathedral.

At the turn of the fifteenth century, it was agreed to replace it with a new cathedral on the same site. It should be 'so beautiful and so grand that those who see it finished will take us for mad', declared those responsible for its plans. And in the ensuing hundred years of its construction they indeed did make it grand and beautiful. The builders retained some features of the original mosque, including its historic minaret, now known as the Giralda bell tower, and perhaps the city's most iconic symbol.

It costs extra to go up the tower, but it's well worth it for both the history and the views of the city from the top. I was first struck with the desire to visit this historic landmark when I watched a three-part BBC documentary by Simon Sebag Montefiore, which is thoroughly enjoyable, called *Blood and Gold: The Making of Spain*.

It's more of a history of Andalucía and its interwoven cultures than an account of Spain's history – although the two are intrinsically linked, of course – but it's still really engrossing. The section concerning Seville and the Giralda tower is in the second episode, and Simon tells us why the internal ramp that ascends to the top of the tower was designed the way it is. Instead of being a staircase that leads you skywards, you follow an anticlockwise ascent up a series of brick ramps, designed so that the Imam, who had to go up and down several times a day to make the muezzin call to prayer, could do so on the back of his donkey. Genius.

At 105 metres, the Giralda stands majestically tall alongside the cathedral and was rightly recognised as a UNESCO World Heritage Site thirty years ago. Its most famous resident is Christopher Columbus – or most of him at least, they believe. Even in death he sailed the Atlantic and Caribbean before returning to Spain. The poor fella (or murderous swine as I maintained earlier) was first interred up in Valladolid – probably alongside a bottle of Ribera del Duero – before being exhumed a number of times on his way to his various temporary resting places of Seville, then Santa Domingo in the Dominican

216

Republic, then Havana, Cuba, and finally back to Seville Cathedral just over a century ago.

When we finally emerged back into the searing heat of a Sevillian summer, we decided to head over to the equally magnificent Plaza de España that sits on one side of the María Luisa Park. This whole area, which includes extensive parkland and the exquisite semi-circular, moat-fringed exhibition hall, was constructed for a World Fair in 1929 to celebrate Spain's industry and technology.

'Wow! It's bloody gorgeous,' Neil said.

'I know,' I said. 'It makes Manchester's GMEX conference hall look like an old railway station.'

Darryl looked at me quizzically. 'But the GMEX *is* an old railway station,' he said.

'Well, that just proves my point then.'

The plaza has been used as a backdrop to films such as *Lawrence of Arabia*, in which I played the starring role, apparently – Chris reckons I used to resemble Omar Sharif before I shaved my tash off … I'll take that. *Star Wars: Episode II – Attack of the Clones* was also filmed in the Plaza de España. Neil was a big Star Wars fan, but he never spotted the connection. Anyway, bringing it back to Manchester, it was also used by Mick Hucknall in Simply Red's 'Something Got Me Started', and the ginger-haired crooner would have gone home even redder if he'd filmed it in this heat.

Every day's a school day, eh?

We were starting to feel parched and ready for lunch, so a quick internet search pointed us in the direction of a fabulous unassuming tapas bar, even if it was a kilometre away. I always think it's worth going the extra mile for a decent lunch, and this was only just over half that distance, so I asked the lads to have faith and follow their tour guide.

Andén 3 (platform 3) turned out to be a real find, although nowhere near a train station, surprisingly. It was situated on a sweeping corner of a large roundabout, well out of the touristy central part of town. It looked like an uninspiring café from the outside, but the chef was playing a blinder inside. They had some really interesting dishes on the menu.

The entertainment was good too. We watched as some unfortunate chap came off his pushbike on the roundabout and had to be carted off in an ambulance. Bloody attention seeker.

'Right lads, we can't sit here and drink all day,' I said.

'Whyever not?' Neil said, who looked like he was enjoying his *vino blanco* a bit too much.

'Where are we off to now?' Darryl asked.

'The Moorish Gardens of the Royal Palace, the Real Alcázar.'

'How far's that from here then?' Neil asked.

'Only a mile away.'

'Should have put my hiking boots on,' he said.

'Well, I told you this morning you'd regret wearing flip-flops.'

The Royal Palace and Gardens were a treasure trove of architectural and horticultural excellence. The place owes much to its original sponsor, Abd al-Rahman III who was a native of Córdoba and a descendant of the influential Umayyad Caliphate who left their architectural mark throughout Andalucía. Old Abd ruled Córdoba for part of the tenth century and was also responsible for the building of a grand Medina outside Córdoba, another location featured in Mr Montefiore's documentary.

After walking ourselves silly all day, we grabbed a beer and went back to freshen up. We dined somewhere unremarkable in the city that evening – well, I just can't remember where we ate is the truth of it, hence why I'm not able to remark on it. We did a few wine bars on the stagger back by the bullring, I do recall, before having a nightcap outside Cervecería La Grande ('the big pub').

'How far have we walked today?' Neil asked.

I got my phone out to check.

'Just over sixteen k, so about ten miles.'

'Not bad, that,' Darryl said.

'I know, considering Neil did most of it in his flip-flops.'

We ate what we could of the overstocked provisions in the morning before checking out of the apartment and driving north out of the city to go and visit the other location featured in Simon's TV documentary, the Anfiteatro de Itálica, a truly splendid and well-preserved Roman amphitheatre that was the handiwork of the Roman general, Scipio. It's easy to get to as it's only five miles outside the city, and it was free entry for EU citizens if you show your passport – glad we got in there before Brexit, then, although it's only one euro fifty to get in otherwise … don't you just love Spain?

The first Roman city to be built outside Italy, Itálica was also the first Roman settlement in Spain, chosen for its important links offered by the Guadalquivir river.

'Hadrian was born here, it says here,' Darryl said.

'The famous Roman brickie?' I said.

'That's him.'

'Aye,' said Neil, unconsciously adopting the Scottish affirmative. 'He built a wall to keep the marauding Scots at bay.'

'Well it didn't work, did it?' I said.

'Why not?' Darryl asked.

'Well, they got out and trashed Wembley in '77.'

'Ha! That's right,' Neil said. 'They beat England 2-1. Gordon McQueen scored the opener.'

'Was he playing for United then?'

'No, he was still at "Dirty Leeds". He joined United in '78 for half a million.'

'Alright Statto. Thanks for that.'

Amongst other things, Neil is our resident football statistician. He can remember what colour underpants he wore to each of Manchester United's FA Cup wins, and he's probably been to nine out of the twelve.

'Anyway,' I said, 'we'll have to dig old Hadrian up to build us another wall if Jimmy Krankie gets her independence wish north of the border.'

'Don't let Chris hear you dissing the Scots,' Darryl said.

'She was only born there,' I said. 'She was in Hong Kong by the time she was a year old. And if she'd been a boy, her Dad said he would have driven south to register the birth so his son could play football for England.'

'Did her Dad play football?' Neil asked.

'Yes. He was quite good, apparently. He had trials for Accrington Stanley before he joined the army.'

'Accrington Stanley? Who are they?'

'Exactly,' I said, closing out our reprisal of the Milk Marketing Board's 1980s' TV ad campaign.

It's funny how some commercials stick in your mind. I suppose that's what they hope for: recall. Well, that one worked a treat, as we're still replaying it in our heads almost thirty years later.

'This place is amazing,' I said, as we wandered around it.

And it really was. It hosted gladiatorial combat to the cheering masses, and excavations in the centre had exposed an area where they used to cage the animals. It was also used as a location for the final episode of season seven of *Game of Thrones*.

'What does it say the capacity was, Darryl?'

'About twenty-five thousand.'

'That's more than Burnley's ground,' Neil said, deadpan.

You're able to wander freely through the passageways and up the stairs to the seating area within the amphitheatre, and you get a real sense of what it must have been like here on a 'matchday'. Afterwards, we wandered round the rest of the grounds where they'd unearthed elaborate mosaics from the floors of some of the Roman villas. All in all, this was the most impressive part of the entire trip for me. My curiosity was sated, and I was ready for the drive home to my lovely Scottish (half English, half German) wife.

We pushed the boat out on their last night with us and went into town to eat in the courtyard garden of Santiago's Kitchen. Then it was time to say goodbye to the lads.

'Make sure you bring Angela and Nathalie with you next time,' Chris said, waving us off to the airport in the morning.

'Ignore her,' I said when we'd shut the car doors. 'Come on your own again so we can have a lads' trip to Granada.'

42

More Local Wildlife

We had ten days to relax before our next guests, and our largest party to date, arrived. Our eldest, Steph, was coming over again, but this time she was bringing her three girls with her, the fourteen-year-old twins and four-year-old Amelia who, unlike the others, was visiting us for the first time. The weather was getting even hotter as the days ticked down to their arrival, and we told them to stock up on sun creams at the airport.

The pool was a blessing in the heat, although the water had now topped thirty degrees. The lawn was also not coping well with the temperatures, despite its nightly sprinklering. It was going bare in some places and brown in others. I was glad we didn't have to pay for the water we used in the garden as that came under the landlady's 'campo water' supply that she paid a nominal amount for. Having said that, our own bills for 'town water' to the house were very reasonable at about two euros per week. Either the grass wasn't performing as it suggested on the box, or our garden was hotter than the Gobi Desert. And as the week wore on, I suspected the latter.

On the thirteenth of July 2017, Spain set a new temperature record in Andalucía. Montoro in Córdoba Province, less than a hundred miles away, recorded 47.3 degrees. On that same day, we stepped out onto the terrace in the morning, then stepped straight back in and put the air con on full blast. And we stayed indoors all day to avoid the heat.

'This is ridiculous,' I said. 'I'm going to make some ice lollies.'

'What flavour?'

'Cuba Libre flavour!'

'Ooh! My favourite. *¡Buena idea!*'

The hot weather was also driving the wildlife crazy as things were popping up all over the garden that week. We'd been plagued by little paper wasps for a couple of weeks. They didn't bother you on the terrace or come and buzz round your food like wasps often do, but they used to come down to the pool edge to drink. If there were just a few of them, I wouldn't have minded, but there were quite a lot of them making frequent visits all day long. I was concerned that they might upset or even sting Amelia when she arrived, so something had to be done.

I jumped in the pool with my trusty fly swatter. At first, I positioned myself in the centre of the shallow end, waist deep, within striking distance of this side of the pool edge and waited until one landed. Then I'd swat it against the surface of the water, and with a second quick flick of the wrist from underneath, sent it arcing over the side of the pool to its final resting place in the shrubbery. My old squash playing days were clearly not wasted. I started counting them as I despatched them. One, two, three … twenty-eight, twenty-nine. I was quite enjoying myself actually.

'What're you doing?' came a familiar cry from the terrace.

'I'm killing the wasps, so they don't sting Amelia.'

'How many have you killed?'

'Thirty-six so far.'

Chris got her phone out and filmed me then put the video on the family WhatsApp group. 'Dad's killing wasps in the pool,' she wrote. 'He thinks he's some kind of waspinator.'

The sun resembled a blast furnace again, and I could feel it burning my shoulders, so I submerged myself up to my mouth with the tip of my killing machine breaking the surface. Then, as another wasp settled down for a drink, I sprung out of the water to swat it like Rambo – or just a crazed idiot, Chris no doubt thought. She'd seen enough and went inside again to get the benefit from the air conditioning. I called it a day at fifty, but resumed the war the next day, making it a round hundred in two days.

The mosquitos were a pain in the summer months too, and unsurprisingly, without nets on the windows, the odd one or two found their way indoors. They had the habit of waiting until you'd got in bed and were about to doze off before making a first tentative buzz past your lughole. And then you had to get up to kill it, of course. My skin didn't react to mozzie bites, but Chris got welts and had to cover herself in Jungle Formula each evening.

We had one of those battery-powered zappers for the mozzies, but as soon as you flicked the light on to find the bugger, it went and sat on the ceiling smirking at you, because it knew I couldn't reach it there. The ceilings in the villa were about thirteen feet high, and even with the stepladders I couldn't quite reach. It usually took me about half an hour of up, down, light on, light off, jumping around the bed before I could finally fry it.

We had a variety of other wildlife visit in the week, including a creepy little jet-black spider scuttling across the patio, and a huge grasshopper that took a shine to our basil plant. But that wasn't the half of it … there was much worse to come.

Steph and the girls arrived for their two-week summer holiday, and were straight in the pool, which in the ensuing heat was the best place to be. The weather was wall-to-wall cloud the day they arrived, which made it very muggy, and even more of a necessity to cool off in the pool. Amelia was having so much fun, with barely a wasp in sight to bother her, but after lunch, the early morning reveille to catch the flight started to wear on her, and she had to go for a siesta.

The first week passed happily without incident, but at the start of their second week, Amelia was playing on the terrace behind the sofa and popped her head up.

'Mum?' she said,

'What, sweetheart?'

'There's a big spider behind the sofa.'

Steph jumped up off the sofa before it could leap three feet in the air and attack her from behind, as it surely would. Amelia had thankfully not developed the arachnophobia bug that cursed her

Mum and other members of the family, including me. Steph trotted round the sofa, giving it a reasonably wide berth.

'It's probably nothing. We haven't seen any big ones over here yet,' Chris assured her.

'Jesus!' Steph screamed. 'It *is* a big one.'

'Don't panic. I'll deal with it,' Chris said, the only one capable of handling the situation rationally.

We both got up and wandered round to see what the fuss was all about, and it was indeed a big one. It was enormous, in fact – or it was in relation to anything else I'd seen up close in the garden, especially compared to UK house spiders. It was light brown in colour, with dark brown markings and really hairy legs … eight of them (which I believe is the full compliment) … and two big hairy front ones for eating you with (or whatever they do with them).

'Wow!' said Chris. 'That *is* big. It looks like a wolf spider.'

'What, that thing eats wolves?' I said.

'No. It's just the name of the species. They hunt on foot like a wolf, rather than lie in wait in a web.'

'I don't care what species it is. Just get rid of it,' Steph cried.

I disappeared inside quickly to get a glass – my little way of helping out in a crisis. Then I handed the glass to Chris, naturally, while she trapped it. She showed it off to us as we all took photos of it. At the time, I'd have sworn blind it was a good six inches from hairy foot to hairy foot, but on reviewing the photo, and after measuring the diameter of the glass, it was probably not much bigger than three inches. That doesn't sound vey big in tarantula terms, but if you don't like spiders, it's a bloody monster.

I looked up arachnophobia and was surprised to find that less than four percent of the population suffer from it. In our family, it's about ninety percent, so we're not going to win any bravery awards. And according to the experts, it's not the fear of being bitten, it's a rather irrational fear of their legginess, sudden movement and speed. And they're probably right, as those little jumpy ones are right buggers. I once caught a snake with a plastic bag in an African hotel room while on safari, and I'd take that any day over a little jumpy spider.

Chris waltzed off down to the bottom of the garden to release the hairy beast anyway, and I made a mental note to watch out for it down there next time I was strimming under the eucalyptus trees.

The twins were spending too much time lolling around with their phones, so I took them into Málaga. I thought they might enjoy an afternoon of culture, so we paid a visit to the Automobile and Fashion Museum, where they had lots of old cars on display along with fashionable outfits of the day. I'm a lover of vintage cars myself, so I was probably going to enjoy the trip more than the girls, but at least it got them out of bed and doing something stimulating.

The exhibition is split into themed rooms, with the cars and fashion displayed alongside each other. It's the number one attraction in Málaga, according to TripAdvisor – and it would have scored highly on ShitAdvisor too if the idea hadn't been left to die in the alcoholic vapours of a certain Dutch bar. It was reportedly one of the top ten museums in all of Spain, so we were in for a treat.

The collection turned out to be larger than I expected, with around ninety vehicles, two hundred Haute Couture pieces and some Contemporary Art installations. And if we'd have come at the weekend, they would have started some of the cars up so we could hear them roar. Amongst the best on display was a 1961 Aston Martin that was the forerunner for the most iconic James Bond car ever, the DB5 that starred in *Goldfinger*. And if you've got a dog, you can take it along on pet-friendly Mondays.

We ended our afternoon at Dunkin' Donuts and rounded off the entire holiday with a Sunday night jaunt into town for cocktails and tapas at Nuevo Y Sur. Amelia made friends with a non-English speaking Belgian girl, and being only four herself, Amelia's Flemish wasn't up to much either. But it's amazing how kids can play happily together when they can't even communicate effectively.

All in all, everyone thoroughly enjoyed themselves: nobody drowned ... nobody got heatstroke ... nobody got stung by a wasp ... and nobody got bitten by a spider. It was great to spend some quality time with the grandkids, as if we still lived in the

225

UK, we might have seen them more often, but perhaps not enjoyed wonderful holiday time together in the sun like this.

After they'd left, we took stock of the damage again. This time, apart from a popped lilo, a broken pool scoop and teenage-size make-up handprints down the twins' bedroom wall, we were left relatively unscathed from the child invasion.

We were also left unscathed by the earthquakes that struck Andalucía that night – I didn't even know we got earthquakes round here. Anyway, this one was sixty miles away and no damage was done on this occasion as the tremors only measured four on the Richter scale. It was a different story on Christmas day in 1884 when the region's most fatal ever quake struck in the same area, killing over twelve hundred people and seriously injuring another fifteen hundred. Bloody hell, if I'd wanted earthquakes, I would have moved to San Francisco.

The biggest ever quake in Spain also struck in Andalucía in 1954 but was less fatal. By my reckoning, the next big one was therefore due in 2024, so we'd better make the most of this early retirement while we can. I made a mental note to run out of the bathroom if I was in there when the next one struck, just in case those heavy ceramic ceiling tiles were shaken down on top of me.

Three days later we were back at the airport collecting our last visitors of our first summer in Spain. Our fourth and final daughter to visit us, Rachel, was coming for a week with her boyfriend.

It was another week of beach visits, eating out, making chocolate and playing golf – that's me crying into my beer on the nineteenth hole again … I really must book some more lessons to arrest the slide. We also had a visit from a praying mantis that came and said the Lord's Prayer in the jasmine on the terrace. At the time, I was watching the footie, and Real Madrid were beating United two-one with five minutes to go, so I said a quick Hail Mary myself (to no avail).

As our guests packed their suitcases on the last evening, so did we. We were off on our own mini holiday in the morning as my favourite (and only) nephew on my side of the family was getting married in Mallorca. We were going to be away nine nights, with two spent celebrating my Dad's eightieth in Barcelona, followed by seven nights in the Balearics for the wedding. Rather than leave the car at the airport, I booked a taxi to take all four of us there. Sadly, I made the fatal mistake of giving the driver four days' notice, and therefore the chance to forget.

Our flight to Barcelona was at 07:10 and Rachel's flight to Manchester was twenty minutes later, so we booked the taxi for 04:30, an ungodly time of day in anyone's book. 04:30 came and went with no sign of our ride, so I rang the driver several times without reply. Living in a sleepy backwater Spanish town rather than a city the size of Manchester, they don't have a cab office you can ring to send another one, so we were stumped.

At 4:45, we hurriedly threw everything into the boot of the Lexus and set off. I was pretty livid, and my mind wasn't a hundred percent on what I was doing, so as our little lane joined the next one at a right angle three hundred yards from the house, I was ill-prepared for it. A scream from Chris as a ditch and a steep bank filled the windscreen seemed to do the trick, and I was able to slam the brakes on just in time.

As we drove towards the airport at speed, Chris was googling which car park we could use. The one we'd used in the past was off the airport and not affiliated with them, but you had to book in advance for that one, so we needed to know where the entrance to the airport's medium-term car park was and what the tariffs were likely to be. We found the entrance but not the tariffs, and parked up anyway, making a dash for the terminal building. I'd never missed a flight yet, despite commuting abroad most weeks for work in the past, and I wasn't going to start now.

As we cleared security and headed for the airside cafés, the taxi driver must have seen the missed calls and checked back on his messages, only to realise he should have been up two hours earlier to run us to the airport. He messaged me and was most apologetic, claiming it had never happened before, and that he must have got his days mixed up. He promised us a free round trip to the airport another time, and we left it at that.

'Do you want a coffee?' Chris asked.

'No. A beer. And make it a large one.'

43

Beautiful Barcelona

Barcelona is our favourite Spanish city – although Málaga is fast catching up with every visit we make – and after landing, we had a short wait for Mum and Dad's flight to arrive.

'Ooh! Guess what?' Chris said, as she returned from the toilet.

'What?'

'There were two Spanish women in the loo, and I could understand what they were saying.'

'Well, you have been learning the language for a while now.'

'I know, but they were speaking really clearly, not with an Andalusian accent. They must have flown in from Madrid.'

'So you want us to move to Madrid now?'

'No, course not. I just wish they'd speak proper Spanish where we live. None of this "*ta luego*" for "*hasta luego*", and how did they say it up in La Rioja?'

'I think it was "*a lugo*", or something like that.'

'Yeah, that was it, "*a lugo*". We'd have a fighting chance if they spoke proper.'

I'm sure she did that last bit just to tease me, as I'm a stickler for using adverbs correctly, but I didn't take the bait.

When the old folks landed, we whisked them off in a taxi to an Airbnb apartment a short walk from the Sagrada Familia in the Eixample district. Gaudí's iconic, jaw-dropping Catholic church was planned as the highlight of our itinerary. Chris and I had been inside once before, and it was the most beautiful thing

I've ever seen in my life. Mum and Dad are churchgoers – in fact, it was always the first thing Dad would do when they took us kids on holiday: pop into the Catholic church to find out what time Sunday mass was – and we knew they'd be as awestruck as we were. I'm a lapsed Catholic, myself, and Chris … well, I'm not too sure what she is, but a churchgoer she isn't.

The apartment was just what we were expecting. We dumped the bags and hailed another cab outside to take us to the top of La Rambla ('the avenue'), the bustling treelined walkway that runs for three-quarters of a mile from the Plaça de Catalunya to the Christopher Columbus monument. On the many prior occasions Chris and I had ambled down this most famous of Spanish boulevards, we'd been entertained by street performers and the occasional sighting of Barcelona's naked rambler, a grey-haired bloke who wanders the streets nude, save for a pair of loafers, ankle socks and tattooed speedos ... with a ring through the end of his willy. I told Mum to keep her eyes peeled for him, but he was conspicuous by his absence. If he did make an appearance, I just hoped it didn't give my Dad any daft ideas.

Halfway down, we decided to stop for refreshments and to watch the world go by on this sun-drenched August afternoon. We found a vacant table at one of the pavement cafés, and when the waiter arrived, I ordered three *cervezas* and a sangria for Mum. The waiter was no fool, and seeing as we didn't stipulate a size and were clearly tourists, he wandered back a few moments later with three litre glasses of beer and a litre glass of sangria, the latter adorned with fruit and some brightly coloured two-foot-long straws. Well, you should have seen my Mum's face when he put it down in front of her.

'I'll never drink all that,' she protested … but she did, with only a little help from Chris. We then had to link arms to get her to the end of La Rambla and find a restaurant for a spot of lunch, after which we got a taxi back to the apartment as there was no way she was going to make it back up La Rambla. She went for a kip when we got back and recharged her batteries for a big night out.

Dad had turned eighty the day before, and so we had to find somewhere special for dinner. On an earlier business trip to this magnificent city, my Spanish hosts had taken me for seafood at the Port Olímpic marina, the location for the sailing events during the 1992 Olympics, so that's where I wanted to take my Dad as he loves his shellfish, and it's a charming place to pass the time of an evening. My Dad is the only person I know that eats prawns without taking the shells off. He must have the constitution of a cuttlefish. Either that, or he's just a bit odd – the jury's still out.

I couldn't remember the name of the restaurant I'd visited on that previous occasion, so I just asked the taxi driver to drop us outside one that he could recommend. Always a top tip to get a recommendation from a local, and it paid off again this time. We dined at Restaurante La Barca del Salamanca, and the staff gave us an excellent night. When the owner found out it was Dad's eightieth, he brought out a slab of cake with two candles in it, an eight and a zero. What a great way to round off the evening.

The following day, we stopped off at a café across from the apartment for breakfast before heading over to the Sagrada Família. What can you say about this place that hasn't been written a thousand times before? You would struggle to run out of adjectives and superlatives when trying to describe Gaudí's masterpiece. The Pope's even been to consecrate it in 2010, which must have drawn a bit of a crowd. Mind you, his predecessor came to Manchester's Heaton Park in 1982 and I couldn't be that bothered going, although a quarter of a million more devout followers than me made the effort. Oasis played to that many people at Knebworth in 1996 … although, admittedly, that was over two nights.

The Basilica de la Sagrada Família is a truly ambitious project. Designed by the legendary architect, Antoni Gaudí, who left his mark all over this glorious city with works including Park Güel and Casa Mila, it was his life's work for forty years before his untimely death in 1926 – he was run over by a bloody tram of all things. And to add insult to injury, he was left dying in the street like the beggar onlookers presumed he was because he was a bit scruffy – nobody recognised him, and he wasn't carrying id. He was taken to hospital but only identified the next day. By that time, without the proper treatment that would have been afforded to the city's favourite native had he been recognised sooner, he was too far gone and passed away a couple of days later, two weeks shy of his seventy-fourth birthday. My Dad's lasted longer than that, and he's a clumsy bugger at the best of times.

Except for a brief hiatus during the Spanish Civil War, building work has been going on ever since, and they might just finish it in another ten years with a bit of luck. Mind you, they've been saying that since we first came to the city in 1998.

We'd booked in for the tour package, so avoided the queues and went straight into the grounds with our radio-controlled earpieces, waiting for the tour guide. Without a guide, you'll leave without a full understanding and appreciation of most of the features of the outer structure.

There are three façades to the building, none of which Gaudí saw to completion. The Nativity Façade is dedicated to the birth of Jesus and is designed in a naturalistic style one might recognise from other gothic cathedrals of the era. It was almost complete when Gaudí walked into the path of the passing number thirty. The Passion Façade is much more striking in its austere design, a design left behind by Gaudí and created to resemble the skeletal features of Jesus in his last moments on Earth. The third façade, the Glory Façade, is reportedly going to be the most striking yet (once complete), dedicated to the road to God and eternal salvation.

When we finally got inside, I was close to tears again myself, even though I knew what to expect. Mum didn't, and she was suitably humbled by the stunningly beautiful and bright interior. It's like walking into heaven. I'm not a religious person (as you might have gathered by now) but I am incredibly moved by architectural works of complete devotion like this – it's difficult not to be unless you've a heart of stone. I would recommend seeing it before some nutjob decides to blow it up.

Six days afterwards, and exactly one week to the day after we had walked the same path on La Rambla, terror did indeed strike at the heart of Barcelona. A Moroccan terrorist drove down the centre of the pedestrian area ploughing down innocent bystanders. In doing so, he killed fourteen people and stabbed

231

another man to death while stealing his car. The youngest victim was only three years old. What a senseless loss of life.

That evening, after a spot of tapas in the Eixample district, we took a cab out to see the musical fountain, which is a magical sight for people of all ages. Built in 1929 for the International Exhibition, the Font Màgica of Montjuïc is Barcelona's largest ornamental fountain, and it comes alive at night, dancing in finely choreographed, brightly coloured jets of water to a musical accompaniment. That night, the water danced to the symbiotic strains of Freddie Mercury's 'Barcelona', on which local girl done good, Montserrat Caballé, unleashes her operatic vocal cords.

A short walk from there, on the corner of Plaça d'Espanya, is the old bullring, which no longer operates as such. Instead, it's been converted to a multi-floor retail and leisure site called Las Arenas de Barcelona, with bars occupying the top level. You get a wonderful 360-degree view of the city from the walkway that circles the bars, and we went up for one last drink before bedtime.

'I'll have a Baileys,' Mum said.

'Now you will remember having it in the morning, won't you?' we all rushed to be the first one to say.

44

Balearic Bliss

Mum did remember having the Baileys, which is an improvement on last time. We packed up and got a cab to the airport for the one-hour flight across the Med to the largest island in the Balearics, Mallorca. My older brother, Mike, used to have an apartment in Pollença, and his daughter, Eleanor, had already married there in 2012. Now it was his son's turn, although Alistair and his bride-to-be, AJ, had chosen to marry on the other side of the island, in Cala d'Or.

It's difficult for UK residents to officially get married in Spain, so the easiest solution is to have a civil ceremony in the UK first, and then have a religious service or symbolic wedding blessing in Spain. Mike had booked a big villa a short walk from the seafront that accommodated ten of us, including my younger sister, Janet, and we were the last to arrive.

The wedding was taking place at the Yacht Club the following afternoon, so after checking out the villa's facilities and grabbing a quick lunch by the pool, we headed down to the front to meet up with some of the other guests. The sun was out, the marina at Cala d'Or was gorgeous, and the drinks were flowing freely. What's not to love about a summer wedding and spending quality time with all the family? You can't put a price on memories like that.

Alistair is one of the nicest lads you could ever wish to meet. He's a big lad, height-wise, and a keen rugby player in his youth, but his size belies his temperament, as he's a big softie inside.

On the eve of Al's wedding, we all met up for dinner down by the marina and afterwards went our separate ways. Everyone was looking forward to the wedding, especially the bride, AJ, who took herself off to bed. Al and his mates decided they'd go on a pub crawl round the town, with Al dressed as the evil Jafar from Aladdin, and some of the girlfriends went with them. After a few too many scoops, Al decided he was going to walk home on his own.

After staggering in the right general direction for ages he arrived at the main roundabout on the edge of town and took the wrong turn, walking instead to the next town of Portopetro, about one and a half miles away. Upon arriving there, he realised he'd gone wrong and walked back to the roundabout. He did a circuit of the roundabout, then took off in the same direction as before. Upon arriving in Portopetro for a second time, he went into the reception of an aparthotel and, with his phone out of charge, picked up the payphone and tried to dial 999 for assistance, obviously drawing a blank there.

Heading back up the road, he lay down on the grass verge for a snooze and woke up covered in ants. He also remembers injuring his hand falling off a garage roof at some point, presumably up there looking for his flying carpet. Eventually, some kindly soul stopped their car when they came across a big bloke dressed as Jafar kneeling in the middle of the road, begging to be rescued. With only the street name in his head, he was dropped outside AJ's villa and woke everyone up. Despite not supposed to be seeing him on the eve of the wedding, she cleaned him up and left him sleeping it off on the sofa ... and then very sportingly agreed to marry him the following day, despite having discovered he'd used her wedding dress as a blanket in the night.

This behaviour was not unusual for Al, which is what makes it all too plausible. I remember him turning up at his sister's wedding on the island a few years earlier having fallen asleep on the beach the day before without any sun cream on, and he was as red as a boiled lobster. Thankfully, he's found someone in AJ that has promised to look after him ... for better or worse.

The sun shone relentlessly on the morning of the wedding, and although the ceremony wasn't till four in the afternoon, it was still cracking the flags. Chris and I had noticed since arriving that the summer heat in Mallorca is a quite different heat to that we experience in Andalucía – it's a lot more humid compared to the dry summer heat of the Costa Del Sol, which isn't great when you're dressed up in your best bib and tucker for a wedding. As it wasn't me getting married today, I decided to forego a jacket and tie and just went with a plain white short-sleeved shirt instead. Chris looked absolutely gorgeous in her dark floral off-the-shoulder dress, and I'd have happily married her again there and then.

AJ only kept us waiting five minutes past the hour, which was considerate of her, seeing as we were all sitting in our own pools of sweat, and she had sensibly opted to wear a wedding dress with a plunging neckline and lots of room under the arms, allowing plenty of air through. The only hitch during the ceremony was the best man forgetting the rings. We thought he was bluffing at first, but we had a five-minute wait while he legged it back to his room.

With the formalities out of the way, we were all back on the cava and beers for a few hours while the photos were taken, and everyone had a good old natter. When we moved indoors for speeches and some food, we were all quite glad of the air conditioning. The speeches were highly amusing, as we might have expected from Al and his mates, and they didn't go on too long. All the same, we were glad when the food arrived.

In keeping with the Spanish wedding, the bride and groom had opted for a typically Iberian spread. Maybe that's all that was on offer, but it was just perfect – I don't think a roast dinner would have been as much appreciated in this heat. We started with tapas and Chris was pleased to see two of her favourites brought out: *tortilla española* (Spanish omelette) and *albóndigas* (meatballs). I was equally chuffed with the *jamón ibérico* (Iberian cured ham) and *calamar* (squid), but the highlight for me was the dates wrapped in bacon (which was written in English). Judging by the spelling mistakes on the other items, I think Al might have knocked up the menus in England himself and brought them with him, and perhaps gave up trying to figure out the translation for dates in bacon.

There was only one main course that could justifiably follow that starter, a paella, and we had a choice of meat or fish. Dessert was *Créme Catalina* (sic), a Catalan crème brûlée. Mum's eyes lit up at the sight of these and quickly hoovered up any spares off our table – she had three of them.

The rest of the evening passed in a bit of a blur if I'm honest, but I do remember Dad falling into the shrubbery on his way out of the venue and claiming he was pushed. And apart from some thieving scoundrel sneaking into the villa one afternoon and nicking a load of euros out of Mike's bedroom, the rest of the week spent in Mallorca was great. We were only a short walk from the town centre and all the fabulous bars and restaurants.

In the words of Rafael Nadal, 'I live in Mallorca, Spain, and I am not sure there are better places'.

45

Doesn't Time Fly?

'How much?!' Chris exclaimed in shock.

'One hundred and seventy-five euros,' I said.

'For ten days' parking? What a rip-off.'

We'd landed back in Málaga to collect the car from the medium-term car park and were paying the price for not booking it in advance … or rather, for our cabbie having a bloody lie-in when he should have been running us to the airport.

'And we're getting a free round trip next time?'

'Yes,' I replied. 'Although he should throw dinner and a bottle of wine in for that price.'

I class myself as a generous man. I'm usually first up to the bar to get a round in, I enjoy going out for dinner with friends, and I'm genuinely happy that our enjoyment provides an income for the hard-pressed locals, but one thing I don't enjoy doing is wasting my money, and that was 175 euros that could have been spent at our local bar. So I wasn't best pleased. There was nothing that could be done about it, and so we drove home to see what state the garden was in.

The villa was still standing, Chris's Mini was still on the drive, and nobody had forced their way in … including the ants, who had been deterred by a liberal spraying of all entrance points before we left this time. I wish someone had broken into the shed and strimmed the garden for me, though, as it was overdue a haircut, and the lawn was badly in need of a drink.

Perhaps I should have taken Graham's advice and put Astroturf down instead, although it might have melted in July.

Fourteen sweaty, back-breaking hours with the strimmer sorted the weeds out, but the lawn would have to revive itself through the autumn. After I'd done the gardening, we went down to the coast. One of my old work colleagues was over on holiday with his family and I said we'd meet up for a beer. Their apartment was in Calahonda, so we parked up in La Cala. The boardwalk from La Cala runs for about three and half miles and takes in Calahonda, so we had a nice long walk beside the beach.

The Senda Litoral de Málaga has been a bold project. It's almost complete now, save for a few small sections to join everything up, but when it's finished it will run continuously for just over a hundred miles and cover the entire length of Málaga Province's seafront, from Manilva up to Nerja. That would make one hell of a pub crawl.

It was good to see a friendly face again and we swapped stories of our vastly different lives since we'd last worked together.

'So, what're you planning to do with yourself now you're not contracting?' he asked me.

'I thought I'd take some time out and write a book.'

'An interesting change in career path. What about?'

'Well, moving over here has been an experience and a half, so I could write about that. But I've had this storyline going round my head for years.'

'Oh yeah, what's that then?'

'I've often dreamt about Chris getting kidnapped.'

'Ha! A happy dream then,' he laughed.

'No, I couldn't live without her. I don't know how to work the washing machine, for one.'

'That makes two of us.'

'No, I thought I'd write a kidnap thriller. In fact, I'm going to make a start next week.'

Before I was able to embark on such a fanciful idea, however, we were back off to the UK a few days later for another brief visit to see all the kids. We hadn't been over there for two months as most of them had come over to see us in Spain over the summer, and we had two birthdays in the family to celebrate.

We booked our usual taxi driver to take us to the airport again, although this time the flight was an afternoon one, so at least he couldn't oversleep. But cabbies in Spain tend to work for themselves and share their cab with another driver, and it was his oppo that took us to the airport. He knew nothing about our free return trip and so I had to fork out for the journey again. Our free rides would apparently only be when the boss was driving, as he couldn't expect the other guy to run us for nothing. Hopefully, it would be free on the way back then.

After a brief three-night stay, we checked in at Manchester for the return journey and were told of a short delay to our 19:55 flight. At 20:42 the delay was upgraded to two hours and I received snack coupons via text message from the airline. That all seemed quite efficiently handled, I thought. No worries. Can't be helped. Back to the bar for two more wines then. We had our cabbie collecting us for a free ride home, but by the time we'd get into Málaga it would be gone 2am, and I thought it wouldn't be fair to keep him up that long, so I told him to get some sleep, and we'd get a cab outside the airport instead.

Two hours became three and a half by the time we were in the air and the pilot didn't spare the horses. It's downhill anyway to Spain, and I think he was desperately trying to get us there inside three hours from our original arrival time, to avoid triggering EU flight compensation payments.

The captain was clearly trying 'to boldly go where no man has gone before', and despite his chief engineer – who may or may not have been called Scotty – 'givin' her all she's got', he knew deep down that you 'cannae change the laws of physics'. The plane was vibrating, and I think Chris was praying someone would beam her up.

'I don't like this,' Chris said, as the plane descended rapidly from the black sky.

'Don't worry, she'll hold together,' I assured her, dropping in a Hans Solo quote.

'I hope so. It feels like we're travelling at the speed of light,' she said, her hand gripping the armrest.

'Don't start throwing Queen songs in the mix,' I said – she either didn't hear me or it just went over her head.

As the pilot threw the plane down onto the tarmac at Málaga, I checked my watch. We were three hours and three minutes late.

'We're in the money,' I began singing cheerily.

'What're you on about?' Chris said, having just rediscovered a faith in God.

'We're quids in,' I said. 'Or eight hundred euros in, to be exact. We've landed more than three hours late.'

'I bet the airline don't agree.'

However, she was wrong. Before the plane had even come to a halt on the stand, an email pinged in from the airline apologising for the late arrival of our flight ... by three hours and one minute (hurrah!) ... and informing us how to make a claim of four hundred euros each in accordance with regulation EU261.

Result!

I'd only paid 461 euros for the flights, which by normal standards was expensive for return flights to Málaga, but it was the bank holiday weekend after all. And now it had cost me nothing. In fact, the extra dosh coming our way even covered the 175 euros we'd blown on parking fees the previous week. It's swings and roundabouts ... or what goes around comes around. Either way, despite it being gone three in the morning, I was as happy as a dog with two ... well, you know how that one ends.

We hailed a cab outside and crashed into bed around 4am, making sure the *persianas* were down fully to block out the morning light. Next day, I filled in the claim form and had the money in our account by the end of the week.

As our first year closed out, we found ourselves on the rooftop café bar of Malaga's premier department store, El Corte Inglés. We were just starting to wind down after a whirlwind summer and were reflecting on what we'd achieved in our first hectic year in Spain. Since we'd driven the Mini off the boat in Santander ... we'd packed our jobs in ... we'd moved to a new house in a foreign country ... we'd rented out our UK house ... the kids hadn't disowned us, and although they miss us terribly, they think we've probably done the right thing ... and we'd navigated an unbelievable level of bureaucracy to obtain Spanish residency, despite it being a process more akin to an egg and spoon race through a minefield.

And in doing so, we'd created some unforgettable memories along the way.

I think we're going to be very happy living in Spain, and especially amongst the charming people of Alhaurín El Grande, who are in general a really sweet and openly generous bunch. In particular, we owe a debt of thanks to our kind landlady, Olivia, and our neighbours for making us feel so welcome.

The way people let on to each other in the street all the time, even to strangers, never feels forced or unnatural. It's sadly something that in the UK has gradually died off in many communities as people don't even know their neighbours' names most of the time.

There is a deep and rich culture running throughout Spain that is a joy to experience and, with the exception of bullfighting, many of the long-standing traditions and festivals are amazing spectacles to witness.

The food is absolutely amazing, and such good value for money, especially when eating out at one of the many *ventas* (roadside restaurants) that offer a ridiculously cheap *menú del día*. The tomatoes are bursting with flavour, and all of the meat we buy in the supermarket is of top quality. For instance, if you want minced beef, you just pick up a pack of minced beef – you don't have to look carefully to see if you're buying the cheap and fatty 'Value' version, or the 'Lean' or 'Extra Lean' version ... it's automatically very lean and of the highest quality.

The weather is unbeatable and very predictable. The Costa del Sol has around 320 days of sunshine every year, and although the villa is bloody freezing in the winter, we can still go outside during the daytime and sit in the warm sunshine in February.

There is hardly any traffic congestion outside the centre of Málaga, and as a consequence, the air is much cleaner. We definitely notice the difference when we get off the plane at Manchester.

The scenery close to where we live is breathtaking, and there are walking trails throughout Andalucía. We haven't really taken advantage of that aspect yet but will rectify that in the coming months.

The pace of life is so much better, and it's wonderful to be sitting outside a restaurant in the evening at 11pm and seeing entire Spanish families out eating dinner with their young children. They really do have a very family-centric lifestyle, and that's very heartwarming to observe.

On the other side of the coin, if I were to change anything about Spain, it would be the idiotic, complex bureaucracy and the inconsistent application of the rules. That and the punitive tax situation, which we're yet to fully experience. Suffice to say, it's something I'm not looking forward to, and future encounters with officialdom may yet fill a second volume.

On balance, however, we feel we've definitely made the right move.

People reckon if you can stick it out for two years, then you're likely to stay longer, so if this next year pans out as we hope, then we may be here for the long run and become just as much a fixture of the town as our Spanish hosts.

And in the last few days of our first year in Spain, I finally put pen to paper and began to write my first novel … it's about an ex-bomb disposal officer from the British Army who emigrates to Spain, from where his wife and son are subsequently kidnapped off La Cala beach. This was it … it was happening … I was going to be a writer.

And with a bit of luck, they might one day name a Spanish street after me.

* * *

About the Author

Before emigrating, I'd lived what most might describe as a pretty unremarkable life: I'm a fifty-odd-year-old musician whose popstar dreams were dashed (more than once) at a young age and who found success ultimately in IT. Resident in Spain now – yes, we're still here 7 years on – I've loved writing funny poems all my life, thanks to the inimitable Pam Ayres, and now I have a bit more time on my hands, I thought I'd turn my hand to a more expansive writing career.

I enjoy the writing process, and like most writers, I don't write to be famous or earn a million – although that would be very nice, of course, even if the Spanish state would end up keeping more than half the proceeds – and so I'm really writing to entertain the reader.

I do hope you enjoyed my debut travelogue, that I put a smile on your face at times – and even raised a chuckle – and I hope I haven't put you off from making a similar move yourself in the near future. In the words of Mahatma Gandhi, *"Live as if you were to die tomorrow. Learn as if you were to live forever."* ...

... And please remember to leave an honest review of my book, as they are the lifeblood of a budding author.

Thanks for accompanying me on this journey. *¡Hasta luego!*

Acknowledgements

Some photos are from www.unsplash.com and are used on the understanding they are "Free to use under the Unsplash License".

In particular, the author would like to thank the following photographers for their work, the use of which the author believes has helped to enrich the book for the reader:

Peijun Song, Anthony Delanoix, Guus Baggermans, Daniil Onischenko, Wesley Tingey, Jon Tyson, Will Stewart, Joe Pizzio, Claudio Schwarz, Jordan Bebek, Leon Oblak, Geetanjal Khanna, Yaoqi, Maddy Baker, Alexander Awerin, Markus Spiske, Brooke Lark, Guillermo Velarde, Quino Al, Tonik, Roman Raizen, Henrique Ferreira, Daniel Corneschi, Vojtech Petr.

In addition, one image is used on the same understanding courtesy of Wikimedia Commons. All remaining photos were shot through the author's lens.

A special thanks too to Alasdair Campbell, author of "Stepping into Darkness", for his frank editorial comments.

Printed in Great Britain
by Amazon